CHALLENGING LIBERALISM

CHALLENGING LIBERALISM

FEMINISM AS POLITICAL CRITIQUE

LISA H. SCHWARTZMAN

THE PENNSYLVANIA STATE UNIVERSITY PRESS
UNIVERSITY PARK, PENNSYLVANIA

Library of Congress Cataloging-in-Publication Data

Schwartzman, Lisa H., 1969–
    Challenging liberalism : feminism as political critique /
    Lisa H. Schwartzman
        p.   cm.
Includes bibliographical references and index.
ISBN 978-0-271-02853-8 (cloth : alk. paper)
ISBN 978-0-271-02854-5 (paper : alk. paper)
1. Feminist theory.
2. Liberalism—Philosophy.
3. Abstraction.
4. Individualism.
5. Feminist criticism.
I. Title.

HQ1190.S37 2006
320.51'3—dc22
2005028568

Contents

Acknowledgments

I am very grateful for the advice and support I received while working on this book. First, I wish to thank Sandy Thatcher, my editor at Penn State Press, who has been supportive and helpful throughout the publication process, as well as the two reviewers, whose comments encouraged me to sharpen and develop my arguments in fruitful ways.

This project began as a doctoral dissertation at the State University of New York, Stony Brook, and I am grateful for the advice and feedback I received from the members of my dissertation committee, especially Kenneth Baynes, who directed the dissertation and provided invaluable questions, comments, and criticisms over the years. In discussions about the value of liberal theory, Ken encouraged me to engage critically debates I otherwise might have dismissed. I am also deeply thankful to Eva Kittay, who has continued to comment on my work well beyond the dissertation years. I owe a great deal to the philosophy department and the other graduate students at Stony Brook, especially the community of feminist scholars with whom I moved through graduate school. This rich intellectual feminist community afforded me the freedom to examine the complex relationship among feminism, liberalism, and radical political critique, as well as other questions in feminist political philosophy that had intrigued me since my undergraduate years.

I am very fortunate to work in a department where feminism and political theory are highly valued, and where I enjoy the intellectual companionship of engaging and supportive colleagues. Michigan State University has provided me with financial support as well, and I am especially thankful to the Office of the Vice President for Research and Graduate Studies, which awarded me an Intramural Research Grant for the fall of 2003. I am also grateful to my students, in particular those in my Philosophical Aspects of Feminism classes, and the graduate students in my seminar Feminism, Equality, and Impartiality and in my course Liberal Theory and Its Critics.

Over the years, many friends and colleagues have read portions of this book and have discussed its ideas with me. Audiences at several conferences that I regularly attend have been very helpful, especially those at the Association for Feminist Ethics and Social Theory, the Society for Women in Philosophy, the North American Society for Social Philosophy, and the Radical Philosophy Association. Without this vibrant intellectual community of feminists and other critical social philosophers, it would have been far more difficult to formulate and develop my ideas. My work has also been significantly enriched by helpful conversations and comments from many friends and colleagues: Barbara Andrew, Claudia Card, Margaret Crouch, Ann Cudd, Faith Danforth, Stephen Esquith, Sara Ferguson, Marilyn Frye, Jean Keller, Bill Lawson, Hilde Lindemann, Bonnie Mann, Sarah Clark Miller, Kathy Miriam, Jim Nelson, Cecelia Ober, Dick Peterson, Gaile Pohlhaus, Nancy Snow, and Allison Wolf.

I owe a very special thanks to Jeffrey Gauthier, who read every chapter of this book, offered insightful and helpful suggestions, and provided unwavering support for my work over the many years that I have known him. I am also very grateful to Jonathan Caver, for reading and commenting on nearly all of the chapters, for stimulating conversations about feminism and political theory, and for his encouragement and friendship over the many years that I was working on this project.

Finally, I want to thank my parents and my sister, Marcy, for their love and encouragement and for their steadfast support for me and my work.

Earlier versions of some portions of this book have been published before. Chapter 1 is a revised version of "Liberal Rights Theory and Social Inequality: A Feminist Critique," which appeared in *Hypatia* 14, no. 2 (1999): 26–47. Chapter 5 is an expanded and revised version of "A Feminist Critique of Nussbaum's Liberalism: Toward an Alternative Feminist Methodology," which was published in *Feminist Interventions in Ethics and Politics: Feminist Ethics and Social Theory*, ed. Barbara S. Andrew, Jean Keller, and Lisa Schwartzman (Lanham, Md.: Rowman and Littlefield, 2005), 151–65. Earlier versions of Chapter 6 and Chapter 7 were published, respectively, as "Feminist Analyses of Oppression and the Discourse of 'Rights': A Response to Wendy brown," *Social Theory and Practice* 28, no. 3 (2002): 465–80, and "Hate Speech, Illocution, and Social Context: A Critique of Judith Butler," *Journal of Social Philosophy* 33, no. 3 (2002): 421–41. I am grateful to these journals and publishers for allowing me to reprint this material here.

Introduction

The ideals and concepts of liberalism have been used in feminist struggles for liberation throughout recent history. From the time of the women's suffrage movement to the more recent battles over abortion, women have formulated their demands in terms of equality, autonomy, and individual rights. Although numerous feminists have demonstrated their value, liberal concepts can work to undermine women's interests, reinforcing not only sexism, but also racism, classism, and other forms of oppression. Examples of this include cases where men have used the "right to privacy" to argue that the state should not interfere in situations of domestic violence and marital rape, as well as more recent cases in which racist hate speech, violent pornography, and sexually harassing speech have been granted protection under the right to "freedom of expression." Why is it that these concepts yield such radically different conclusions? When and why do liberalism's central ideals work to oppress, and when and why do they function as tools of liberation?

In this book, I do not undertake an empirical investigation into the ways that rights, equality, privacy, autonomy, and individualism have been used throughout history, nor do I offer a simple answer to the question of whether liberal terminology should be employed in feminist arguments. Rather, I begin with the question of *why* it is that liberal concepts function in such seemingly contradictory ways. Part of the answer, of course, is that liberal concepts are indeterminate and thus can be used in different sorts of arguments—arguments by feminists and antiracists, on the one hand, and arguments by those who seek to maintain and uphold structures of power, domination, and privilege, on the other. But this is not the only reason these concepts can function in such radically different ways. Many liberal theorists acknowledge this indeterminacy and are fully aware that "rights" and "equality" (for instance) can be used to uphold oppression and to promote injustices. Although the issue of how one applies indeterminate concepts is important, it is also useful to focus attention on the methodology typically employed in liberal theory. In this volume, I examine (1) the attempted *abstraction* of liberalism, which leads liberals to set aside or "bracket" important information about particular social structures and (2) the *individualism* of liberalism, which suggests that people are independent, autonomous choosers rather than members of social groups on which systems of oppression are based. These two related but distinct features of liberalism—abstraction and individualism—are responsible for many of the problems I discuss.

Although their arguments are not always framed as critiques of liberal abstraction or individualism, contemporary feminists often question the role that liberal ideals and concepts should continue to play in feminist theory and practice, and many object to specific aspects of liberalism. In particular, feminists criticize the way in which liberal theorists draw a sharp line between the public and private spheres, a line that relegates women to the "private" sphere of the home and family while allowing men the freedom to dominate the "public" arena.[1] Furthermore, feminists question the liberal view of persons as rational, self-interested individuals motivated primarily by autonomously formed preferences. Some argue that this ideal is "abstract" insofar as actual persons typically do not possess merely self-interested and rational desires, and others claim that the liberal ideal of the rational, economic "man" fails to pay adequate attention to other important human qualities, such as affection, care, and concern for one's family and community.[2] Noting that care and affection are typically associated with women, some feminists argue that liberal political theory ought to value such qualities more highly.[3]

Without entirely dismissing these problems, some argue that liberalism's strong emphasis on individualism, autonomy, choice, rights, and equality makes it a promising theory for feminists. For instance, Martha Nussbaum offers a feminist defense of a version of liberal individualism, arguing that "where women and the family are concerned, liberal political thought has not been nearly individualist enough."[4] In addition to supporting certain forms of individualism, some feminist liberals promote liberal abstraction as central to the pursuit of justice, and some offer feminist arguments for the contractarianism of liberal political philosophy.[5]

Other feminists defend specific aspects of liberal theory, while acknowledging the troubled history of the liberal tradition. For instance, in a recent essay that highlights the problematic ways that "autonomy" has been associated primarily with men, Marilyn Friedman nonetheless argues that this concept holds great potential for feminists.[6] Likewise, some feminist legal theorists argue that "privacy" and "rights" can be refashioned in feminist ways. For instance, Elizabeth Schneider takes what she calls a "dialectical" approach to rights and argues that when rights discourse and rights claims emerge from political struggle, they "can help to develop political consciousness which can play a useful role in the development of a social movement."[7] Elsewhere Schneider argues that the right to privacy can take on new meaning in the context of feminist struggles for freedom and equality. Although privacy is typically associated with the right to be left alone, this concept has "radical potential" if understood as "affirmatively linked to liberty and the right to autonomy, self-expression, and self-determination."[8] Situating her analysis in the context of a discussion of domestic violence, Schneider urges feminists to challenge the strict separation between the public and the private and to develop a right to privacy that is not "synonymous with the right to state noninterference" but that instead recognizes the affirmative role that privacy can play in the lives of battered women. Thinking about privacy in this way encourages us to recognize the importance of its social and material preconditions, and it enables us to understand this concept in a more radical and less individualistic way.[9]

Throughout this book, I build on the critical analyses of feminists who have been working to identify and challenge these problematic aspects of liberal theory. My two central charges against liberalism—that it employs a problematic form of abstraction and that it sets out an ideological account of individualism—are certainly not new ones. Moreover, a number of feminist liberals have responded to the charges of abstraction and individualism, claiming either that liberalism is not abstract or individualist in the ways that some critics contend or that the best interpretation of liberalism is one that would not suffer from these problems.[10] What is needed in this debate is an emphasis on method: most versions of liberalism—including those promoted by some liberal feminists who explicitly address these charges—suffer from certain methodological problems. I do not claim here that liberalism cannot be reformed, nor do I suggest that liberal concepts are useless for feminists. Rather, my assertion is that the methods of abstraction and individualism typically employed and often championed by liberals (including feminist liberals) are problematic. Feminist theory and practice embody an alternative methodology, one that does not eschew all abstraction and individualism but reformulates these concepts and situates them in a critical analysis of women's oppression, thus avoiding some of the problematic aspects of contemporary liberalism.

Defining Liberalism

Although liberalism can be defined in various different ways, contemporary liberal philosophers often focus on three defining features: first, liberalism holds that all persons have an essential interest in leading a life defined in accordance with their own conception of what is valuable—that is, with their conception of "the good." Liberals debate the extent to which this requires the state to remain entirely "neutral" between individuals' conceptions of the good, but most endorse some form of state neutrality.[11] Furthermore, although the conception of value that an individual holds at any particular time is not necessarily what is best for that person, liberals generally do not support a situation in which the state, or any other coercive body, tells individuals what is best for them. Rather, liberals typically argue that one's life is best led "from the inside," according to one's own beliefs about value.[12]

A second component of liberalism follows directly from the first: because all persons have an interest in leading life according to their own conception of the good, all persons have an interest in the freedom and liberties that are needed to develop a conception of the good and to deliberate about questions of value. Thus, most liberals emphasize the importance of civil liberties and freedoms, such as freedom of expression, that guarantee the conditions under which individuals can devise and revise their conceptions of the good.[13]

Third, and perhaps most important, liberals hold that all persons are of equal moral worth and that the state must treat persons with "equal concern and respect." Like other components of liberalism, this central tenet is interpreted in different ways by different theorists, both in terms of its justification and in terms of its implications for social policy.[14] For some liberals, the reason that people deserve equal treatment is that they all have the capacity to form and revise their conception of the good. For instance, according to Martha Nussbaum, the "equal dignity" each person possesses is rooted in the "power of moral choice" within each individual, "a power that consists in the ability to plan a life in accordance with one's own evaluation of ends."[15] Nussbaum echoes Rawls's claim that the basis of equality is the "capacity for moral personality," which involves the capacity to form a conception of the good and the capacity to have a "sense of justice."[16] Other liberals, such as Ronald Dworkin and Will Kymlicka, suggest that the basis of equality is not this *capacity* but rather the *interest* that underlies it. Kymlicka, citing Dworkin, argues that although the capacities described by Rawls are central, "our interest in them stems from our higher-order interest in leading the life that is good."[17] In any case, although liberals offer slightly different justifications for the claim that individuals are of equal moral worth, most seem to agree on the centrality of this idea. From this claim about equal moral worth it follows that the state must treat persons with "equal concern and respect," as Dworkin puts it.[18] How the state goes about treating persons "as equals" is the subject of further disagreement within liberalism, but most liberals contend that the government need not treat each person in exactly the same manner to treat them "as" equals. Furthermore, within liberalism, theorists also debate the question of *what* is to be equalized in order to ensure that individuals are treated as equals: should the state seek to equalize the welfare of individuals (for instance, as measured by the degree to which their preferences are satisfied)? Or should it seek to measure resources, capacities, opportunities, or some other variable? While I do not engage the details of this particular debate, I do critically examine the theories of two prominent liberals, Dworkin and Rawls, who argue that some version of "equality of resources" is the best interpretation of the liberal principle of equality.

In short, liberalism can be understood as holding that (1) all persons have an essential interest in leading a life in accordance with their own conception of value, (2) all persons have an interest in freedoms and liberties needed to develop and revise their conception of the good, and (3) the government must treat individuals with equal concern and respect.

The Problems of Individualism and Abstraction in Liberalism

Some of the most common objections to liberalism involve claims that liberal theory is too "abstract" and too "individualistic." Before considering the feminist objections to these aspects of liberalism, it is worth noting that both communitarians and conservative critics of liberalism also object to liberalism's abstraction and individualism. The substance of these criticisms, however, is very different from that of the feminist critique.[19] Nonetheless, theorists who respond to the feminist objections to liberalism sometimes fail to distinguish feminist objections from communitarian ones.[20] The responses that feminist liberals make to such objections suggest that liberalism is a better theory for feminists than is a traditional, values-based communitarianism. This is a problematic and false dichotomy: feminists need not choose between liberalism and communitarianism. Although some feminist critics of liberalism endorse certain aspects of communitarianism (for instance, some care-based versions of feminism celebrate women's traditional roles as mothers and as members of families and other traditional communities), placing more attention on traditionally defined "communities" is not the goal of most feminists who criticize liberalism. Rather, many feminist critics of liberalism—and the ones whose work most interests me—call attention to the collective nature of women's oppression and to the concrete experiences of women's lives under sexist social structures.

Discussions of the "feminist critique of liberalism" often begin with a consideration of Alison Jaggar's examination of liberal political theory in her 1983 book, *Feminist Politics and Human Nature*. Jaggar's work is cited both by feminists who endorse her critique of liberalism and by theorists (feminist and nonfeminist) who argue against it.[21] According to Jaggar, many problems with liberalism stem from a flawed conception of human nature that involves an individualistic understanding of human rationality. Calling this "metaphysical assumption" of liberalism "abstract individualism," she explains:

> The assumption in this case is that human individuals are onto-logically prior to society; in other words, human individuals are the basic constituents out of which social groups are composed. Logically if not empirically, human individuals could exist outside a social context; their essential characteristics, their needs and interests, their capacities and desires, are given independently of their social context and are not created or even fundamentally altered by that context. This metaphysical assumption is sometimes called abstract individualism because it conceives of human individuals in abstraction from any social circumstances.[22]

Defenders of liberalism have responded to Jaggar by claiming that liberalism is not—or need not be—committed to these (or any) metaphysical assumptions. Contemporary liberal equality theorists such as Rawls, Dworkin, and Kymlicka argue that individuals are socially situated and that the social context must be one in which individuals are free to develop their life plans and choose from a range of attractive options. Nonetheless, these liberal theorists continue to emphasize the importance of individual choice and freedom to pursue one's own conception of the good. The freedom of individuals—and the need for the state to respect individuals' choices—is central to the theories of Rawls, Dworkin, and other contemporary liberal egalitarians. Thus, I argue that liberalism continues to emphasize "individualism," though not in the narrow sense described by Jaggar in her 1983 work. The individualism that I criticize does not entail a metaphysical assumption about human nature, but it does involve a commitment to a problematic methodology: the methodology of focusing primarily on each and every individual as an individual, rather than also calling attention to the social context and to the relations of power in which individuals live.[23] Beginning from the assumption that it is the needs and interests of individuals that are primary, liberals have a difficult time detecting and analyzing cases of oppression.[24] Because oppression is based on one's membership in a social group, understanding how social power and oppression work requires an adequate understanding of the significance of group membership.

In addition to adopting a methodology that focuses on individuals *as individuals*, rather than as members of social groups, liberal theorists often construct highly abstract models of political and social justice. Although Jaggar describes the individualism of liberalism as "abstract," abstraction and individualism are separate but related problems. To elucidate the problems with liberal abstraction, I consider the work of two prominent contemporary liberal political philosophers, Rawls and Dworkin, both of whom rely heavily on the use of abstract ideals to illustrate their conceptions of justice. In his groundbreaking *Theory of Justice*, Rawls argues for principles of justice that would regulate a "well-ordered" society, and he employs the abstract ideal of the "original position" to make his case for this view. Defending his emphasis on an abstract ideal, Rawls writes, "The reason for beginning with ideal theory is that it provides, I believe, the only basis for the systematic grasp of these more pressing problems. . . . I shall assume that a deeper understanding can be gained in no other way, and that the nature and aims of a perfectly just society is the fundamental part of the theory of justice."[25] Although Rawls's more recent work in *Political*

Liberalism may seem less "abstract," insofar as he more explicitly situates this project in the context of contemporary liberal democracies, he nonetheless continues to emphasize the role of abstraction in normative theorizing:

> The work of abstraction . . . is not gratuitous: not abstraction for abstraction's sake. Rather, it is a way of continuing public discussion when shared understandings of lesser generality have broken down . . . the deeper the conflict, the higher the level of abstraction to which we must ascend to get a clear and uncluttered view of its roots . . . formulating idealized, which is to say abstract, conceptions of society and person . . . is essential to finding a reasonable political conception of justice.[26]

Thus, throughout his writing, Rawls stresses the importance of abstraction and the need to devise and justify abstract, idealized models of society and of individuals.

Dworkin differs from Rawls in a number of ways, but the former too believes that political theories should be abstract; like Rawls, he constructs an abstract ideal to illustrate and defend his conception of distributional equality, which he calls "equality of resources."[27] In Dworkin's ideal, immigrants on a desert island must decide how to distribute the island's resources. Dworkin argues that people in such a situation would choose to employ an auction, an "envy test," and a hypothetical insurance market, and he suggests that this idealized model can guide assessment of our current society's distributive mechanisms and social institutions. For both Rawls and Dworkin, the ideal and allegedly abstract scenarios are intended to illustrate fundamental ideas that we have about equality and justice, and they are supposed to help us clarify our views about what is just and unjust in our own society.

In my critical analysis, I argue that theorists who aim to construct highly abstract models succeed in abstracting only from certain features, while other aspects of our social world remain unchallenged and often unacknowledged. Thus, liberalism's "abstract" models are not in fact as abstract as they purport to be. Ultimately, the important work of identifying and challenging oppressive structures of social, political, economic, and sexual power is best accomplished by methods that do not aim for this sort of abstraction. Feminist theory, by paying close attention to structures of power and to social context, and by examining the concrete experiences of women living within these structures, suggests a method of theorizing that moves beyond the forms of individualism and abstraction that are prominent within liberalism.

• • •

In the first three chapters (Part One), I critically examine the work of Dworkin and Rawls in order to illustrate problems that arise from liberal individualism and abstraction. In Chapter 1, I analyze Dworkin's liberal rights theory and argue that rights should be reconceptualized so that they focus on the interests of persons who are understood as members of oppressed and oppressor groups, rather than simply as individuals. Although all persons should be entitled to certain rights, rights can conflict with other sorts of claims (including claims to equality), and they can also conflict with other rights. Making decisions about whose, and which, rights should prevail involves a careful, contextual understanding of social power structures, including those of racism, sexism, and classism. Rather than viewing rights as entitlements that can only be possessed by individuals, I argue that many rights should be seen also as "goals" that need to be sought after and achieved through structural changes in social power structures. The efforts of oppressed groups to reconceptualize rights in ways that work to challenge various forms of unjust domination are central to this struggle. Thus, specifically, women may need to obtain certain particular rights (such as the right not to be raped, the right not to be harmed by pornography, and the right to control one's own reproduction) in order to achieve freedom and equality.

I critically analyze the issue of abstraction in liberal theory, focusing particular attention on Dworkin's theory of distributional equality (Chapter 2) and on Rawls's original position (Chapter 3). In both cases, an abstract ideal is supposed to guide assessment of our own society's distributive mechanisms and institutions. Although one obvious problem with such ideals concerns the difficulty of knowing how to apply them in a non-ideal context, the issue of application is not the central focus of my critique. Rather, there are deeper problems with the very models themselves: often, liberal political theories that claim to be abstract are actually concrete and particular in ways that the theorist fails to recognize. Assumptions about individuals, and about the surrounding social context, are often built into the theory and function as background assumptions that the theorist does not acknowledge, articulate, or defend. In other words, what appears to be an abstract ideal may actually embody many of the same relations of power and oppression that are present in our own society. Thus, a critical awareness of oppression is essential to theorizing and attempting to abstract from questions of gender, race, and class will not work to eliminate these oppressive structures.

Having explained in Part One the limitations of a liberal framework, in Part Two (Chapters 4 and 5) I draw on the work of feminist moral, political, and legal theorists to argue for a feminist approach that does not eschew ideals such as rights, equality, and autonomy but rather employs them within a critique of social relations of power. Here I consider two liberal feminist defenses of abstraction and individualism: Onora O'Neill's suggestion that liberalism must be more—not less—"abstract," and Martha Nussbaum's contention that liberalism often fails women when it is not "individualist" enough. Although O'Neill and Nussbaum belong to very different theoretical traditions (neo-Kantian and neo-Aristotelian, respectively), both argue that feminism could be accommodated within liberalism if liberalism more consistently adhered to its principles: employing methods of "mere abstraction" (O'Neill) and paying attention to each and every individual, as an individual (Nussbaum).

Rather than emphasizing the merely individual perspectives of specific women, and rather than attempting to be as abstract as possible, I advocate a feminist methodology that begins by examining the lives, experiences, and interests of women. This feminist methodology is not anti-individualist, nor does it eschew abstraction. It does, however, pay careful attention to the ways that individuals are embedded in social contexts, ones often characterized by power and domination. With this awareness, feminists should employ concepts such as rights, equality, liberty, and autonomy in ways that emphasize women's perspectives; what women need in order to live free from the oppressive structures of male domination can, to some extent, be articulated through reformulating these ideals and using them in ways that avoid the pitfalls of liberalism.

As examples of the sorts of feminist reformulations I have in mind, I note cases in which an oppressed group argues for a social policy on the basis of its right to equality. For instance, for feminists, women's right to workplace and educational settings that are free from unwanted sexual attention is a matter of equality. Similarly, antiracist activists demand certain restrictions on hate speech, claiming the right to equality for members of historically oppressed racial groups. In both cases, the experiences of oppressed groups serve as the basis for understanding what is required by such concepts as rights, equality, and freedom. The analyses of sexually harassing behavior as "sexual harassment," and of certain racial epithets as "racist hate speech," rely upon a critical understanding of social structures; such analyses do not derive from the mere perspectives of individuals or from abstract ideals. In fact, the development of such critical perspectives often comes about through methods that examine the experiences common to members of a certain social group, such as women or people of color. Viewed separately as the merely personal experiences of individuals, cases of sexual harassment might initially appear to be mere flirtation or "harmless fun," and incidents of racist hate speech might seem to be "isolated incidents." Understood this way, neither of these actions seems to have the power to seriously harm an individual or negatively affect the well-being of an entire social group. Considering these incidents in the context of structural and entrenched relations of domination and oppression, however, engenders another analysis. For the right to equality, autonomy, or freedom to be meaningful for members of historically oppressed groups, a liberal approach that attempts to abstract from social relations of power and focus only on individuals is inadequate. Thus, an analysis of social structures of power must supplement discussions of rights, equality, liberty, and autonomy and these concepts must be situated within a more radical social critique than the one provided by liberalism.

In Chapters 6 and 7 (Part Three), I contrast my own analysis with the postmodern feminist critique of liberalism offered in the recent work of Wendy Brown and Judith Butler. In their discussions of rights and hate speech, Brown and Butler criticize liberalism for both its abstraction and its individualism, though their understanding of its inadequacies, as well as their proposed alternatives, differ sharply from my own approach. Specifically, Brown and Butler argue that because liberal concepts such as rights and equality are inherently abstract and inevitably universal, feminists and antiracist activists should avoid these concepts rather than reformulate them to embody the perspectives of oppressed groups. They argue against the sort of analysis I advance, contending that references to social systems of power risk "reifying" and making permanent precisely those structures they wish to overturn. As an alternative, Brown and Butler advocate engaging in open contests for meaning without any recourse to normative claims or to generalized analyses of social and political power. There are, however, a number of ways in which their postmodern alternative ultimately resembles the very liberal theory they set out to attack.

First, Brown and Butler mistakenly contend that liberal concepts actually are "abstract" and "universal." Although they offer this view as a critique, concluding that feminists should avoid appealing to these concepts, their critique essentially accepts liberalism's description of itself as abstract and universal. As I lay out in preceding chapters, this claim of abstraction is in fact false: such concepts actually embody the interests of particular groups of people, those who have power in a given social context. Thus, attempts to reinterpret liberal concepts so that they come to embody the interests of the subordinated and the oppressed (such as women, people of color, workers, and lesbians and gays), is one way of shifting their actual content.

Second, Brown and Butler's approach, in the end, maintains a problematic form of individualism similar to that of liberalism. Although they acknowledge the pervasiveness of power in society, they refrain from describing the systematic ways in which power works, claiming that such an analysis would "pin down" or "reify" current power relations.[28] Despite this position, a critique of oppression requires an examination of social relations of power. While any such account would be subject to change and revision, understanding who has power over whom is essential to theorizing about justice, rights, and equality. Without engaging in systemic analysis, Brown and Butler are left only with individuals, each striving for merely personal goals and attempting to preserve only his or her own individual interests.

Finally, Brown and Butler implicitly endorse the liberal commitment to some kind of neutrality between different conceptions of "the good." Because they dismiss all "moral" discourse, claim to refrain from "normative" analysis, and leave discussions about the good up to individuals and those who engage in "politics," they end up with a view that shares certain features with a libertarian version of liberalism. Moral norms, however, are already functioning in the world of politics and attempts to avoid discussion of them can easily result in the implicit endorsement of oppressive and unjust norms, ones that are often not made explicit but nonetheless continue to function and affect people.

• • •

Feminist philosophers and social theorists need to critically examine both the social context of male power and the relationship of this context to the development and application of liberal theories. In this volume, I use feminist theory to suggest that certain aspects of liberalism need to be reconceptualized if liberalism is to be useful for feminists and other advocates of justice. Social understandings of power, whether explicit or implicit, are always employed in the articulation and application of normative theories and ideals; feminists must acknowledge and understand the workings of such power structures in order to challenge and change them. By situating discussions of rights, equality, and freedom in the context of a critique of oppressive structures of power, feminists can avoid the problematic forms of abstraction and individualism that plague many liberal theories.

PART ONE

A Feminist Critique of Liberalism

1

Individualism, Oppression, and Liberal Rights Theory

In recent years, a number of feminist scholars and activists have examined the function of rights in liberal political theory and have raised questions about how rights should be defined and understood.[1] Some claim that although rights can be used in arguments for women's equality, they can also function to uphold the power of privileged groups. For instance, in *Pornography and Civil Rights*, Catharine MacKinnon and Andrea Dworkin point out that rather than winning equality for oppressed minorities, rights often function in ways that uphold current power structures: "Those who have power over others tend to call their power 'rights.' When those they dominate want equality, those in power say that important rights will be violated if society changes. . . . Law protects 'rights'—but mostly it protects the 'rights' of those who have power."[2] MacKinnon and Dworkin go on to describe the specific ways that powerful groups have used rights to maintain their positions of dominance in society. For instance, they note that white supremacists in the segregated South used rights such as the "right to association" to argue against demands for integration: "Forced to integrate . . . whites lost the power to exclude Blacks. This they experienced as having lost the 'right' to associate with whom they wanted, that is to say, exclusively with each other."[3] In other words, it is often the powerful groups in society who succeed in using rights to protect the advantages that they have.

What is to be made of the fact that liberal rights theory can function in support of hierarchies of power? Do cases in which this occurs merely involve improper *applications* of liberal rights theory, or is the liberal conception of rights flawed in a more fundamental way? If so, should feminists and other social justice activists avoid all reference to rights, or is there an alternative to the way that liberals define and use rights? Rather than undertaking a more general investigation and critique of liberal rights, in this chapter I have a somewhat narrower focus. I concentrate specifically on the works of Ronald Dworkin, Rae Langton, and Catharine MacKinnon to construct a feminist argument that liberal rights-based approaches to the law are problematic for three reasons: first, those taking a liberal approach typically define *rights* as rights against majoritarian decisions in a democratic society; second, they claim that rights are possessed by people as individuals; and third, they see a fundamental distinction between rights and goals. It is not the case that rights must be rejected entirely; rather, these shortcomings indicate certain problems with liberalism's assumptions and methodology. In the final section of this chapter I suggest an alternative, more radical, way of conceiving of rights. Linked to arguments for equality, and in particular to forms of equality needed to eradicate systems of oppression, rights can function in a more liberatory fashion.

Dworkin's Liberalism and the Importance of Rights

Ronald Dworkin is one prominent legal theorist and philosopher who articulates clearly and concisely both the main tenets of liberalism and the fundamental importance of rights.[4] According to Dworkin, the "fundamental distinction within political theory" is between arguments of principle, which are "arguments intended to establish an individual right," and arguments of policy, which are "arguments intended to establish a collective goal."[5] Although acknowledging that any complex political program is likely to make use of both rights and goals, Dworkin argues that if someone has a right to something, this can override the community's goal: "Rights are best understood as trumps over some background justification for political decisions that states a goal of the community as a whole."[6] In other words, if an individual has a right to something, this right is maintained even if it conflicts with the goals of the community or government. Thus, a government may not act simply according to whatever will produce overall benefits for the community; it must respect the rights of individuals as fundamental, and it must allow these rights to act as restricting conditions on the majoritarian goals of society.

According to Dworkin, the most basic right of individuals is the right to be treated with "equal concern and respect."[7] Because individuals are said to differ in their conception of the good life, treating each with "equal concern and respect" requires that the government remain "neutral" on these questions.[8] The best mechanisms for ensuring equal treatment are the two main institutions of our own society—democracy and the economic market (66). In themselves, however, these institutions are not sufficient to guarantee the rights of individuals to be treated equally. For instance, as Dworkin notes, in a democracy the government could legislate, according to the majority's preferences, to ban certain sexual practices or the expression of certain forms of unpopular political opinions. While this would be permitted according to democratic norms (because it is simply enacting the majority's preferences), it would nonetheless "invade" rather than enforce "the right of citizens to be treated as equals" (69–70). Such policies appeal to people's "external preferences," which are not strictly "personal" but actually "about what others shall do or have" (70). To prevent this sort of problem (which is likely to arise in a democracy), a society must somehow "determine those political decisions that are antecedently likely to reflect strong external preferences" and "remove those decisions from majoritarian political institutions altogether" (70). Thus, with this system of rights (specifically, the Bill of Rights) in place, the institutions of our society—democracy and the economic market—will be best able to protect the rights of individuals to act on their own preferences about "the good life" and to ensure that the government treats individuals with "equal concern and respect."

Given Dworkin's argument for the importance of rights, several questions arise: What exactly are the rights of individuals that must be recognized to ensure that they be entitled to pursue their conceptions of "the good" according to their "personal" preferences? Specifically what must a government do to ensure that it is treating its citizens with equal concern and respect and that it is not inadvertently endorsing people's "external" preferences? How can a government guarantee that it remain "neutral" on questions of "the good life"? Dworkin admits that his theory of liberalism is abstract; in fact, he suggests that it must be so if it is to remain "neutral" and not favor any particular preferences. His theory of rights "does not, of course, tell us exactly what rights men do have against the Government."[9] This is a question about which "reasonable men disagree."[10] Nor does his theory of rights detail exactly how the lines are to be drawn between "personal" and "external" preferences.[11] The answer to this question "will depend on general facts about the prejudices and other external preferences of the majority at any given time, and different liberals will disagree about what is needed at any particular time."[12] Dworkin does not consider this to be a problem, however; he trusts that the majority will answer these questions in ways that will recognize the minority's right to equality: "The institution of rights is therefore crucial, because it represents the majority's promise to the minorities that their dignity and equality will be respected. . . . The institution requires an act of faith on the part of the minorities, because the scope of their rights will be controversial whenever they are important, and because the officers of the majority will act on their own notions of what these rights really are."[13] In other words, he acknowledges that although there is a "promise" of equal concern and respect, minorities will have to rely on the good faith efforts of those in power to recognize their rights as individuals.

It seems then that one initial problem for Dworkin's theory may be the indeterminacy with which specific rights are delineated and justified according to his system. How could there ever be any assurance that the rights of all individuals would be protected equally? In theory, the rights that are encoded in the Bill of Rights are supposed to guarantee that this happens, but what is to stop the governmental and judicial officials from interpreting these unfairly, from importing their own "external" preferences into the law (with or without realizing that they are doing so)? In other words, what is to guarantee that the mechanism that is supposed to guarantee neutrality is not misused and applied in a nonneutral way, according to preferences of the majority or of the officials in power? Clearly, these are only some of the questions that arise when one considers the application of Dworkin's rights-based strategy.

In *Taking Rights Seriously* (1977) and *A Matter of Principle* (1985), Dworkin discusses some particular conclusions that he reaches through applying his rights-based arguments to political and legal issues. In *A Matter of Principle*, for instance, he argues that a rights-based approach to pornography yields the conclusion that restrictions on pornography are unjustified. He explains that even though "[t]he majority of people in both countries [Great Britain and the United States] would prefer (or so it seems) substantial censorship," this would violate the right to "moral independence" (which is rooted in the right to equal treatment) of individuals.[14] Thus, because individual rights trump the majoritarian goals of the community, Dworkin's rights-based strategy prohibits banning or restricting pornography.

Feminists can argue against Dworkin's defense of the "right to pornography" in different ways. In the following section, I focus on MacKinnon's critique of this sort of argument; Rae Langton suggests another response: one could disagree with Dworkin's conclusion about the question of pornography yet maintain that the problem lies not in his theory of liberalism but instead in the particular way that he applies this theory in the case of pornography. In her essay "Whose Right? Ronald Dworkin, Women, and Pornographers," Langton brilliantly illustrates that Dworkin's conclusion about pornography is *not* the only one that follows from his approach. She demonstrates how it is possible to employ a different definition of "external preferences" (one he uses elsewhere), along with some empirical facts that Dworkin does not consider, to reach the opposite conclusion about pornography. In discussing the *Sweatt* decision, as Langton notes, Dworkin explains that in any community where there is a strong prejudice against a particular minority, "the personal preferences upon which a utilitarian argument must fix will be saturated with that prejudice," and this will make it difficult, if not impossible, to reliably determine whether these preferences are really "personal" or whether they are actually "external" preferences. Thus, in such cases, "no utilitarian argument purporting to justify a disadvantage to that minority can be fair." For such a disadvantage to be fair, one would have to prove that the same disadvantage would have been justified in the absence of the prejudice; in cases where "the prejudice is widespread and pervasive, as in fact it is in the case of blacks, that can never be shown."[15]

Employing this expanded (but nonetheless "Dworkinian") definition of external preferences, along with some additional background information that Dworkin seems not to consider, Langton demonstrates that Dworkin's own rights-based approach can lead to the conclusion that pornography *should* be restricted. It is not necessary, she claims, to provide conclusive evidence that pornography causes violence, but rather simply that it conflicts with women's right to "equal concern and respect." Langton constructs her argument to parallel Dworkin's: she sets up a utilitarian argument and then shows how it can be "trumped" by the rights claims of individuals whose right to equality it would otherwise threaten. Although Langton's argument has the same basic structure as Dworkin's, she begins with the utilitarian argument *in favor of permitting* pornography (the argument that "most people would prefer that pornography be permitted, and so our policy should be to permit pornography"), and the rights to which she refers are the rights of women to be treated with equal concern and respect.[16] According to Langton, Dworkin fails to apply his own method properly in part because he starts with the wrong utilitarian argument and in part because he does not take into account the empirical evidence of how pornography affects women's right to equality.

Thus, on one reading of Langton's work, Dworkin's major error is that he does not sufficiently evaluate the context in which individuals' rights are situated. Had he paid more attention to the fact of women's inequality and understood individuals' "preferences for pornography" in this context, he would have come to very different conclusions.[17] In fact, at the end of her essay, Langton suggests that it would be possible to apply the same Dworkinian strategy that she employs here to questions that arise concerning other civil liberties that liberals typically defend; for instance, because racist hate speech violates the right that members of certain racial minorities have to "equal concern and respect," an effort to limit or ban it could be supported by this approach. In other words, it seems that one can begin with a liberal rights approach and arrive at nonliberal, "radical" conclusions. Because the liberal rights approach does not specify details such as *whose* rights are to be made central to the argument and *which* utilitarian argument is most plausible (nor does it suggest *what* is necessary for individuals to be treated with "equal concern and respect" in particular contexts), it can lead to different conclusions depending on the context in which it is employed.

Perhaps the "context" in which debates about pornography occur has changed sufficiently in recent years to require Dworkin to take feminist concerns into account when discussing pornography (which he does not even attempt to do in his 1981 piece, "Do We Have a Right to Pornography?"). Unfortunately, despite increased public awareness of the systematic sexual abuse of women, and despite his having had ample opportunity to consider pornography in the context of questions about women's oppression, Dworkin's analysis does not seem to be evolving. In a 1993 review of MacKinnon's *Only Words*, Dworkin is very critical of MacKinnon's advocacy of a law that would empower women who claim that they were abused sexually as a result of the making or use of pornography to bring civil suits against pornographers. Although presumably aware of the evidence of the widespread sexual abuse of women (he does not *deny* that many women are abused and suffer from sexual harassment, assault, and rape), Dworkin has not altered his views on pornography. He continues to view pornography as if it were the mere "expression of the *idea* feminists most loathe"; moreover, he specifically rejects several of MacKinnon's main arguments, for instance, her claim that pornography silences women.[18] He maintains that while the First Amendment can protect freedom of speech, it cannot offer any positive guarantees about the conditions under which one makes use of this right. MacKinnon's claim that it is women, not pornographers, who are in need of freedom of speech is "premised on an unacceptable proposition: that the right to free speech includes a right to circumstances that encourage one to speak, and a right that others grasp and respect what one means to say. These are obviously not rights that any society can recognize or enforce."[19] Furthermore, Dworkin defends the right of pornographers to publish pornography by suggesting that pornographers are merely expressing their "hostile or uncongenial tastes" and by claiming that they should be free to express or indulge these tastes. Referring specifically to the tastes and views of sexists and racists, he explains, "In a genuinely egalitarian society, however, those views cannot be locked out, in advance, by criminal or civil law: they must instead be discredited by the disgust, outrage, and ridicule of other people."[20] In other words, Dworkin claims that the state must be neutral about the different "tastes" and "preferences" that its citizens express and that it must therefore recognize people's right to pursue these preferences.

Thus, in contradiction to Langton's suggestion, it seems that Dworkin's reasons for rejecting restrictions on pornography might not be limited to the fact that he does not consider the evidence of women's subordination. Rather, certain characteristics of liberal thought seem to lend themselves to rejecting the arguments made by more radical theorists, such as MacKinnon. In the remaining part of this chapter, I draw on MacKinnon's work to analyze critically some of the basic tenets of Dworkin's theory and to show why liberal, rights-based approaches tend to lead to conclusions that support the status quo.

Critique of Liberal Rights-Based Approaches

Rights as "Rights Against the Majority"

In her many feminist writings, Catharine MacKinnon develops a critique of liberalism that calls into question Dworkin's claim that it is primarily the government (which expresses the majority's will in a democracy) against which people can be said to have rights.[21] Her work illuminates the ways that other structures of social power operate to oppress and exploit people. The structure of male dominance, for instance, while often working in conjunction with state power, is not entirely dependent on or derivative of it, in that "men's forms of dominance over women have been accomplished socially as well as economically, prior to the operation of law, without express state acts, often in intimate contexts, as everyday life."[22] Because the government is not the sole source of power in a society, it is not the only power that is capable of depriving people of their rights. (To assume that it is only the government that can deprive one of power, suggests MacKinnon, is to assume the position of one who is already socially privileged in every other way.) Given that a nongovernmental hierarchy such as gender involves relations of power, it seems that individuals should also be entitled to rights against systematic sexist harms, whether or not the government explicitly instigates these harms.

While MacKinnon focuses primarily on the ways that liberal conceptions of rights and equality do not adequately address issues of gender injustice, similar arguments can and have been made about race and class and about various combinations of gender, race, and class oppression. Because liberal theory tends to focus on the ways that the government can infringe on people's rights through its explicit policies and procedures, liberal legal theory often leaves relations of class, race, and gender hierarchy unaddressed, especially when these three hierarchies are intertwined in complex ways. A number of feminists of color argue that when the oppression that women undergo is not only based on gender but also on race, class, or both, the law has an even harder time acknowledging and addressing the problem. For instance, because the law typically recognizes discrimination based on deviance from a standard, the claims of white women have been taken as definitive of discrimination based on sex, and the claims of men of color have been taken as definitive of discrimination based on race.[23] According to liberal legal theory, white women and Black men are the prime candidates to represent "sexual" and "racial" discrimination because persons in these categories are said to differ from the white male standard in only one way. The problem with this is that under conditions of racial and gender hierarchy, these phenomena are intertwined and their effects are compounded. For instance, as Helen Zia notes, racist hate crimes committed against women of color are often also sexual crimes, and yet they tend to be prosecuted as either one or the other and not both—if they are prosecuted at all.[24] Describing this phenomenon, Zia details a number of cases in which white men have targeted Asian women for brutal acts of sexual violence. None of the cases that she describes was prosecuted as a racially motivated hate crime, even though the victims were targeted specifically because they were Asian. In these cases, the presence of gender as an element in the crimes was seen as somehow negating the possibility that the incidents were also racist.

A similar problem can be seen in the portrayal of people of color in pornography. If pornography is understood as reinforcing relations of power at all, it is typically thought to reinforce gender hierarchy. Nonetheless, studies have shown that a great deal of pornography that uses women and men of color depicts them in ways that reinforce racial and ethnic stereotypes. MacKinnon offers several examples of how pornography can sexualize racial hatred or turn racial stereotypes into sexual fetishes: "Asian women are presented so passive they cannot be said to be alive, bound so they are not recognizably human, hanging from trees and light fixtures and clothes hooks in closets. Black women are presented as animalistic bitches, bruised and bleeding, struggling against their bonds. Jewish women orgasm in reenactments of actual death camp tortures."[25] Thus, for women of color, pornography can simultaneously be a vehicle of both racial and gender oppression. Unfortunately, the rights that people are granted formally under liberalism do not provide much in the way of protection from these types of oppression.

In response, a liberal might counter that because there are laws—both criminal and civil—preventing harms perpetrated by the government or by individuals, protection already exists against the systemic harms of racism, sexism, and other forms of oppression. Whether an individual, group, or government commits these harms, laws already exist to address them. Focusing on civil law, and on constitutional law in particular, MacKinnon notes that the law provides a formal guarantee to respect and protect the rights of individuals to be treated "equally." Nonetheless, the way that liberal theorists interpret and employ these rights often renders them ineffective in bringing justice to people whose oppression is constituted through the operation of racial, sexual, and economic power structures. Without these power structures being addressed and altered, the formal granting of the rights to free speech, privacy, freedom, and equality are not going to succeed in bringing about justice and equality for women, or for other members of oppressed groups. Although recent laws that recognize sexual harassment as a problem of sex equality are one exception to this, for the most part the law does not acknowledge explicitly the oppression of women and attempt to remedy it. Rather, the rights of women and members of other oppressed groups are recognized to the extent that the persons in these positions resemble white, upper-middle-class men. Offering several examples of this, MacKinnon explains, "Rape law assumes that consent to sex is as real for women as it is for men. Privacy law assumes that women in private have the same privacy men do. Obscenity law assumes that women have the access to speech men have. Equality law assumes that women are already socially equal to men." [26] In other words, mainstream equality law seems to require women already to have achieved social equality before recognizing their claims of inequality.

Note that I am not suggesting that these structures of power are wholly independent of the state or that they will not change unless structures outside the realm of the state change first. State power works in conjunction with specific hierarchies, in both overt and covert ways. Thus, rather than interpreting liberal rights and freedoms as simply rights against government intervention, one should understand these also as rights against various forms of oppression and against agents of oppressive systems of power (including individuals and groups). Rights must be interpreted in such a way that they can begin to alter structures of oppression and thereby make it possible for people to exercise the formal rights that the Constitution legally grants them.

Furthermore, the liberal understanding of rights as claims *against the government* is problematic because it focuses too narrowly on "negative," as opposed to "positive," liberty. In this liberal view, rights are violated only when the state acts to deprive a specific individual of his or her rights. Not only does this imply that there are no other, nongovernmental, structures of power (against which individuals should also be entitled to rights); it also suggests that the state need not do anything actively to ensure that people have rights. By declaring that individuals *have* rights *against* the government, liberals suggest that everyone already enjoys a basic equality before the government and before the law. One specific manifestation that this takes involves the right to free speech. As MacKinnon explains, "The most basic assumption underlying First Amendment adjudication is that, socially, speech is free. The First Amendment says, 'Congress shall not abridge *the freedom of speech.*' Free speech exists. The problem for government is to avoid constraining that which, if unconstrained by government, *is* free. This tends to presuppose that whole segments of the population are not systematically silenced *socially*, prior to government action." [27] In other words, by interpreting the First Amendment in this way, the liberal approach to the law presupposes that everyone already has basically equal access to speech. Challenging this assumption, MacKinnon argues that given the pervasiveness of gender inequality, as well as the additional hierarchies of race and class (which further disadvantage many women as well as some men), it is not the case that all individuals really have "freedom of speech." For groups that are excluded from access to the power that would otherwise enable them to enjoy this right, freedom of speech is not really about "the avoidance of state intervention as such" but is instead a matter of "finding an affirmative means to get access to speech for those to whom it has been denied."[28] However, according to the liberal "constitutional invocation of the superiority of 'negative freedom'—staying out, letting be—over positive legal affirmations," this is precisely what socially subordinated groups are not allowed.[29] Without the social conditions and institutional power arrangements needed to exercise rights, oppressed people are not able to use their rights in the same way that powerful groups do.

Moreover, the harm from which oppressed groups suffer (as a result of this "negative" formulation of rights) is not limited to their frequently being unable to exercise their rights in any meaningful way. In an unequal society, the power that one group enjoys is often power over another group; as a result, the second group may suffer whenever the first group exercises its rights. Thus, the assertion of negative rights by members of the powerful group may further solidify the inequality: "If one group is socially granted the positive freedom to do whatever it wants to another group, to determine that the second group will be and do this rather than that, no amount of negative freedom legally guaranteed to the second group will make it the equal of the first. For women, this has meant that civil society, the domain in which women are distinctively subordinated and deprived of power, has been placed beyond reach of legal guarantees."[30] By granting negative rights to the dominant group—men, in this case—and depriving the subordinated group of access to any rights that would bring about change, the law can function to cement inequality. Offering an example of the way this works, MacKinnon discusses the law of privacy. Because this law, formulated as a negative right, "restricts intrusions into intimacy," it "bars change in control over that intimacy." In this way, the right to privacy works to uphold the "existing distribution of power and resources within the private sphere . . . the legal concept of privacy can and has shielded the place of battery, marital rape, and women's exploited labor."[31] Thus the laws and rights of a "negative" state not only prevent women—and other oppressed groups—from achieving the "positive" freedom necessary to exercise their rights; they may also reinforce the rights of the powerful to continue to exploit and oppress.

Interestingly, although MacKinnon faults liberal theorists for focusing on negative (as opposed to positive) rights, it is not clear that she really finds this distinction useful. In fact, her work seems to call into question the idea that a person could have a "negative" right. How is it that someone could have a right that others (including the government) not interfere with him or her—the right simply to be "left alone"? Such a right does not make sense if one understands individuals as always embedded in social structures and networks of power. Thus, when the government acts as if it is leaving a person "alone" to do as he or she pleases, it is really merely surrendering its authority to other institutional arrangements of power. In other words, one is in a sense never really left alone, because social and political institutions always limit and shape an individual's activities and possibilities.

In response to the charge that liberal rights are conceived primarily as negative rights against the government and not against other powerful institutions, liberals might contend that I fail to distinguish the position of contemporary liberals from that of classical liberals. While Dworkin is a "liberal" in terms of the contemporary liberal/conservative split, he is at least less explicitly wedded to the "negative freedom" conception of liberty and rights than are classical liberals such as Robert Nozick. Nonetheless, contemporary liberal political theorists, including Dworkin, still place far too much emphasis on negative liberty and far too little emphasis on the social conditions that are necessary to make use of it. For instance, as I noted earlier, Dworkin maintains that the right to free speech does not include the "right to circumstances that encourage one to speak" or "a right that others grasp and respect what one means to say."[32] Dworkin seems to think that for MacKinnon the law can force people to listen to, respect, or understand one another, and he ridicules her for holding this position. This misrepresents her; she never claims that people should be legally *forced* to respond in this way. Nevertheless, both MacKinnon and Dworkin clearly hold that people have a right to "equal treatment." Dworkin explicitly states that everyone has not only a right to "equal treatment"—that is, the right to an equal distribution of some opportunity, resource, or burden—but also a right to "treatment as an equal." It is this latter right that Dworkin considers "fundamental"; it is supposed to guarantee that each individual "be treated with the same respect and concern as anyone else."[33] Unfortunately, when Dworkin articulates specifically what the government must do to ensure that everyone has the right to "equal concern and respect," he too often assumes that the state need not do much of anything to bring these conditions about for those who suffer from gender, race, and class hierarchies. To the extent that Dworkin takes these conditions for granted and assumes them to be beyond the realm of government responsibility, his position bears an unfortunate similarity to that of classical libertarian liberalism. By assuming that a strategy of official "neutrality" will best respect the rights of individuals to free speech and privacy, for instance, Dworkin fails to acknowledge the ways that the state is (and historically has been) complicit in various forms of oppression, and he fails to note the crucial role that positive rights and freedoms need to play in securing these opportunities for all.

Rights as "Individual Rights"

Not only is the "negative" construction of liberal rights an unsatisfactory construct; the liberal conception of rights as properly belonging only to individuals is questionable also. According to Dworkin, people are entitled to their rights not because of their membership in this or that group, but because of their status as "individuals."[34] Examining this claim through a feminist lens, however, reveals a problem: because liberal theory grants rights to individuals *as individuals*, it primarily recognizes violations of rights that occur one at a time, to individuals *as individuals*. MacKinnon explains that liberal theory has difficulty identifying the sexist harm of pornography because its conception of injury is "individuated, atomistic, linear, exclusive, isolated, narrowly tortlike [and] positivistic" and that "discrimination does not work like this."[35] While pornography does harm individual women, it does not always operate on them one at a time; rather, it harms them *as women*, that is, as members of that group. In part, this occurs because pornography "purports to define what a woman is," which it does "on a group basis, including when it raises individual qualities to sexual stereotypes."[36] By defining women in this way, pornography encourages male sexual violence and contributes to an atmosphere in which women's consent is inferred from their silence. In other words, liberalism's conception of harm focuses on the individual as an isolated person and thereby fails to see that individual, personal events can manifest and replicate societal structures of inequality.

According to a nonliberal, group-based conception of harm, the harms women suffer are not reducible to the sum of the harms each individual woman suffers; to understand the harm of particular incidents of sexist oppression, something must be known about the conditions of women's lives under male dominance. Until such conditions have been identified and analyzed, one cannot understand the full meaning of the harm that individual women suffer from domestic violence, sexual harassment, pornography, rape, or other abuses. In other words, the context of male dominance is part of what constitutes the meaning of particular incidents of sexist harm. Without accounting for this context from the perspective of women who are affected by sexism, legal and political theorists tend to assume that all individuals enjoy the same basic circumstances—roughly those of white, upper-middle-class men. Of course, once it has been pointed out (for instance, by feminists, antiracist activists, or workers struggling for justice) that the life circumstances of oppressed individuals differ from the conditions enjoyed by members of the dominant class, liberal theorists are eventually able to incorporate these criticisms into their theories. In other words, while liberalism can accommodate more radical critiques after these alternative descriptions of society have been articulated and accepted, liberalism is not itself sufficient for generating such critiques. It typically places too much emphasis on the individual and on the personal circumstances of the individual; thus, liberals such as Dworkin initially tend to overlook the significance of the social circumstances in which individuals are constituted.

Furthermore, the fact that group-based injuries tend to coincide with larger structures of social, political, and economic power creates additional problems for the liberal view of harm. Because racism and sexism are embedded in society, the harm of racist and sexist practices often cannot be isolated easily from the social organization of society and, as a result, may not even be recognizable as harm. MacKinnon elucidates how the liberal conception of harm (based on a model of "individuals" whose rights can be violated) may make the harm of pornography impossible to detect: "If pornography is systemic, it may not be isolable from the system in which it exists. This does not mean that no harm exists. It does mean that because the harm is so pervasive, it cannot be sufficiently isolated to be perceived as existing according to this model of causality."[37] Dworkin's discussion of pornography exemplifies this problem with the liberal conception of harm. When he attempts to defend his position against the feminist claim that pornography harms women's "equality," he takes issue with the notion that pornography could be "an important cause or vehicle" of the construction of women's identity, responding, "That seems strikingly implausible."[38] As evidence of this implausibility, he offers the following comparison: "It seems unlikely that it [pornography] has remotely the influence over how women's sexuality or character or talents are conceived by men, and indeed by women, that commercial advertising and soap operas have."[39] As I argued earlier, however, the fact that other pervasive social practices and institutions reinforce the harm of pornography does not mean that pornography "causes" no harm. Rather, it is a part of the sexist structures that harm women's right to equality; the fact that its harm cannot be isolated should not lead one to conclude that it causes no harm, but rather that the harm that it causes is pervasive and systemic.

Of course, one could question why MacKinnon objects so strongly to pornography if it is not the only social practice that harms women. For instance, if soap operas and commercial advertising also harm women's equality, why does MacKinnon not call for restricting them, too? First, it seems unlikely that MacKinnon would agree with Dworkin's simple assertion that pornography has comparatively little influence on women's equality. Although commercial advertising and soap operas promote sexist norms for women and define and limit the mental, emotional, and physical qualities that are considered attractive in women, these ads and programs do not deal with sexual practices as explicitly as pornography does. Given the significant role that sexuality plays in women's subordination, MacKinnon would argue that an industry that explicitly perpetuates and constructs sexual norms is harmful in a way that other industries and institutions are not.[40]

Second, for MacKinnon, the harm of pornography is not limited to its effects on "how women's sexuality or character or talents are conceived." Rather than merely arguing against this sort of abstraction, MacKinnon is also condemning the actual physical and sexual abuse that arises out of the production and use of pornography. For MacKinnon and other feminist antipornography activists, the industry of pornography harms women's equality not only because it affects the social perception of what is "sexual" but also because it has actual consequences for the lives of many women who are used in its making and who are abused as a consequence of its consumption. MacKinnon details numerous examples of women being targeted for rape and other sexual abuse and torture as a result of the consumption of pornography, and she notes that "[l]aboratory experiments showed that pornography that portrays sexual aggression as pleasurable for the victim—as so much pornography does—increases the acceptance of the use of coercion in sexual relations."[41] Thus, pornography helps create a context in which sexual abuse is more likely to occur, even if it does not directly lead men to go out and commit rape. MacKinnon also objects to the violent and coercive conditions that exist within the industry. She argues that pornography is not just an "idea," because actual women must be used to produce it:

[I]t should be observed that it is the pornography industry, not the ideas in the materials, that forces, threatens, blackmails, pressures, tricks, and cajoles women into sex for pictures. In pornography, women are gang raped so they can be filmed. They are not gang raped by the idea of a gang rape. It is for pornography, and not by the ideas in it, that women are hurt and penetrated, tied and gagged, undressed and genitally spread and sprayed with lacquer and water so pictures can be made. . . . It is unnecessary to do any of these things to express, as ideas, the ideas pornography expresses.[42]

Thus, MacKinnon seems to suggest that women are hurt more seriously and more directly in the production and use of pornography than they are as a result of commercial advertisements and soap operas.

Responding to this point about actual harm, a liberal might object that MacKinnon's approach is unnecessary and that her condemnation of the industry of pornography is misplaced: why not simply prosecute specific abuses as they occur, rather than condemn pornography as inherently abusive? In other words, why not simply use existing laws to prosecute those who rape, coerce, and abuse the women who are used in the making of pornography? The problem with this approach is that it is unlikely to succeed. On MacKinnon's analysis, one of the main functions of pornography is to portray women as enjoying their own violation and as desiring their own subjection to men's sexual demands. This makes it extremely difficult for the women who work in pornography to prove that they were not simply consenting to "rough sex," since it is their job to appear as if they really *do* enjoy similar acts when they are being filmed.

Another liberal response might be to claim that no one should be involved in pornography unless she is a willing participant who has made a rational career decision. This position, however, simply assumes an acontextual individualism that fails to recognize the impact of the social, political, and economic conditions of male dominance. It is these conditions that lead women to be coerced into accepting jobs in the sex industry (as well as other jobs in which they are subjected to exploitation, sexual harassment, and abuse), even though this is not necessarily what these women would choose to do under conditions of freedom and equality. The coercion that leads women to these jobs may be more or less explicit, but it is seen most clearly when one takes a "group-based" approach to harm. A similar point can be made about prostitution. Women who "choose" to work as models in the pornography industry, or as prostitutes, do not make these choices in a vacuum. The fact that some women are used to make pornography affects the conditions of life—and the options available—for *all* women. Without pornography, this path would not exist for women. But because it does, women who find themselves in dire poverty can always "choose" to work in the sex industry. The fact that this same option does not exist for men (it is at least not nearly as widespread, nor is it really the "same" option), makes the circumstances of women, as a group, very different from those of men. However, if one assumes that individuals are only harmed as individuals, it is much more difficult to understand the ways in which the conditions of one's life *as a woman* affect the decisions and choices available to her.

Critique of "Rights" Versus "Goals"

Not only does Dworkin's liberal rights theory focus insufficient attention on social groups and on the structures of power that exist between these groups; his theory also promotes a problematic dichotomy between "rights" and "goals." In describing Dworkin's theory of liberalism, I noted that he divides political arguments into two fundamentally different kinds—those intended to establish a collective goal, defined as a goal of the "community as a whole," and those intended to establish an individual right. On the one hand, Dworkin would surely acknowledge that a society can change and come to recognize certain rights that it formerly did not acknowledge. Nonetheless, his manner of distinguishing rights from goals suggests that rights are that which people already have; they are not goals that a society must attempt to achieve by developing institutions and practices that embody them. Thus, when he discusses the right to "equal concern and respect," he cannot suggest that it is a goal that all *should* have this right— nor even that the state must aim to create a situation in which each individual can actually enjoy this right. Rather, he must be describing a right that all individuals already possess.

In other words, one serious problem with Dworkin's way of separating rights from goals is that "equality" ends up becoming a right, the "right to equal treatment," rather than also being considered a goal. On this view, the liberal state attempts to protect and maintain equality by adopting procedures that treat the expressed preferences of individuals with "official neutrality." Such procedures, however, maintain the status quo, and social power structures must be changed if people's right to equality is to be achieved. If the state wants to promote this right for all its citizens, it must concern itself specifically with the goal of rectifying current (and pervasive) inequalities. In the absence of such concern, current hierarchies are reinforced and perpetuated. As MacKinnon and Andrea Dworkin explain, "We need to establish a legal imperative toward equality. Without equality as a fundamental value, 'rights' is a euphemism for 'power,' and legally protected dominance will continue to preclude any real equality."[43] In other words, the state must actively attempt to achieve equality and not simply presuppose its existence. Achieving equality must be of constant concern as the state works to define and enforce the other rights of its citizens.[44] Thus, the *goal* of equality is not only significant in and of itself, but is also relevant to the way in which other rights are socially defined, granted, and enforced.

In suggesting that equal concern and respect be considered a goal, I am not proposing that it be considered a goal *instead of* a right. Rather, I am addressing the problem of Dworkin's distinguishing rights from goals as if they were mutually exclusive. Viewing rights also *as goals* (and not in opposition to them), one faces the need to strive to achieve the conditions in which all people can exercise rights—conditions under which rights are possessed in more than a merely formal sense. Furthermore, I do not mean to suggest that the Constitution should not protect the goal of equality or that equality should be left up to the whims of whoever is currently in power. Although this would be the consequence of arguing that equality is a goal instead of a right, this is not my claim.

Moreover, my critique of Dworkin—that he does *not* consider rights to be goals, that he regards rights and goals as entirely separate—should not be understood as a claim that he *actually* advocates rights that really do not involve any goals at all. On the contrary: it is not the case that liberal rights are too abstract and that they need to be made more concrete by tying them to actual goals. Rather, liberal rights already advocate particular goals without claiming to be advocating anything in particular. One goal that they advocate implicitly, at least according to MacKinnon, is the maintenance of current hierarchies of social power.

Situating Rights in the Context of Inequality

To understand how equality might be incorporated into the definition of certain specific rights, consider the debate over the right to free speech and its relation to pornography. On the one hand, because liberals such as

Dworkin assume that equality involves neutral treatment of expressed preferences, they do not necessarily view the facts of women's current inequality (evidenced by widespread sexual abuse and exploitation) as relevant to questions of free speech. On the other hand, MacKinnon views equality as a goal that society must aim to achieve; it is not merely a matter of treating people's preferences "neutrally." Thus, given the state's responsibility for creating equality (where everyone would be treated with equal concern and respect), it must actively work to ensure that the rights that people are granted do not further entrench already existing inequalities. To pursue equality, the law must view many different issues and rights in an equality context; discussions of the general rights to free speech and privacy, as well as discourse about more specific issues such as abortion, sexual harassment, and pornography, must all take place in the context of questions about equality and what is needed to achieve it. Unfortunately, these issues—and many others that concern equality—are often treated in a legal rubric that attempts to be neutral and that assumes an already existing basic equality. For instance, MacKinnon notes that questions about equality have rarely been considered in cases involving campus harassment policies and their relation to free speech: "[T]he virtual absence of discussion of equality in recent litigation over discrimination policies that prohibit group-based harassment and bigotry on campuses was astounding. . . . In challenges to these regulations under the First Amendment, which have been successful so far, the statutory equality interest is barely mentioned."[45] Unless rights are viewed in an equality context, it can too easily be assumed that all individuals have equal access to these rights when they do not; such assumptions work against the equality interests of socially disadvantaged persons.

Moreover, it is this dismissal of concern for equality—and this misunderstanding of *equality* to mean mere *neutrality* among expressed preferences—that is largely responsible for the liberal assumption that rights are separate from goals, that individuals already possess them and they need only be preserved and protected. Rather than understanding rights in this way, MacKinnon holds a view of rights that is much more in line with the way that activists of the civil rights movement conceptualized civil rights. According to this view, rights are not abstract and general, but are tied closely to political struggle and to the undoing of social inequality. In a discussion of civil rights, MacKinnon and Andrea Dworkin note: "Ever since Black people demanded legal change as one means to social change, civil rights has stood for the principle that systematic social inequality—the legal and social institutionalization of group-based power and powerlessness—should and would be undone by law."[46] In other words, the notion of "civil rights" that came out of the civil rights movement embodies a view of change; rights are that which need to be achieved through altering the social structures of inequality. In *Pornography and Civil Rights*, MacKinnon and Andrea Dworkin argue that because pornography is "a practice of civil inequality on the basis of gender," it is a violation of women's "civil rights."[47] However, the right to be free from pornography (and from a pornographic world) is clearly not one that women currently enjoy. Nor is this right considered inherent in the abstract conception of rights to which all individuals are said to be entitled in our liberal society. In contrast, the right to be free from pornography has arisen out of political struggle; it has been articulated and put forth as the result of a specific analysis of the social structures of power, and it is linked inextricably to a desire to change those structures, a desire to achieve equality. In this way, the very meaning of "rights" is expanded to include the interests and perspectives of those groups who were formerly denied them.[48] In other words, for rights to be meaningful, and not empty abstractions that support the status quo, they must be linked both to an analysis of the social structure and to some sort of goal with regard to changing it.

Conclusion

In this chapter, I have criticized adherents of liberal rights theory—and Dworkin in particular—for conceiving of rights as individual rights against the government (and not instead as rights that members of oppressed groups hold against whomever oppresses them), and I have argued against the liberal separation of rights from goals. Given these problems, Langton's suggestion that it is easy to make Dworkin's liberal theory yield nonliberal conclusions seems incorrect; liberalism is plagued with problems more serious than the mere fact that it does not take certain empirical information into account and that it begins with the wrong utilitarian argument.[49] Nonetheless, does identifying these more fundamental problems in liberal theory require that one reject the notion of rights?

Clearly, it would be easy to interpret my objections to liberal rights theory as a simple rejection of certain rights, among them the right to privacy or the right to free speech, if not all rights in general. In his review of *Only Words*, Dworkin seems to view MacKinnon as rejecting the right to free speech: "[MacKinnon] and her followers regard freedom of speech and thought as an elitist, inegalitarian ideal that has been of almost no value to women, blacks, and others without power; they say America would be better off if it demoted that ideal as many other nations have."[50] Dworkin also suggests that MacKinnon sees equality and liberty as opposed to each other, that she sees them as "competing constitutional value[s]."[51] On the one hand, Dworkin might be right: MacKinnon seems to dismiss many of the rights that are currently discussed in liberal political debates. She argues that these rights function to uphold the status quo, to obscure relations of power, and to prevent equality from being achieved. What I have suggested, however, is that her arguments do not entail a rejection of rights per se. Although she writes harshly about rights, MacKinnon is criticizing the way that these rights have been formulated—and the way that they currently function—outside a critical analysis of society's structures of power and apart from questions of equality. Only by critiquing social hierarchies and questioning structures of power (in ways that go beyond the simplistic individual/government dichotomy) can one develop a new conception of rights that would not suffer from the problems of liberalism.

The criticisms of liberal rights theory that I have articulated do point to the need for an alternative conception of rights. Although I have not developed this alternative conception, I have suggested that it would specify concretely the needs and interests of groups of oppressed people. Because liberals define rights abstractly (and because they tend to focus on individual, negative rights), they often take for granted social relations of power. As a result, the rights of people of color, women, working-class people, and other members of oppressed groups tend to be overlooked. The allegedly abstract way that liberal theory formulates and describes the rights to which individuals are said to be entitled often conceals the more concrete content that these rights actually embody in our society. In this way, the rights that upper-middle-class white men value and already enjoy are protected under the guise of treating individual preferences *neutrally* and protecting *abstract* rights. To change a system in which certain groups of people already have powers and freedoms that are—at least in practice—unavailable to others, an alternative theory of rights would have to include an analysis of who has power over whom, and it would have to concern itself with attempting to remedy these inequalities through changing society's institutions, practices, and structures of power.

2

Abstract Ideals and Social Inequality:
Dworkin's Equality of Resources

Although political philosophers, feminists, and ethical theorists often employ abstract ideals to argue for social change, these ideals can also work to support and perpetuate hierarchical relations of social, political, and economic power. In the previous chapter, I demonstrated how liberal rights theory can function in support of such hierarchies and argued that this problem relates to a number of assumptions about individuals that are often embedded in liberal theory. In Chapters 2 and 3, I consider the issue of abstraction in liberal theory by focusing particular attention on the abstract ideals put forth by Ronald Dworkin (in Chapter 2) and John Rawls (in Chapter 3). Although there are certainly differences between their theories, both Rawls and Dworkin construct abstract scenarios to illustrate their conceptions of justice and equality. As we shall see, examining an ideal scenario central to the work of each reveals that both theorists import problematic assumptions into their allegedly abstract ideals and that they avoid important questions about the generation of social power structures, focusing instead on remedying the resulting distribution of goods. In contrast, feminists (and others who are concerned with social justice) must also examine the ways that structural hierarchies are established and perpetuated. In overlooking the significance of these structures, liberal theorists may unwittingly import them into their theorizing and fail to achieve the abstraction for which they aim.

In this chapter, I critically examine Dworkin's theory of distributional equality, which he calls "equality of resources," and the idealized situation that he constructs to explain it. One important preliminary question raised by Dworkin's work, and by other abstract political theories, is that of how such an ideal should be interpreted and applied in the context of current social structures. Although Dworkin touches upon this question, the links between the abstract conditions of the ideal and the concrete realities of our own society are not entirely clear. In fact, some, including Will Kymlicka, have argued that the reforms that follow from Dworkin's theory are more radical than the ones that he himself articulates: "Dworkin often writes as if the most obvious or likely result of implementing his conception of justice would be to increase the level of transfer payments between occupants of existing social roles. . . . But his theory entails a more radical reform— namely, a change in the way existing roles are defined."[1] Despite the indeterminacy of Dworkin's theory, however, there are general features of his liberalism, as well as specific features of his theory of distributional equality, that lead him *not* to endorse more radical reforms, but instead to generally support the institutions of the status quo. Furthermore, these general features give rise to problems *within* Dworkin's ideal prior to the additional problems of application.

After summarizing the main points of Dworkin's theory, I articulate three specific criticisms. First, in putting forth his theory, Dworkin relies on background assumptions—about matters such as the economy, social circumstances, and political relations—that are neither made explicit nor given justification by his theory. Specifically, the hypothetical situation he constructs requires that individuals possess knowledge that would be unavailable to them under the conditions he describes. While this is an objection to his particular ideal, and not to liberal theory generally, it does suggest that it is extremely difficult to construct abstract ideals without embedding assumptions that are characteristic of our own society and that are not necessarily ideal. Second, Dworkin assumes that the actual inequalities in our society result mainly from two types of factors, lack of resources and lack of "natural endowment." Thus, he considers inequality to be primarily a question of one's personal circumstances, not a matter of larger systems of oppression, and he underestimates the role of hierarchical systems of power (such as race, class, and gender) in reinforcing and perpetuating inequalities. Third, Dworkin fails to address important questions about the motivation behind his ideal, the desire to come up with a theory that is sensitive to individual ambition but insensitive to endowment or circumstance. While this may be an appealing goal, any program or procedure used to pursue it would work only if it were possible to isolate one's ambitions from one's circumstances. Rather than discussing and questioning how this distinction is made, Dworkin proposes a theory that takes the distinction for granted. In other words, his theory seems simply to accept as given whatever ambitions, preferences, and personalities individuals currently happen to have, without questioning to what extent these were formed in response to specific circumstances. As a result of his failure to make this important distinction, Dworkin's theory tends to function ideologically, thereby lending support to hierarchical structures of power rather than challenging them.

Dworkin's "Equality of Resources"

In explaining "equality of resources," Dworkin's central concern is to articulate an ideal of distributional equality that is both "ambition sensitive" and "endowment insensitive," and he claims that this distinguishes his own theory from others that are welfare based as well as from theories that hold that there must be an absolute equality at all points in time.[2] He argues that his is the best theory of distributional equality because it does not penalize individuals for their lack of natural endowments or for their unfortunate luck, but it does hold them responsible for all the *decisions* that they make about how to use their resources.

Dworkin begins by constructing a hypothetical scenario involving immigrants stranded on a desert island. Assuming that talents and wealth were initially equal, how would the immigrants go about dividing up the island's resources? According to Dworkin, they would choose to divide their resources through the process of an auction. In describing this auction, Dworkin dismisses the question of whether the immigrants would choose to hold some resources in common, simply putting aside this possibility: "They [the immigrants] do not yet realize, let us say, that it might be wise to keep some resources as owned in common by any state they might create."[3] Similarly, he sets aside questions of political power. While he notes that questions of distributional equality are not entirely independent of questions of political equality, he suggests that these two issues are best analyzed separately.[4] Thus, he proceeds to outline his theory by focusing specifically on the resources that are owned privately by individuals.[5]

In the desert island scenario that Dworkin describes, each immigrant receives an equal number of clamshells, which are used as currency in an auction. During the auction, the immigrants all place bids on the island's available resources, taking into account both their own individual ambitions and desires and the likely effects their plans will have on the resources left over for others. The auction is run again and again until the "envy test" is satisfied—that is, until the point at which no one prefers anyone else's bundle of resources to his or her own.[6] Dworkin notes that this test does not insist that individuals must be equal in resources only at one point in time; rather, the envy test "requires that no one envy the bundle of occupation and resources at the disposal of anyone else over time, though someone may envy another's bundle at any particular time."[7] For instance, although Susan may envy the current bundle of resources that Maria has right now, if the envy test has been met, she would not envy Maria's bundle when considered over time, perhaps because this bundle includes years of hard work at an occupation that Susan finds undesirable. As long as their talents and resources are equal initially, then it is only fair that individuals should be held responsible for the consequences of their ambitions and choices about how to live their lives and what to do with their resources. Because people have different ambitions, choices, and preferences, a theory of distributional equality treats individuals unfairly if it demands a constant level of resources for everyone at all times.

After describing the auction that would take place among immigrants who had initially equal talents and resources, Dworkin acknowledges that this hypothetical example is inadequate to the conditions of the actual world, and he attempts to compensate for these inadequacies by adding hypothetical "insurance markets" that could be used to model schemes for taxation and redistribution of wealth in our own society. Explaining the need for these insurance markets, Dworkin notes that while the auction seeks to equalize "external resources," it fails to account for two other kinds of factors that inevitably affect the success that individuals have in pursuing their ambitions: luck (especially "brute luck") and "personal resources." Even if individuals were to begin with equal external resources (money, land, and so on), it would be difficult to imagine a scheme that would equalize their "personal resources"—their natural talents, skills, and capacities of physical and mental health. Thus, once the auction is complete and the envy test is satisfied, the initial equality would soon be disturbed and inequalities would arise. While some inequalities would be caused by differences in effort and ambition, others would result simply from factors that are not a part of an individual's personality but are merely the results of natural endowment or brute luck, factors for which it is unfair to hold individuals accountable.

Dworkin is fully aware that it is, in actuality, impossible to include personal resources (such as natural talents and health) and brute luck in any kind of an auction, and that it is also impossible to simply "redistribute" them in the ways that one might redistribute wealth or other impersonal resources. Nonetheless, there must be some way of equalizing circumstances, or of at least partially compensating people who are "unequal" in terms of their circumstances. To accomplish this, Dworkin proposes a hypothetical situation, similar in some ways to Rawls's "original position," in which people do not yet know whether they will lack certain natural endowments. The individuals in this situation would each be given a certain number of resources and asked to decide exactly how much they would be willing to spend on insurance that would protect them from various natural disadvantages. A similar hypothetical auction would be conducted to determine how much insurance such individuals would purchase against the possibility that they would have bad brute luck.[8]

Assuming that specific amounts can be determined through this hypothetical situation, these amounts can then serve as the basis for a system of taxation and income redistribution in the real world. While we would not want to compensate fully those who are born into unjust circumstances, since this would involve the transfer of more resources than the people in this hypothetical situation would agree to spend, certain amounts of taxation would be justified in order to compensate those who are less well off in terms of their natural endowments. Despite endorsing this theory, Dworkin notes that, in actuality, it is nearly impossible to distinguish the effects of one's natural talents from the effects of one's ambitions; thus, he suggests that the best way to apply this in the real world would be to tax the rich to help compensate the poor, even though this does not really succeed in identifying the exact effects of natural disadvantage.

Assumptions About "Background Institutions"

In describing the ideal scenario that illustrates his equality-of-resources theory, Dworkin makes a number of assumptions that he does not justify (or even identify). In this section, I will briefly explain how these assumptions function in Dworkin's theory and show that they are linked to his implicit acceptance of the basic institutional structures of our own society. Assuming background information from our own society—about the market and about the ambitions and circumstances of "normal" people—without acknowledging that he is employing such information, Dworkin suggests that certain facts about our own society would not radically change even if we were to begin from an ideal of initial equality.

In *Social Justice Reconsidered*, David Mapel writes that in order to make sense of the situation of the immigrants on the desert island, it must be assumed that they possess a great deal of information that they could not have had unless they already knew more than they supposedly know in Dworkin's initial situation. In order to place bids in the initial auction, for example, the immigrants must somehow have the power to predict the future value of their resources. However, this cannot be determined until after the auction ends and production begins. Similarly, because the insurance scheme models current ambitions in order to come up with a premium rate structure, Dworkin must import from our own society complex cultural assumptions about matters such as family structure, occupational choice, and desires for wealth.[9] Presumably, some of these structures must be open to change, and yet this will be difficult if these sorts of assumptions are incorporated into the ideal.

Furthermore, it seems that the hypothetical persons in Dworkin's discussion of the insurance scheme would have a hard time making decisions about how much insurance to buy against certain risks without their simply assuming many things about the society that has not yet developed. In order to think about how much money I would be willing to pay to insure against the possibility that I would be blind, I would need to know a great deal about the prospects of blind people in society: How are they treated? What are their chances for being able to function independently? Furthermore, my decision would also depend on many facts about the social structure: would I have supportive family and friends? Questions about the amounts people would pay for certain types of insurance only make sense in the context of much other information about society. Without being able to envision more specifically the sort of society that would develop out of his abstract model, Dworkin ends up simply assuming that many aspects of our own society would remain unchanged in his ideal.

Of course, every ideal theory must make use of *some* information from one's own society. Dworkin never suggests that his ideal would be appropriate for everyone, in any time period, under any conditions, but rather that it is supposed to serve as an ideal for societies much like ours in the modern world. Nonetheless, when the information taken in by the ideal and the background assumptions employed reflect precisely the relations of power that a theory of equality should be used to challenge, this is a serious problem.

Social Structures and Sources of Inequality

A second important problem with Dworkin's theory is that it treats equality as if that quality were simply a matter of individual resource holdings and not of how institutions and systems of power are organized. Viewing inequality as a matter of personal misfortune, Dworkin presupposes that the roles and institutions of our own society are not major sources of inequality and, thus, need not be substantially altered.

Although Dworkin does not explicitly discuss the social systems of power in our own world, his general discussion of what is involved in equality suggests that he does not take inequality to be rooted in these structures. After Dworkin describes what would be involved in the hypothetical auction of "impersonal resources," he points out that this simple auction would not work in the real world. In our own world, if such an auction were to occur among individuals who landed on a desert island, as soon as the envy test was met and the bidding ended, the immigrants would quickly become unequal. According to Dworkin, this is because individuals in the real world have varying degrees of natural talents and luck, and these factors lead to inequalities. Thus, the desert island scenario is very different from the circumstances of our own world in ways that could not possibly be dealt with in an auction (and, for this reason, an insurance scheme is needed).

While Dworkin is surely correct to point out that individuals in the real world have differing degrees of natural talent and brute luck and that these differences can lead to inequalities, it nonetheless seems odd that they are identified by him as the main (if not the only) sources of inequality aside from initial resource distribution. What exactly does Dworkin think falls under these categories? Are individuals who inherit large sums of money simply "lucky"? And are those who are born into racial and ethnic groups that are subject to discrimination and economic subordination merely unlucky? Underlying much of what might be seen simply as luck or talent, and in addition to any manifestation of either of these, there are larger structural patterns that play an enormous role in determining which individuals end up suffering from particular inequalities.[10] While anyone *could* have a "natural talent" for nuclear physics, such a talent is unlikely ever to develop if a person is not sent to good schools and encouraged to excel in math and science. Such opportunity and encouragement are not equally available to everyone; in reality, they are more commonly offered to students who are white, upper middle class, and male. Thus, it seems that while Dworkin focuses on the ways that natural talents and luck affect the distribution of resources in our own world, he does not pay sufficient attention to the effects of structural hierarchies of social power (those of race, class, gender, and other factors). These structures play a powerful role in determining who actually ends up with what may, from an individualistic perspective, look like mere luck or natural talent.

In overlooking the significance of structures of power while attending to the forces of luck and nature, Dworkin fails to acknowledge the extent to which the actual inequalities in our own society are rooted in these structures. Rather than questioning the very existence of the positions of power in which individuals happen to find themselves, he simply asks how much insurance hypothetical persons would choose to purchase against the possibility that they would end up in such circumstances. Illustrating his hypothetical insurance argument, he compares two worlds:

> In the first those who are relatively disadvantaged by the tastes and ambitions of others, vis-à-vis their own talents to produce, are known in advance and bear the full consequences of that disadvantage. In the second the *same pattern of relative disadvantage holds*, but everyone has subjectively an equal antecedent chance of suffering it, and so everyone has an equal opportunity of mitigating the disadvantage by insuring against it. . . . The hypothetical insurance argument aims to reproduce the consequences of the second world, as nearly as it can, in an actual world.[11]

One problem here is that Dworkin fails to question why any particular "pattern of relative disadvantage" holds. Feminists and other social justice theorists argue that many "patterns" of advantage and disadvantage are the effects of social hierarchy and oppression and must be changed if justice is to be achieved. Dworkin's theory merely seems to equalize individuals' chances of ending up in certain unchosen circumstances, rather than examining and altering the hierarchical ways in which many circumstances are structured.

Ambitions, Circumstances, and the Formation of Preferences

Dworkin's assumptions about background institutions and his treatment of inequality as a matter of personal resource holdings may both be related to a third, more fundamental, problem with his "equality of resources" and his liberalism generally. While his claim that a theory of equality should be sensitive to ambition but insensitive to endowment is compelling, he fails to address one very important practical consideration: in order to make sense of this ideal in the actual world we must be able to clearly distinguish ambitions from circumstances. By focusing on an abstract ideal, Dworkin fails to examine questions about how an individual's ambitions and preferences might be shaped by social circumstances, and in particular how they might be "adaptive" to situations of oppression. In an example of how ideal theories can function ideologically, Dworkin's envy test reinforces sexist ideology when employed without a critical analysis of the circumstances of male dominance. For Dworkin, a theory of distributional equality should respect individual differences in ambitions, preferences, and life plans. After the initial auction, "since people are different it is neither necessary nor desirable that resources should remain equal thereafter. . . . If one person, by dint of superior effort or talent, uses his equal share to create more than another, he is entitled to profit thereby, because his gain is not made at the expense of someone else who does less with his share. . . . superior industry should be rewarded."[12] While surely correct in stating that individuals are "different," Dworkin neglects to consider the nature and origin of these differences. There are enormous differences not only in people's ambitions, but also in their circumstances, and it is not always easy to separate one from the other. Dworkin's argument makes sense only if we assume that we know which differences result from a person's individual ambition and which from circumstances. Thus, to reward someone's "superior industry," we first must know that we are rewarding something for which this individual is actually responsible and not something that he was able to achieve because of his position in an unjust social structure—for example, by profiting from the exploitation of others or by benefiting from a privileged upbringing. Because Dworkin fails to address this matter, his theory seems to operate as if the differences that people end up exhibiting are actually caused by factors that arise out of their individual personalities and ambitions and not out of their circumstances.

In fact, Dworkin suggests that circumstances matter mostly because they determine how easy it will be for an individual to *achieve* her ambitions, not because they play a role in her ambition and preference *formation*. However, Dworkin runs into problems if the social, political, and economic circumstances in which an individual lives affect not only the "resources" she has available to her in *pursuing* her ambitions but also the very ambitions and preferences that she *develops*. For instance, consider Dworkin's discussion of the significance of one's economic circumstances. Noting that individuals can be harmed by the fact that they own less property than they might, he explains, "[t]he economic environment may frustrate my efforts to raise my children to have the values I might wish them to have; I cannot, for example, raise them to have the skills and experience of collecting Renaissance masterpieces."[13] This response trivializes the importance of having just and equitable economic institutions as the background circumstances in which a person is raised. A child growing up with insufficient material resources might suffer because she goes to school hungry and cannot concentrate, because her parents cannot afford to buy her any books to read, or because she has to work in order to help support her family and thus has little time to develop interests of her own. Problems such as these can permanently and negatively affect the development of an individual's preferences and ambitions. And yet Dworkin's example of how such an individual might be harmed seems to belittle this point.

Recall that Dworkin aims to devise a theory of distributional equality that is "ambition sensitive" and "endowment insensitive." However, if personality (ambition) and circumstance (endowment) intertwine in complex ways, he faces a serious problem. Because his theory rests on a very strong distinction between ambition and circumstance, and because individual preferences and ambitions play an important role in his envy test, he ends up simply accepting the expressed preferences of individuals at face value without asking how these might be different if they were developed under drastically different circumstances.[14]

While Dworkin does not explore the ways in which preferences form or change in response to one's social circumstances, other political theorists have raised and discussed this issue. In *Sour Grapes: Studies in the Subversion of Rationality*, Jon Elster considers several cases in which a person's preferences change based on his circumstances.[15] He focuses particular attention on the "sour grapes" phenomenon, in which a person's inability to obtain something he desires causes him to give up that desire. Elster contrasts this "purely causal process of adaptation," which takes place "behind the back" of the person concerned, with the related but distinct phenomenon of "character planning," which he finds less problematic.[16] Character planning also involves adjusting preferences in response to circumstances, but unlike the sour grapes phenomenon, it is a process that the individual himself controls by intentionally engineering the adaptation of his preferences to his possibilities.[17] Because it is directed by the person's own "meta-desires," Elster contends that character planning is compatible with autonomy, while the "causally induced" phenomenon of sour grapes is guided by mere "drives," and is thus less compatible with autonomy.[18]

Although Elster's work itself raises interesting questions, here I am concerned with its connection to Dworkin's discussion of the need to distinguish preferences from circumstances. While Dworkin does not explicitly consider the possibility that one's social circumstances could *cause* one to have certain preferences, like Elster he aims to isolate the *choices* that a person makes, since it is these choices for which the person is responsible. (In contrast, one should not be held responsible for circumstances that are beyond one's control.) Notably, Dworkin does describe two different ways in which people adjust their preferences, both of which he finds unproblematic; although they involve preference adjustment, both differ significantly from the nonintentional adjustment that Elster calls "adaptive preferences." First, consider Dworkin's treatment of "expensive tastes." Dworkin argues that people should be held responsible for cultivated tastes and preferences that they have developed in certain controlled ways, such as tastes for fine food and wine. In fact, one significant objection he raises against "equality of welfare" is that it cannot account for the problem of expensive tastes and thus ends up granting people with such tastes an excessive amount of resources (since this is what such persons require if they are to achieve the same level of welfare as persons who desire less expensive goods).[19] Yet his discussion of expensive tastes differs significantly from Elster's account of adaptive preferences (in the sour-grapes sense), since having expensive tastes is not adaptive in the negative sense, wherein one convinces oneself that one is happy with less than what one previously desired. Second, Dworkin emphasizes the importance of people considering the amount of resources left over for others, and thus it seems he would think it acceptable if one were to adjust one's desire for a particular delicacy upon realizing that it was scarce.[20] Although this involves a negative adaptation (whereby one's desire for something is lessened upon realization that it is unobtainable), if it happens as a matter of conscious choice, it would not fall into the category of adaptive preferences that most concerns Elster, and it would likely be unobjectionable in his view.

In fact, it seems that Dworkin has not considered the possibility that one's preferences can be adaptive in the nonintended sense that Elster describes. While Elster notes that it may, in practice, be difficult to distinguish the intentional from the nonintentional (or "causal") adjustment of preferences to possibilities, he nonetheless believes that this distinction is important and that the issue of nonintentional preferences must be addressed by any theory of justice that makes central the issue of individual preferences.[21] Although Dworkin is not a utilitarian, and he is not defending a welfare-based theory, his discussion of the envy test, and his aim to devise a theory that is ambition sensitive and endowment insensitive make clear that the preferences and choices of individuals are central issues in his conception of equality. As a result, his work suffers for not considering and addressing the issue of nonintentional adaptive preferences, especially in cases where such adaptation occurs in the context of oppressive power structures.

Although a detailed consideration of this matter is beyond the scope of this chapter, I question whether so much emphasis should be placed on the notion of one's conscious intentions in determining whether the preference adjustment was autonomous. Especially in cases of oppression, it seems at least possible that one could make a conscious decision not to pursue something that is unavailable (or that is nearly impossible for one to achieve) under the oppressive system, and this could still be problematic. If, knowing that women suffer from discrimination in the upper levels of scientific study, I decide to pursue a career as a high school science teacher instead of following my dream of becoming a brilliant physicist, my choice would be a conscious decision, and yet it still seems that it is not entirely "free." The problem here is that the circumstances themselves are problematic, and it may be that any choice made within such oppressive structures would itself be constrained by them.

Interestingly, Dworkin avoids directly dealing with these complex questions about preference formation by focusing his theory on the abstract situation of the immigrants stranded on a desert island. While he suggests that these immigrants are very much like "real people," he never discusses the society or circumstances in which they developed their preferences and personalities. Although their resources are said to be equal when they land on the island, he leads us to believe that they are otherwise "normal" people from a society much like our own, a society marked by class, gender, and race privilege and other forms of unjust social power. Given the fact that the immigrants developed their current desires, personalities, and preferences within particular social and cultural institutions, these preferences are likely to reflect (at least to some extent) the relations of power in those contexts. Hence, inequalities may be built into Dworkin's theory without his ever having to make any statements or direct claims about the social arrangements of power. If hierarchical systems of power are embedded in the preference structures of individuals, then it is not necessary for him to acknowledge their existence in order for his theory to work in a way that reinforces them.

While Dworkin never directly addresses the problem that I raise, he does at one point bring up an objection that touches on this important matter of the origin of individuals' preferences: some might argue, he notes, that the "auction supposes that the preferences people bring to the auction, or form in its course, are authentic—the true preferences of the agent rather than preferences imposed upon him by the economic system itself."[22] Unfortunately, rather than responding by discussing the question of whether the immigrants' preferences are "authentic," he seems to conflate this matter with another objection altogether: he continues, "Perhaps an auction of any sort, in which one person bids against another, imposes an illegitimate assumption that what is valuable in life is individual ownership of some-thing rather than more cooperative enterprises of the community." This is "an objection against the idea of private ownership," and it is "better consi-dered under the title of political equality."[23] Regardless of what the best response to this second objection is, Dworkin evades the question of whether the preferences that individuals bring to the auction are "authentic." One could certainly argue that they are not, or that there is a good chance they will reflect ideological systems of power, without raising the further objection to private ownership that Dworkin notes here.

One example of how Dworkin's theory could work in a way that rein-forces current hierarchies of power can be illustrated through considering Dworkin's envy test. Even in the initial auction for resource bundles on the desert island, the individuals bidding possess preferences based on who they already *are*, which is in large part who they came to be in the former society in which they lived. They do not suddenly become new people who make radically different decisions about value. For instance, suppose that Sally and Joe are two of these immigrants, and that they both came from a society marked by a patriarchal gender structure. Given the sorts of lives to which they were accustomed, compared to Joe Sally is happier with much less. In fact, it would make Sally happy if Joe had more than she does, since she believes that her interests are best served when men have more resources so that they will be wealthy, strong, and well equipped to offer protection and support to women. In this situation, people like Sally will be satisfied (the envy test will be met) when their bundles of resources are significantly smaller than the bundles that some others have.

In response to this objection, Dworkin might claim that I make illegitimate reference to Sally's "external preferences."[24] The auction should take into account only what individuals want for themselves; Sally's desires regarding others' resources must be excluded from consideration. Nonetheless, this requirement poses a problem in a society in which individuals are not equally self-interested: some classes of people are taught to believe that their own interests are best served by promoting the interests of others. Sally might honestly describe her preferences in a way that made no reference whatsoever to the preferences of others—"I simply prefer to have the small bundle," she could say. While this may appear "irrational," Dworkin must consider this possibility, if this is indeed how some members of oppressed groups form their preferences. Furthermore, although Dworkin discusses the illegitimacy of external preferences in his work on rights theory, he does not mention them in his discussion of equality of resources, and thus he never specifically prohibits them from the auction. Furthermore, he provides no mechanism for identifying external preferences and distinguishing them from personal preferences. He explains that personal and external preferences are often "so inextricably combined . . . that the discrimination is psychologically as well as institutionally impossible."[25] Thus, there are several reasons why he cannot simply dismiss my example for relying on external preferences.

In short, Dworkin seems to assume that all individuals already enjoy the basic freedom needed to autonomously develop their preferences, desires, and personalities. By assuming that social conditions do not have much impact on individuals' preference formation, Dworkin can describe individuals as wholly responsible for their preferences and choices, regardless of the social context. For instance, note his discussion of an individual's "choice" not to work: "to the degree that I have less because I have chosen to spend on expensive luxuries that I have consumed, or because I have chosen not to work, I am responsible for that circumstance, and it makes no difference whether I made those choices out of a strong taste for those luxuries, or out of a sense that work is degrading, or for some other reason."[26] Dworkin states unequivocally that to the extent that one has "chosen not to work," one is responsible for this choice, regardless of the reasons that the choice was made. But what if the only jobs available were in a dangerous factory that pays extremely low wages? Are there no conditions under which one could be held less "responsible" for such a choice? Dworkin seems to assume that safe, well-paying jobs are available to everyone and that if an individual "chooses" not to work, this must be the result of some characteristic of that individual person, and not, instead, a response to unjust social circumstances.

Dworkin's assumption that individuals develop preferences independently from social systems of oppression is problematic not simply because it treats the expressed preferences of oppressed individuals as if they were their *actual* preferences, but also because it treats the social pattern of preferences as if it were something to which individuals must adjust when considering the impact of their choices on the larger community. Rather than questioning the larger social patterns of "preferences" and their ties to unjust forms of social power such as racism, sexism, and classism, Dworkin seems to assume that society is basically fair, or that it is at least not characterized by pervasive forms of oppression. At several points in his work (on equality and elsewhere), Dworkin writes as if cases involving racism, for instance, are unusual and must therefore be treated as exceptions. He argues that we must decide for ourselves "what an appropriate way to live is . . . by taking the tastes and convictions of others as among the parameters of our situation."[27] If people's tastes and preferences are different from my own in a way that works to my disadvantage, I must adjust to this, and it would be wrong for me to protest that I deserve to be compensated. "There is, anyway, something seriously wrong with regarding other people's tastes and attitudes as compensable bad luck, except under special circumstances, like those of racial prejudice. In most circumstances, we take the mix of attitudes and tastes given in the community to *decide* what is fair. . . . It may be bad luck that I live in a community of people whose needs are very different from mine. But that is not compensable bad luck, not a case of injustice."[28] But why assume that a case in which people's preferences have been affected by hierarchical systems of power is an exception? If racial, sexual, and class structures affect people's preferences, then relying on such preferences to determine what is "fair" seems highly problematic. In a racist, sexist, and homophobic society, the preferences people develop will likely embody and reinforce these systems of power, at least in certain ways. Only by assuming that these systems of power are not present, or that they only rarely affect people's preferences, can Dworkin take the given structure of expressed preferences to be a fair way of determining the "parameters of our situation."

Conclusion

Many of the problems I have identified with Dworkin's theory concern his inattention to the effects of institutional power relations and his assumptions about the individualistic nature of preference formation. Interestingly, Dworkin purports to be making certain assumptions about individuals and their social circumstances, but he ends up making quite different (unacknowledged) assumptions about each of these. According to his own description of his methodology, he is taking individuals—people not much different from those of our own world—and placing them on a desert island, where they do not yet know what kind of social, political, or economic circumstances they will be creating. His theory attempts to focus on the "circumstances" of the individuals in order to equalize them. In other words, it seems that Dworkin has stated that he will assume that the individuals in his scenario are basically as we know them to be in our own world, but that their circumstances—their patterns of resource distribution—have yet to be determined.

Unfortunately, as I have argued, in the end Dworkin makes the opposite assumptions. Instead of portraying the individuals in his scenario as regular people, he suggests that they are far more "ideal." They seem to form their preferences autonomously, and their "personalities" are relatively unaffected by their social, political, and economic circumstances. Moreover, rather than suggesting that social conditions have yet to be determined, he assumes that the basic roles, positions, and institutions would remain quite similar to those of our own society. As I stated earlier, however, striving for "equality" requires calling into question the very existence of the roles and positions of current hierarchies. Dworkin, instead, mostly aims to equalize the chances that individuals have of ending up in these roles.

By examining Dworkin's ideal, equality of resources, I hope to have demonstrated that the problem with abstract liberal theories is not merely that they are difficult to *apply* to our own situation, but that they are often also internally flawed. In other words, the assumptions in Dworkin's theory are embedded within the theory itself and do not merely arise at this secondary level of "application." Allegedly abstract liberal ideals cannot simply be applied to current social conditions and be made to yield radical conclusions, since these allegedly abstract theories often need to assume certain things about a society's "background institutions" in order to get off the ground. When such institutions involve oppressive relations of power, this becomes a problem. Furthermore, liberal theorists frequently presuppose too sharp a distinction between the preferences of individuals and the societal circumstances in which these preferences are situated. When social institutions are hierarchical and oppressive, it cannot simply be assumed that individuals are making choices and developing preferences autonomously. By not paying sufficient attention to the influence that institutional power arrangements have on the development of individual preferences, "abstract" liberal theories can unwittingly lend support to oppressive structures.

3

Rawlsian Abstraction and the Social Position of Women

Whereas Dworkin's writings have not attracted much attention from feminists, the work of John Rawls has been the subject of considerable feminist debate.[1] In fact, some claim that a reformulated version of Rawls's theory of justice holds great potential for feminism. Unlike many liberal theorists who focus narrowly on equalizing the resources or the welfare of individuals and place a great deal of emphasis on individual preferences, Rawls purports to concern himself with the justice of society's "basic structure," which makes his theory appealing to feminists seeking to rectify inequalities in society's institutions and structures of power.

In this chapter, I address a number of problems with feminist attempts to use Rawls's work to argue for feminist conclusions. My specific interest is in the question of whether an abstract, ideal theory such as Rawls's, in which we are instructed to think from the "original position," is an effective feminist strategy, and I conclude that it is not. I begin by examining Susan Okin's suggestion that Rawls's theory of justice can be reformulated in ways that hold great potential for feminism.[2] I argue that Okin's feminist reformulation of Rawls depends on two assumptions: (1) The parties in the original position must think from the perspective of persons living in the actual social positions of our own current society; and (2) The parties know that women are subordinated in current society and recent history, and they understand the experience of gender oppression. Not only are these assumptions contrary to Rawls's own description of the original position; they also are precluded by the sort of idealized theorizing that

Rawls—and many other liberals—advocate. While Okin is correct to suggest we learn a great deal by thinking about what would be agreed to by women, and by persons thinking from the perspective of the most subordinated social groups, her arguments that Rawls provides us with many resources to aid in this project are unconvincing. In the final sections of this chapter, I discuss further problems with assumptions made by both Okin and Rawls about the "pluralism" of views that would exist in a well-ordered society, and I suggest that some of these assumptions take for granted the continuation of structures of oppression. Feminism requires identifying and challenging socially generated hierarchies of power, which Rawls's methodology—like that of many liberal political theorists—is ill equipped to do, given his understanding of power, equality, and social positionality.

Okin's Feminist Reformulation of Rawls

Although Okin acknowledges many problems with Rawls's more recent *Political Liberalism*,[3] she believes that some of the basic ideas presented in *A Theory of Justice* hold great promise for feminism: "The feminist *potential* of Rawls's method of thinking and his conclusions is considerable. The original position, with the veil of ignorance hiding from its participants their sex as well as their other particular characteristics, talents, circumstances, and aims, is a powerful concept for challenging the gender structure."[4] According to Okin, because persons in the original position know that they could end up as women, they would not agree to women's subordinate status in the family, in the workplace, or in any other sociopolitical institutions. In fact, she contends that "a consistent and wholehearted application of Rawls's liberal principles of justice can lead us to challenge fundamentally the gender system of our society."[5] She notes that although Rawls does not mention ignorance of one's sex in his initial description of the veil of ignorance, he adds sex—along with race—to the list of unknown features in his 1975 essay "Fairness to Goodness," which suggests that his theory could be used to challenge sex and race inequalities.[6]

Departing from Rawls's communitarian and feminist critics, Okin argues that his theory does not require an egoistic and individualistic subject who thinks only about impartial and universalistic principles.[7] Although Rawls's use of the language of rational choice suggests this reading, "the original position and what happens there are described far better in other terms."[8] In particular, the parties in the original position would have to act out of "equal concern for others," which would involve paying careful attention to the specific experiences of persons living in the various different groups to which one must imagine oneself belonging.[9]

> [T]he only coherent way in which a party in the original position can think about justice is through empathy with persons of all kinds in all the different positions in society, but especially with the least well-off in various respects. To think as a person in the original position is not to be a disembodied nobody. This, as critics have rightly pointed out, would be impossible. Rather, it is to think from the point of view of everybody, of every "concrete other" whom [*sic*] one might turn out to be.[10]

Since the parties in the original position would understand the "general facts about human society," they would know that society is "gender-structured both by custom and still in some respects by law" and "that women have been and continue to be the less advantaged sex in a great number of respects."[11] This knowledge, along with the requirement that they think about justice from the point of view of "everyone," would lead the parties in the original position to consider the possibility that they could be women and to choose principles that would bring about gender justice.

The Centrality of Economic Categories in Rawls

Although Okin believes that Rawls's theory can be made to take gender into account, it is important to note that in the articulation of the difference principle, and in his treatment of equality more generally, Rawls refers almost exclusively to income, class, and economic status, paying far less attention to other forms of social inequality. While he claims that his second principle of justice (which includes both the difference principle and the principle of fair equality of opportunity) applies to all social and economic inequalities, in actuality it is the class positions defined by income and wealth that are of most concern to him.[12] For instance, explaining the requirement that those in the original position evaluate the basic structure from the point of view of equality and from the point of view of representative citizens who occupy "relevant social positions," Rawls contends that each person must consider two perspectives: the position of "equal citizenship" and the perspective "defined by his place in the distribution of income and wealth."[13]

This is troubling for feminists, as well as for those who are concerned about racism, heterosexism, and other forms of oppression, since Rawls seems to focus his discussion of inequality on questions of economic class, thereby rendering other forms of social power invisible. He also emphasizes economic class in his account of the difference principle and in his explanation of how we are to determine which group is the least well off.[14] While this may not be easy to establish, the difficulties, as he explains them, concern questions about average versus relative income and wealth and other, similar questions that arise within a class-based analysis. The difficulties that feminists might have in defining the "least well-off" involve important questions about how racial, class, and gender oppression should be weighed and balanced; Rawls, however, does not even consider such questions.

In *A Theory of Justice*, Rawls does include one passage where he explicitly raises the possibility that social positions other than "the various levels of income and wealth" may sometimes need to be taken into account:

> If, for example, there are unequal basic rights founded on fixed natural characteristics, these inequalities will single out relevant positions. Since these characteristics cannot be changed, the positions they define count as starting places in the basic structure. Distinctions based on sex are of this type, and so are those depending upon race and culture. Thus if, say, men are favored in the assignment of basic rights, this inequality is justified by the difference principle (in the general interpretation) only if it is to the advantage of women and acceptable from their standpoint. . . . Such inequalities multiply relevant positions and complicate the application of the two principles. On the other hand, these inequalities are seldom, if ever, to the advantage of the less favored, and therefore in a just society the smaller number of relevant positions should ordinarily suffice.[15]

This passage is interesting because it is one of few places in *Theory* where Rawls explicitly mentions sex as a possible "relevant social position." Within a sentence or two, however, he concludes that since inequalities based on sex and race are seldom to the advantage of women or people of color, these would not *be* relevant social positions in a just society. In a just society, there would be a group of people who would be the "least well off" and they would be the ones whose interests must be taken into account when justifying social and economic inequalities. Yet women, people of color, and others who suffer from various noneconomic inequalities seem not to be included in this group, because (presumably) these would not be politically relevant positions *in a well-ordered society*. In contrast, Rawls does assume that some class differences are justified by the difference principle and that the well-ordered society would therefore contain economic classes. Although he seems to simply assume that a well-ordered society would have some class distinctions, he suggests that these would be justified because they would benefit the least well off class through advantages such as increased incentives and greater productivity.

In response to my argument, one might argue that Rawls's theory precludes sexual and racial inequalities because it is an abstract ideal that prohibits inequalities based on features that are not morally salient. Not only does Rawls guarantee that people have equal basic liberties; he also writes about the importance of ensuring the "fair value" of these equal liberties, which must be more than merely formal guarantees.[16] Thus, one could defend him by arguing that his theory requires women's equality, as well as the equality of various racial groups, and that it is only certain kinds of class inequalities that are permissible (those benefiting the least well off economic class). The problem with this argument is that it suggests that omitting any discussion of sex and race is a way of ensuring sexual and racial equality. However, insofar as sex and race define socially salient categories in a basic structure, these are important social markers of inequality. Although an abstract ideal can—and should—posit a world in which sex and race no longer categorize people into socially subordinated groups, a theory that simply makes no (or very little) reference to these social categories effectively suggests that they are unimportant in theorizing about justice and equality. What feminists and antiracist critics of Rawls emphasize is that because gender and race are socially salient categories that affect one's ability to enjoy a range of basic liberties and powers, theories of justice and equality must acknowledge, address, and remedy forms of subordination based on these categories.

On a similar note, a Rawlsian might argue that because *A Theory of Justice* deals mainly with ideal theory, that is, with a world in which there is "full compliance" (as opposed to "partial compliance") with a theory of justice, Rawls need not address the specific forms of injustice based on factors such as gender and race.[17] In other words, his silence on these matters in a discussion of *ideal theory* need not indicate that he views these as insignificant forms of injustice; rather, the appropriate place for a discussion of these injustices would be in the context of nonideal theory, which involves a world in which there is partial compliance with the ideal of justice. There are several problems with this line of argument, however. First, as I contend throughout this book, the process of devising an ideal is never entirely independent from the context of one's own (nonideal) society. Rawls's understanding of the different social positions present in his ideal theory of justice is necessarily affected by his view of the current social positions in our own society. It would be impossible to come up with the "relevant social positions" to which Rawls refers without employing some information from our own society. What is problematic is that Rawls focuses selectively on factors that determine one's social position, viewing class and economic position as significant and overlooking the ways that factors such as sex also affect one's social power and positionality. Moreover, by offering an account of "justice" that fails to address the *injustice* of sexism, Rawls's theory seems to overlook the significance of this problem.

Second, it is not clear that the issues of gender and race oppression would in fact be part of Rawls's "nonideal theory." In *A Theory of Justice*, when Rawls departs from ideal theory, his brief discussions of nonideal theory do not treat the oppression of women or people of color as primary examples. He notes that nonideal theory should be understood as consisting of distinct "subparts"; one involves "principles for governing adjustments to natural limitations and historical contingencies," and the other consists of "principles for meeting injustice."[18] In a subsequent discussion of this second subpart, that of injustice, Rawls states more specifically what this part of nonideal theory covers:

> It includes, among other things, the theory of punishment and compensatory justice, just war and conscientious objection, civil disobedience and militant resistance. These are among the central issues of political life, yet so far the conception of justice as fairness does not directly apply to them. Now I shall not attempt to discuss these matters in full generality. In fact, I shall take up but one fragment of partial compliance theory: namely, the problem of civil disobedience and conscientious refusal. And even here I shall assume that the context is one of a state of near justice, that is, one in which the basic structure of society is nearly just, making due allowance for what it is reasonable to expect in the circumstances. An understanding of this admittedly special case may help to clarify the more difficult problems.[19]

Although Rawls does not explicitly mention gender or race oppression, it is of course *possible* that he meant to include them among the types of injustice with which "nonideal" theory would have to deal. Nonetheless, the sorts of injustice on which he focuses seem rather different from the systematic injustices of gender and race oppression. On the one hand, theories of punishment and compensation typically focus on individuals; on the other, theories about just war primarily focus on states. Questions about relations between different groups *within* a single society seem to fall between the cracks. Moreover, in discussing the one example, Rawls states that he "shall assume that the context is one of a state of near justice." Why make such an assumption? Rawls does not give this as his reason, but it may be that he assumes that our own society is one of near justice, and that a discussion of these phenomena in the context of a society not too different from our own will be most useful.

In his more recent work, *Law of Peoples*, Rawls offers a lengthier discussion of nonideal theory. Here he focuses more on entire societies and divides nonideal theory into two types (which correspond to the distinction discussed above). The first is that which deals with "unfavorable conditions," that is, societies "whose historical, social, and economic circumstances make their achieving a well-ordered regime, whether liberal or decent, difficult if not impossible."[20] These are also called "burdened" societies. The second is concerned with "conditions of noncompliance, that is, with conditions in which certain regimes refuse to comply with a reasonable Law of Peoples." These societies are called "outlaw states," and Rawls's discussion of them focuses on what measures other societies "may justifiably take to defend themselves against them."[21] What I find interesting—and troubling—about this more detailed discussion of the two kinds of nonideal societies is that Rawls draws such a sharp contrast between the two. In the first case, the "burdened" society is not to blame for its misfortune. But Rawls's description of the second case, that of "outlaw" societies, suggests an image of people who are radically unjust, who engage in various forms of morally egregious behavior, and whom others need to decide how to reform. Thinking about the current social context of the contemporary United States, one is left wondering: where does our society fit into this picture? It seems as if Rawls does not have in mind the United States when he describes unjust societies as outlaw states; rather, he appears to regard the United States as basically just. However, what feminists (along with many antiracism activists) argue is that sexism and racism are rampant in our society;

it is thus plagued by injustice, even though it does not seem to fit Rawls's description of an outlaw society. In other words, by making his distinction in the way that he does—between burdened and outlaw societies—Rawls implies that the United States is not plagued by injustice. Given these remarks, it appears that the injustices of sexist oppression do not fit easily into Rawls's discussion of either ideal or nonideal theory.

Relevant Social Positions and Knowledge of Oppression

To address Rawls's relative silence on the issue of women's oppression, Okin argues that his theory should be amended to include women as a "relevant social position" in the original position and as a potential group among the "least well-off." She explains that "once we challenge Rawls's traditional belief that questions about justice can be resolved by 'heads of families,' the 'least advantaged representative woman,' who is likely to be considerably *worse* off, has to be considered equally."[22] Making a similar point, Eva Kittay suggests that the social positions of both dependents and those who do "dependency work" (most often women, in our current society) should be included as "relevant social positions" in Rawls's original position.[23] Like Okin, Kittay concludes that the group of "least advantaged" citizens should be defined not solely in terms of economic class, but as including dependency workers.[24] Other feminist analyses of Rawls draw similar conclusions, arguing that the social positions of men and women both need to be considered by the parties in the original position, but I focus here on Okin and, to a lesser extent, Kittay.[25]

One could object to this feminist revision of Rawls by pointing out that it directly contradicts his own claim that the least well off is not to be defined in terms of gender; this he states clearly in a recent book even after acknowledging that the parties in the original position should not be understood as heads of families, but as persons who are ignorant of their gender.[26] Nonetheless, this is not my objection to Okin and Kittay, since they offer only an interpretation of Rawls's theory and argue that it holds potential for feminists, not that it can be applied without revision to bring about gender justice. My objections to the inclusion of gender as a relevant social position in the original position are more fundamental and concern the very meaning of a "relevant social position" in an ideal theory.

On the one hand, most feminists would agree that because of the impact of sexism, combined with other forms of structural oppression, many women in our society are part of what we would consider the least well off social group, as are many of those persons Kittay describes as dependency workers and dependents. Nonetheless, Kittay, Okin, and other feminists seem to be misinterpreting Rawls when they suggest that the relevant social positions in the original position are patterned on the actual social positions in our own society. According to Rawls, the original position is a thought experiment whose relevant social positions are generated by thinking reflectively about, and using our considered judgments to determine, what the relevant social positions would be in an abstract ideal, which Rawls calls a "well-ordered society"; they are not determined by looking around at persons in our own society and deeming the various social groups that we find relevant social positions.

Of course, one might claim that when Rawls himself discusses what would count as relevant social positions, he cannot help but consider the social positions of our own society and import these into the original position. To envision what these social positions would be, we must employ our own considered judgments, which are not entirely abstract or free of bias. Nonetheless, it is noteworthy that Rawls focuses almost exclusively on economic classes, which he claims would continue to exist in a well-ordered society. He argues (however unsatisfactorily) that because of increased incentives and productivity, some class-based inequalities benefit the least well off and thus would persist in a well-ordered society. For instance, in the following passage, Rawls discusses the possibility that inequalities increase incentives, which lead to increases in productivity: "If there are inequalities in the basic structure that work to make everyone better off in comparison with the benchmark of initial equality, why not permit them? . . . If, for example, these inequalities set up various incentives which succeed in eliciting more productive efforts, a person in the original position may look upon them as necessary to cover the costs of training and to encourage effective performance."[27] Although Rawls does not state explicitly here that inequalities *do* work in this way (as incentives), this appears to be because he does not know whether they function this way in any particular case. But throughout his work he suggests that the difference principle works because economic inequalities will sometimes be justified.[28] Whether or not feminists find these arguments about class convincing, most would object to the continuation of inequalities based on gender. Yet the claim that women, dependency workers, or any other currently oppressed group, should be considered a relevant social position in the original position seems to imply that inequalities based on gender, dependency status, or some other such feature would

continue to exist in a well-ordered society. Such an assumption is problematic for feminists who envision a world in which gender does not
determine social status. Similarly, in terms of dependency work, an ideal,
"well-ordered" society might involve the elimination of *classes* of people
who do this work; it is at least possible to imagine that the work of caring
for dependents would be much more evenly spread throughout the population, or that certain people would engage in dependency work for short
periods of time and yet not have their social role defined by it in the way that
many people (and, specifically, many women) currently do. Interestingly,
Okin herself argues in the conclusion of her book that "[a] just future
would be one without gender. In its social structures and practices, one's
sex would have no more relevance than one's eye color or the length of one's
toes."[29] And earlier, she claims that "our current gender structure is incompatible with the attainment of social justice" and that "the disappearance of
gender is a prerequisite for the *complete* development of a nonsexist, fully
human theory of justice."[30] Thus, Okin posits a category in the original
position (gender) that she ultimately believes must be eradicated in a just
society. Not only does this go against what it means for something to be a
category in the abstract ideal of the "original position," but it also has the
very troubling implication that gender is a legitimate category of social
status and that it will continue to be a marker of inequality in a well-
ordered society.

A second way in which Okin departs from the abstract idealization of
Rawls's original position is in her discussion of the knowledge possessed
by parties behind the veil of ignorance. As I noted earlier, Okin claims that
because Rawls grants that the parties would "know the general facts about
human society," they would know that society "is gender-structured both
by custom and still in some respects by law" and "that women have been
and continue to be the less advantaged sex in a great number of respects."[31]
The question of what falls under the "general facts about human society"
is a tricky one, as Okin herself explains in a footnote.[32] Rather than offering
an argument for her interpretation, however, she simply assumes that knowledge of gender oppression would be included in these "general facts."

In describing the original position, Rawls provides a list of what would
and would not be known to the participants; the parties would be denied
knowledge of their place in society, their social status or class position, their
natural abilities and assets, their personality and talents, their conception of
the good, and their own psychological features.[33] He adds that the parties
"do not know the particular circumstances of their own society, . . . its

economic or political situation, or the level of civilization and culture it has been able to achieve."[34] While they would know the "general facts about human society," Rawls takes this to mean is that they would understand "political affairs and the principles of economic theory" and "the basis of social organization and the laws of human psychology."[35]

Looking carefully at this list, it seems that Okin has read too much into the "general facts" that Rawls attributes to the parties in the original position. Facts about current and historical patterns of social domination and oppression—whether racial, gender, or any other sort—are precisely the type of information Rawls excludes. In his view, general facts encompass only basic, generic information: laws of psychology and principles of social and economic organization that would apply generally and would be widely accepted and relatively uncontroversial. While general facts about the oppression of women in current and recent history may be unobjectionable and obvious to feminists, they are controversial and—more important— not the generic type of knowledge of human society that would be known from the perspective of an abstract ideal.[36] They seem more akin to the knowledge that Rawls prohibits: facts about the "particular circumstances" of our own society and its "economic or political situation" and culture. Yet without this specific, historical information about oppression being included in the original position, the thought experiment would not generate the feminist conclusions that Okin desires.

Accommodating "Pluralism" of Views About Gender

Whereas Okin seems to depart from Rawls by including women as a relevant social position and attributing knowledge of gender oppression to the parties in the original position, she sticks closely—perhaps too closely—to him in the matter of accommodating the actual "pluralism" of views found in our own society. Although she believes that a just future would be genderless, out of respect for the pluralism of current views about gender, she argues that "when we think about constructing relations between the sexes that could be agreed upon in the original position . . . we must also design institutions and practices acceptable to those with more traditional beliefs about the characteristics of men and women, and the appropriate division of labor between them. . . . Gender-structured marriage, then, needs to be regarded as a currently necessary institution (because still chosen by some) but one that is socially problematic."[37] This element of Okin's work is troubling, since it seems to conflate the need to respect a diversity of views in general with the need to respect the *particular* diversity of views found in our own society.

In *Political Liberalism*, where he discusses pluralism more extensively, Rawls argues that any just society will continue to have a variety of different views, and he emphasizes that this diversity—and specifically that of "reasonable comprehensive doctrines"—is not something that would disappear in a just society.[38] While he is certainly correct to suggest that a free society would manifest a variety of reasonable views on many different questions of social and political significance, it seems illegitimate to assume that the pluralism of our own society resembles the pluralism that would result from "just" or "free" institutions. Although Rawls does not explicitly state that he means to preserve the actual diversity of perspectives in our own society (in fact, he distinguishes the fact of "reasonable pluralism" from the fact of "pluralism as such"),[39] he often writes as if the current comprehensive doctrines—such as those of the major religions—are acceptable as part of the reasonable pluralism that naturally would develop in free institutions. For instance, he states that "the diversity of reasonable comprehensive religious, philosophical, and moral doctrines *found in modern democratic societies* is not a mere historical condition that may soon pass away; it is a permanent feature of the public culture of democracy."[40] Okin seems to follow Rawls in sliding from the abstract fact of "reasonable pluralism" to the assumption that the pluralism of views in our own society must be respected. In fact, she states quite bluntly that we must "respect the current pluralism of beliefs" about gender and include in the original position "a wide variety of beliefs" about social arrangements based on gender.[41] As she explains, "We may, once the veil of ignorance is lifted, find ourselves feminist men or feminist women whose conception of the good life includes the minimization of social differentiation between the sexes. Or we may find ourselves traditionalist men or women, whose conception of the good life, for religious or other reasons, is bound up in an adherence to the conventional division of labor between the sexes."[42] However, understanding the original position as an ideal theory, it seems highly problematic to simply import views that are based on the specific social and historical developments of our own, nonideal society. Although there would be a diversity of perspectives in the original position, we have no reason to think this diversity would include "traditional" views about gender. "Traditional" views arose in a particular social context, characterized in part by a history of various forms of oppression; such views are not merely the natural byproducts of a free and just society.

Ideal Theory and Reasonable Pluralism

While many feminist objections to *Political Liberalism* pertain to the problematic ways in which issues of importance to feminism, such as the family, child care, reproduction, and sexuality, are relegated to the "nonpublic" and "nonpolitical" sphere and are therefore seen as outside the scope of justice, feminists have focused less attention on the problematic way in which Rawls's recent work waivers between idealized discussions of a well-ordered society and actual descriptions of our own society. Even if we were to accept the problematic public/nonpublic and political/nonpolitical distinctions, it seems that we still would not know—in the abstract—what sorts of views would develop in the nonpublic and nonpolitical realm of a well-ordered society. If there were a truly democratic society with "free institutions," what kinds of reasonable comprehensive doctrines would its citizens hold? This is a difficult question that arises when one is doing abstract, ideal theory, but it is not one that Rawls directly considers. Instead of exploring the question of what sorts of comprehensive doctrines persons might develop in a just, democratic society with free institutions, in *Political Liberalism* Rawls seems more interested in arguing that the actual comprehensive doctrines that people currently hold are acceptable as part of the "overlapping consensus."

In the introduction to *Political Liberalism*, Rawls explains that his earlier work in *Theory* offered an "unrealistic idea of a well-ordered society."[43] Although he views the two books as compatible in many ways, he now argues that "justice as fairness" was presented in *Theory* as if it were a "comprehensive philosophical doctrine" and not instead a more limited "political conception of justice" (xvi). In *Political Liberalism*, Rawls introduces and emphasizes the importance of the political/nonpolitical distinction, and he demonstrates how the revised theory incorporating this distinction can promote stability. As he explains in the introduction, "[T]he problem of political liberalism is: How is it possible that there may exist over time a stable and just society of free and equal citizens profoundly divided by reasonable though incompatible religious, philosophical, and moral doctrines?" (xviii). To elucidate his revised theory, Rawls introduces a number of new ideas: a political conception of justice (as opposed to a comprehensive doctrine), an overlapping consensus, public reason, a political conception of the person, and reasonable as opposed to simple pluralism (xvii). On the one hand, none of these concepts themselves entails the acceptance of the actual plurality of views in our own society. For instance, Rawls explains reasonable pluralism as the "normal result of the exercise of human reason within the framework of the free institutions of a constitutional democratic regime" (xvi). On the other hand, although this explanation sounds abstract and makes no explicit reference to our own society, as Rawls fleshes out his motivations for writing *Political Liberalism* it becomes clear that he is in fact talking about our own society. Consider the following passage: "Now the serious problem is this. A modern democratic society is characterized not simply by a pluralism of comprehensive religious, philosophical, and moral doctrines but by a pluralism of incompatible yet reasonable comprehensive doctrines. No one of these doctrines is affirmed by citizens generally. Nor should one expect that in the foreseeable future one of them, or some other reasonable doctrine, will ever be affirmed by all, or nearly all, citizens" (xvi). In this passage, Rawls implies that actual "modern democracies" are in fact the background context for his own discussion of pluralism. In other words, he suggests that our own modern democratic society is characterized by reasonable pluralism, and the problem for *Political Liberalism* is to explain how it is that we can maintain most forms of pluralism (with the exception of some extreme views that are "unreasonable," such as religious fundamentalism) and still agree on the political ideal of "justice as fairness." Although he claims to be doing abstract theory, it seems that his intention in *Political Liberalism* is to show how the "pluralism" of our own society— especially religious and moral pluralism—is compatible with justice, despite initial appearances to the contrary.

Thus, one problem with the way that Rawls presents and discusses the issue of pluralism is that his blurring of the ideal and the actual makes it difficult for one to object to the specific forms of pluralism of our own society without objecting to the very idea that a plurality of reasonable comprehensive doctrines would result from the normal functioning of human reason under free and democratic institutions. Clearly, most feminists do not object to this abstract point; we have no reason to believe that everyone would think alike or would hold the same values and commitments in a just and free society, nor do we want to promote a uniformity of viewpoints. Yet believing that a just society would be pluralistic does not entail support for the current pluralism of values and perspectives in our own society, which has a history and present marred by various forms of social, political, and sexual oppression.

Of course, the feminist endorsement of plurality is not limited to the claim that there *would be* a plurality of reasonable comprehensive doctrines if we lived in a just and free society (that is, in an "ideal" world). Most feminists also believe that we must respect and even promote certain forms of diversity and pluralism in our own society, especially diversity of the sort that is unjustly marginalized in a culture dominated by men, whites, heterosexuals, and other socially privileged groups. Yet the way to do this, according to many feminists and other social justice activists, is to acknowledge that the state already promotes and encourages certain viewpoints while silencing and repressing others. Because the state is not actually "neutral" toward all possible forms of reasonable pluralism, promoting pluralism will sometimes require measures that support the development of perspectives that tend to be silenced in a racist and sexist culture. Questions of how the state can encourage and promote pluralism without permitting the continuing predominance of oppressive and hierarchical perspectives are very difficult ones that Rawls does not directly answer. In fact, because he fails to question and challenge the comprehensive doctrines of our own society (at least those associated with the major moral and religious perspectives, excluding some forms of fundamentalism), he might even appear to be justifying them. In claiming that these views are "reasonable," he offers "justification" of a sort: he rationalizes their inclusion in the sphere of politics, as part of the "overlapping consensus." Effectively, this legitimates some comprehensive doctrines that feminists define as oppressive. Although Rawls would plead that this legitimization is limited to the claim that such views have a role to play in the "political" sphere, feminists who question Rawls's political/nonpolitical dichotomy might find this response inadequate.

Initial Social Positions as "Arbitrary"

In the preceding sections, I have argued that Rawls too narrowly focuses his discussion of inequality on economic issues, that his methodology is not amenable to the addition of women as a relevant social position, that his theory denies parties in the original position information about issues of oppression, and that his defense of reasonable pluralism ultimately works to justify the continuation of current social structures rather than promoting a just social ideal. In addition to these problems, and in a sense underlying them, is a more basic problem with how Rawls conceptualizes social power and inequality. In this section, I argue that Rawls's discussion of inequality seems to focus on mitigating the effects of the "arbitrariness" of natural advantage and disadvantage rather than on altering the structures of power that generate and perpetuate various forms of social hierarchy and oppression.

Several times in his writings, Rawls describes the "initial social position" into which one is born as "arbitrary," just as the natural talents and abilities that people are born with are so. In fact, he frequently lumps together in his writing the "distribution of natural talents" and the "contingencies of social circumstance" without any suggestion that there may be important differences between them.[44] Like Ronald Dworkin and other liberals, Rawls seeks to separate the effects of one's choices from those of one's endowments and circumstances, since people cannot be held responsible for their natural endowments or for the social circumstances into which they are born. From Rawls's perspective, both these factors—natural endowment and social circumstance—seem arbitrary; it is a matter of luck whether one is born with certain natural endowments, just as it is a matter of chance whether one is born into a wealthy or poor family. At one point, Rawls declares, "The natural distribution [of talents] is neither just nor unjust; nor is it unjust that persons are born into society at some particular position. These are simply natural facts."[45] From the perspective of the individual agent, these facts may seem "natural" and entirely arbitrary. Yet when considered instead from a larger perspective, the issue of social circumstance is anything but natural or arbitrary. The social and economic forces that create and maintain structures of power and oppression—including class, race, and gender—are not governed by luck or accident. It is not merely a matter of luck or chance that men have more power than women, that whites are the dominant race in the United States, or that heterosexuals have more rights and privileges than gays and lesbians do. These are social facts rooted in history and supported by intricate webs of power and privilege. Lumping the effects of socially generated hierarchies with the effects of natural endowment makes it seem as if these structures were not produced by social and political forces.[46]

Although Rawls focuses less on satisfying individual preferences (for welfare, resources, or some other good) than do many liberal theorists, he does not go far enough in addressing the social forces that shape the choices, preferences, and "chances" of individual persons. He seems to follow other liberal theorists in conceptualizing "equality" as a matter to be considered only after individuals are socially situated in various different positions, as though the positions themselves were not sociopolitical creations. In an essay criticizing the way in which many contemporary political philosophers conceptualize equality, Elizabeth Anderson objects to what she refers to as luck egalitarianism: "Recent egalitarian writing has come to be dominated by the view that the fundamental aim of equality is to compensate people for undeserved bad luck—being born with poor native endowments, bad parents, and disagreeable personalities, suffering from accidents and illness, and so forth."[47] What is wrong with the notion of luck egalitarianism, according to Anderson, is that it treats equality as if it were a matter of remedying unluckiness, rather than of eliminating socially generated forms of oppression and creating a just and democratic society. She presents an alternative conception: "The proper negative aim of egalitarian justice is not to eliminate the impact of brute luck from human affairs, but to end oppression, which by definition is socially imposed. Its proper positive aim is not to ensure that everyone gets what they morally deserve, but to create a community in which people stand in relations of equality to others."[48] Although she criticizes the "luck egalitarianism" of those who advocate "equality of resources" as well as those who promote "equality of welfare," she does not specifically state that Rawls is subject to her critique. Nonetheless, to the extent that being born into some particular "initial social position" is for Rawls a matter of luck, and to the extent that this is compared to the arbitrary nature of one's natural talents, Anderson's criticisms also seem to apply to Rawls.

Like other prominent liberal theorists, Rawls pays little attention to the group-based nature of oppression and to the importance of creating cultural contexts in which people can develop and use their moral powers. If we want to alter the power dynamics that create and sustain male dominance, racism, heterosexism, and other forms of oppression, we must view these social hierarchies as human creations that are not "natural" or inevitable. Thus, while it is laudable that Rawls does not merely want to accept whatever effects come about from one's being born into a particular social position, his theory does not go far enough in identifying and challenging the social structures of power that generate these initial positions.

Conclusion: Social Injustice and the Limitations of Rawlsian "Abstraction"

In contrast to the focus that both Rawls and Dworkin place on the perspective of individuals, feminist discussions of justice and equality typically center on relationships between social groups and on the power structures that generate unjust hierarchies within society. Remedying social injustice requires attention not only to the differences between individuals at any given point in time, but also to the social forces and relations of power that perpetuate and sustain these differences. According to Iris Marion Young, many liberal political theorists describe justice as being solely a matter of "distribution" and fail to analyze the institutional context in which patterns of distribution are created and sustained. Young contends that this "distributive paradigm" takes nonmaterial social goods and treats them as if they were material things to be possessed.[49] While it is important to note differences in the rights, opportunities, and self-respect of individual persons, the suggestion that these are things to be possessed distorts the relational character of these "goods." For instance, the degree of a person's self-respect cannot be measured in the same way that other, tangible goods (such as money or property) can be, and it is likely to depend on the social context and web of relationships in which the person lives. Furthermore, subtle changes in these relationships may affect one's self-respect in ways that cannot be detected or fully observed from the perspective of a strictly distributive paradigm.

Young's critique of the distributive paradigm also emphasizes the importance of examining the social processes and culture of the institutional context. On the one hand, it might seem as if Rawls's discussion of the importance of opportunities and self-respect, as well as his claim that people deserve the "fair value" of their equal political liberties, would work to ensure basic equality in the larger culture. Despite this appearance, however, in both of his major books, as well as in his essays and subsequent writings, he fails to describe in much detail the cultural and social forces that create and sustain social hierarchies. For Rawls, power dynamics in the "background" culture are beyond the scope of his theory, since his formulation allegedly concerns only the "basic structure" of society.[50] The ideas and values that people hold—such as their moral views or their religious beliefs—are typically understood by Rawls to be matters of their own personal perspectives and are not considered "political." Thus, many elements of culture and institutional context are relegated to the periphery and seen as separate from the "political" conception of justice that he offers. Instead of challenging the cultural and institutional context that generates and perpetuates various forms of oppression, he leaves this context aside in favor of remedying the unfair advantages and disadvantages associated with various social positions within this context.

Thus, although Rawls—like Dworkin—claims to be offering a theory of justice based on an abstract ideal of a just basic structure, there are a number of ways in which his "ideal" fails to question, and even implicitly assumes, the power structures of our own society. On the one hand, there are several ways in which gender is absent from his discussion: he does not include women as a relevant social position, nor does he grant the parties in the original position knowledge of gender oppression. While some feminists (such as Okin) suggest that these problems with his theory of justice can be remedied by including women, the problems with Rawls are more fundamental and are linked to an underlying failure to question—and even to identify—socially created and maintained structures of hierarchy. Feminists argue that male dominance is not a natural outgrowth of men and women's "differences." To challenge sexist structures, we need to do more than compensate women who are born with the "disadvantage" of being women in a sexist society. We must look more deeply at the causes of women's oppression and at the structures of power that create and sustain it.

While the aim of my criticisms is to undermine the claims to abstraction made by both Rawls and Dworkin, I do not mean to suggest that political theory simply needs to be more "abstract." Feminist change requires envisioning some other alternative society—one where the institutions of the basic structure do not take gender oppression, or other forms of unjust hierarchy, as a given. Such radical envisioning requires a careful, contextual analysis of the mechanisms of domination and oppression in our own society, and this sort of analysis seems to fall well outside the framework of liberal theories such as those of Rawls or Dworkin. Thus, while critical attention to the work of these liberals may be useful in understanding some of the problems with contemporary liberalism, feminists ultimately must move beyond the confines of liberal abstraction to construct theories that illuminate current relations of power and privilege and that envision more radical alternatives.

PART TWO

Abstraction, Ideals, and Feminist Methodologies

4

Idealization, Abstraction, and the Use of Ideals in Feminist Critique

In Chapters 2 and 3, we have seen that both Rawls and Dworkin construct abstract ideals in order to develop and defend their theories of justice and equality and that various problems arise from their attempted abstraction. As feminists, critical race scholars, and other social justice theorists have illustrated, the social context is characterized by various hierarchies, such as those of gender, race, sexuality, and class, and individual agents are affected by these structures in powerful but often invisible ways. Because the effects of oppression can be deep seated and yet invisible, attempts to simply "abstract" from all knowledge about the social structure may backfire and implicitly endorse the effects of dominant ideologies. Nonetheless, because theories consist of generalized claims that transcend the particularities of any given situation, theorizing seems to require some form of "abstraction."

In this chapter, I further explore the issue of liberal abstraction by examining the arguments of Onora O'Neill, a neo-Kantian moral theorist who is aware of some of the problems I note but nonetheless defends the use of highly abstract methods in normative theorizing. According to O'Neill, it is not abstraction that is responsible for these problems, but the use of "idealized" accounts of matters such as human agency, rationality, and independence that often appear in allegedly abstract theories, including those of Rawls and Dworkin. Abstraction can and should proceed in the absence of any idealized account of such matters, notes O'Neill, and it should be done without employing any particular normative "ideals."

After explaining O'Neill's defense of "abstraction without idealization," I present a number of criticisms of this view. In the context of oppression, I contend, methods of abstraction often involve the bracketing of information that is crucial to understanding the nature and sources of subjugation. In the later sections of this chapter, using the work of Susan Babbitt and Elizabeth Anderson, I make the case that normative ideals—which O'Neill rejects—may play an important role in understanding oppressive social structures and envisioning democratic and nonoppressive alternatives. Rather than setting up unattainable ideals for how individuals *should* be, Babbitt and Anderson put forth feminist ideals in an effort to transform society. I conclude by suggesting that normative ideals may be unavoidable in theorizing and that feminist theory can benefit from ideals that aim to challenge and creatively transform social structures of power.

Abstraction and Idealization: O'Neill's Account

At various points in her writing, O'Neill defines abstraction as merely a matter of "bracketing" certain predicates or "detaching certain claims from others"; it is "a matter of selective omission, of leaving out some predicates from descriptions and theories."[1] In this sense, abstraction is "theoretically and practically unavoidable. . . . All uses of language must be more or less abstract; so must all reasoning."[2] Thus, O'Neill claims there is an important sense in which criticism of abstraction is misdirected.

Examining the attacks on abstraction, she isolates two criticisms: the charge of empty formalism and the objection to abstract views of agents. In response to the first charge, which alleges the "formalism and emptiness of all practical reasoning that invokes principles or rules," she writes that while it "is true that principles underdetermine decisions," this is not a reason to reject them.[3] Principles and rules must be supplemented by good judgment; they are never sufficient determinants of action. In other words, principles need not be understood in an algorithmic fashion.

The second charge, that abstraction in ethical reasoning is problematic because it relies on "abstract views of agents" or on "idealizations" of human agency, is more complex. According to O'Neill, proponents of this critique, which she associates with Hegelian and Marxian attacks on "abstract individualism," assert that abstract ethical and political theories make assumptions that actual human agents do not satisfy. For instance, many abstract theories assume that individuals have capacities to reason, choose, or form preferences that only idealized agents possess. While O'Neill agrees with the substance of this criticism—she concurs that people do not have "transparent self-knowledge" or "archangelic insight into others' preferences"—she does not conclude that this is a problem with *abstraction*.[4] Rather, it is a problem with *idealization*: "The objection is not just that much (too much) that is true of human agents is *omitted* in some accounts of agents, but that much (too much) that is false of human agents is *added*. Descriptions of agents in much post-Enlightenment ethical and political theory are often *idealized*; they are satisfied only by hypothetical agents whose cognitive and volitional capacities human beings lack."[5] In objecting to what she refers to as idealization, O'Neill seems to agree with at least some aspects of the feminist critique of abstraction. For instance, some feminist objections to liberalism can be understood as objections to the ways that allegedly abstract theories actually make certain assumptions that are not abstract at all but instead presuppose particular conceptions of human rationality, independence, preference formation, or some other capacity. These assumptions (or "idealizations") tend to privilege men, whites, upper-middle-class people, and others who have power within sociopolitical structures. Although O'Neill focuses less on this aspect of the problem, she does note that idealization tends to favor the more privileged members of society. In a discussion of justice, gender, and international boundaries, she suggests that the problem with idealizations is not simply that they are false, but also that they tend to favor "specific conceptions of the human agent and of national sovereignty which are often more admired and more (nearly) feasible for developed rather than developing societies and in men rather than in women."[6] In this same article, she also admits the scope of this problem: it is not just a couple of theorists who engage in this sort of idealization. Rather, "[m]uch contemporary moral reasoning, and in particular 'abstract liberalism' (whether 'deontological' or utilitarian)" suffers from this problem.[7]

In addition to this first type of idealization (which posits agents with superhuman capacities), O'Neill describes and criticizes a second sort: many moral and political theorists "treat enhanced versions of certain capacities as *ideals* for human action."[8] According to O'Neill, positing ideals of "[r]ational economic men, ideal moral spectators," and "utilitarian legislators" ends up suggesting that these superhuman qualities are ones for which actual people should strive.[9] She objects to this because such ideals are simply unachievable and are often "irrelevant to human choosing." There are many domains where we do not want people to be rational calculators;

for instance, she points out the absurdity of "ideal rational friends and lovers."[10] In other words, these particular ideals may seem "ideal" for the purpose of certain theories but may not be ones that we actually would want people to embody in all realms of human activity. Moreover, O'Neill objects to reliance on ideals, since there is no way to justify them without falling back on assumptions about metaphysical truths: "Writers who start by assuming 'ideals' cannot justify them as mere abstractions, and need to supply appropriate justifications: this may be uphill work if they hope to reject metaphysical certainties that might ground demanding conceptions of the objectively good, or of the person."[11] Thus, O'Neill concludes, moral theory should not rely on idealized assumptions that are not really true of actual people (the first sort of "idealization"), nor should it aspire to particular ideals that it posits as worthy and desirable goals but that are unproved and merely assumed from the start.

After describing these two types of idealization, O'Neill proposes what sounds like a simple solution: moral and political theorists should reject idealization, in both its forms, but they should not reject abstraction. Referring to her solution as "abstraction without idealization," she argues that the problem with the critics of abstraction is that their failure to separate idealization from abstraction leads them, wrongly, to reject abstraction: "The lack of justification for starting with such 'ideal' conceptions of persons, reason or autonomy provides good reasons for querying these positions, but no reason for being suspicious about mere abstraction. . . . The many convincing criticisms of the idealized conceptions of persons, reason and action, on which one or another ethical universalist has in fact relied, while claiming only to abstract, do not show that there is anything wrong with abstraction."[12] In other words, these theorists highlight the problems of idealization and then make the mistake of assuming that such problems are inherent in any theory that uses abstraction. However, according to O'Neill, in order to draw this much more drastic conclusion, one would have to show that similar problems arise with "approaches that abstract, but do *not* invoke unvindicated ideals."[13] Yet this has not been established. She thus concludes that much criticism of abstraction has been seriously misplaced.

Reexamining Abstraction and Idealization

A careful reexamination of the objections to "abstraction" suggests that O'Neill may be misconstruing at least some of these criticisms. While she is right to note that it is difficult to object to abstraction itself when abstraction is defined as the mere "bracketing" of certain predicates (or "detaching certain claims from others"), this is not what the critics of abstraction are attacking. Many of their objections can be understood as objections to certain types of bracketing, and some seem to be arguing that abstract approaches attempt to bracket too much. The problems these critics raise often pertain to the degree or the form of bracketing, not to the act of bracketing itself.

Moreover, O'Neill's definition of abstraction as bracketing or as the "selective omission" of certain predicates makes it an odd candidate for praise. She suggests that as long as idealizations are avoided, "genuine abstraction" (abstraction that does not idealize) can serve as the foundation for moral theory. Given her definition of abstraction, however, it is not at all clear what this would involve. If the omissions are to be "selective" and are to focus on certain predicates rather than others, decisions must be made about what should be bracketed and what should be included. Unfortunately, she does not say much about the details of abstraction; nonetheless, she argues that normative theory needs more abstraction, not less.

A number of problems also arise with O'Neill's rejection of what she considers to be the two different types of idealization: (1) idealized assumptions that are false of actual agents, such as assumptions about human agency, rationality, and relationships; and (2) ideals posited by the theorist—that is, ideals that the theorist acknowledges are not yet descriptive of actual persons but are offered as goals to be achieved. O'Neill rejects both sorts of idealization and suggests that both can be avoided by pursuing a strategy of "mere abstraction."

O'Neill objects most strongly to the first type of idealization she describes. When idealized assumptions about such matters as human agency and human rationality turn out to be false, the models and theories that arise from these assumptions have no real application in the actual world. Furthermore, these theories are not only false but also dangerous; attempts to apply them often work in favor of the most powerful members of society (upper-middle-class white men, for instance) since the lives of the privileged are most likely to embody these idealized assumptions.

Although O'Neill's initial (and most forceful) objection to these idealized assumptions is that they are false of actual agents, her proposed solution suggests that it is not merely their falsehood to which she objects. For instance, in a discussion of justice, gender, and international boundaries, she argues that we must "resist the temptation to rely on idealizing models of human agency or national sovereignty. We should instead consider what sort of theory of justice we would have if we abstracted but refused to idealize *any one conception* of rationality or independence, and so avoided marginalizing or excluding those who do not live up to *specific ideals* of rationality or of independence from others."[14] Elsewhere in the same article, O'Neill suggests that we can—and should—proceed without any particular conception of gender or national sovereignty. First, we must devise abstract principles that do not idealize—that is, that do not assume any specific conception of the human agent. Next, we apply these principles without relying on any specific ideals. Explaining this second move, the one of application, she states that "justice can take account of *certain* differences by applying abstract principles to determinate cases" without "tacitly rein-troducing restricted ideals (e.g., by privileging certain views of gender and sovereignty)."[15] In other words, ideals can be avoided not only in the construction of abstract principles but also in their application. Thus, O'Neill is not suggesting that we simply replace false or oppressive con-ceptions of rationality, independence, gender, and national sovereignty with ones that are more accurate or less oppressive, but rather that we attempt to theorize without employing *any* particular conceptions at all.

This reading is supported by O'Neill's discussion of this problem in *Constructions of Reason*, where she explicitly criticizes Rawls's constructivism for relying on a "certain ideal of the moral person" that she claims is "built into the original position."[16] Specifically, O'Neill objects to the way that Rawls constructs agents so that they are motivated only by the "highest-order interests in their moral powers" and by their "concern to advance their determinate but unknown final ends" (210). For O'Neill, this account of the original position "explicitly bases principles of justice not on a concep-tion of the person that abstracts from the diversity of human agents, but on one that idealizes a certain sort of agent" (210). The problem, she suggests, is that Rawls does not abstract sufficiently; he imports a particular conception of the person when he should have relied solely on an abstract account of agency. This could have been avoided if he had employed "a more Kantian constructivism," one that began "from the *least determinate* conceptions both of the rationality and of the mutual independence of agents" (212). While this abstract version of constructivism could not guide us in choosing principles as concrete as Rawls's, it could justify our ruling out principles that any "abstractly characterized" plurality of agents would reject (218). For instance, O'Neill explains that her version of constructivism, based only on an abstract account of the person, entails the following: "No plurality can choose to live by principles that aim to destroy, undercut or erode the agency (of whatever determinate shape) of some of its members" (213). Or, as she puts it elsewhere, "if a plurality of agents is to share principles, action on the principles must leave the agency of each member of the plurality intact."[17] What this means, more specifically, is that agents must avoid coercion and deception, since these are ways of "destroying and subverting others' agency."[18] Of course, how one interprets these principles, and understands them to apply in any particular case, depends on many features of the circumstances, society, and context. O'Neill does not seem to worry about this problem, and she does not view this as an attack on the principles themselves, since it is not the job of principles to include specific rules for their application.

Although one could object to O'Neill's somewhat hasty dismissal of this problem of the interpretation and application of principles, I leave this matter aside and move on to two other problems with her objection to idealization (and with her defense of "mere abstraction"). In order to show that normative theorizing must do without any particular conceptions of matters such as human agency, rationality, or dependence, O'Neill would have to show both (1) that it is the use of these conceptions themselves that is problematic and (2) that it is possible to do without any such conceptions. However, she fails to establish either of these claims. With respect to the first matter, it is at least possible that the particular problems with the idealizations she discusses could be solved by replacing the idealized assumptions with ones that are more accurate and are less ideological. For instance, the assumption that agents are fully rational, mutually independent decision-makers may be problematic not because it involves a *particular conception of human agency*, but rather because it is *false* of most actual human agents. Moreover, it is "ideological" in the sense that it obscures relations of power that exist between human agents and it often works to bolster the status of oppressive groups. A more direct solution to the problem of false and ideological conceptions of human agency and functioning would be simply to replace these false conceptions with more accurately descriptive ones. Likewise, rather than suggesting that theory should proceed without any particular conception of gender (as O'Neill does in "Justice, Gender, and International Boundaries"), one might instead address the problem by replacing sexist and ideological assumptions about gender with a more accurate conception, one that does not presume women's inferiority.[19] O'Neill has shown only that the particular conceptions employed in the theories she discusses are objectionable. She has not established that all such conceptions—of gender, national sovereignty, and the person in general—are problematic.[20]

For the second point, it may also be the case that normative theory cannot do without some conception of the subject—for instance, an account of human rationality or of relations of dependence. As I noted earlier, because abstraction always abstracts from something in particular, the characterization that one gives to human agents can only be "abstract" in certain respects. The features that remain in O'Neill's account can therefore be said to be forms of idealization, which O'Neill should oppose if her account is to be consistent.

On the surface, O'Neill suggests only that her abstractly characterized agents are "diverse," but it may be that a more substantive form of idealization is lurking in her allegedly abstract account. In focusing on *rational agency*, rather than on other aspects of personhood, she seems to privilege a certain ideal of the person, one centered on agency and rationality as the defining features of personhood. Her focus on agency can be seen in her statement that "if a plurality of agents is to share principles, action on the principles must leave the agency of each member of the plurality intact."[21] For O'Neill, as well as other Kantian liberals, this may appear not to be an "idealization," but rather a mere "abstraction": rational agency is simply what one is left with when one brackets all the particular features of human beings. However, this conception of what defines personhood is not uncontroversial. For those who were not raised in the liberal tradition, or for those who do not subscribe to liberalism's individualism or to its emphasis on reason and rationality, *personhood* may be defined somewhat differently. For instance, Marxists emphasize the centrality of what persons *do*, and they thus define one's labor and activity as central to personhood. Likewise, some feminists contend that while persons are "rational," they are also caring, emotional, and embodied subjects. While not many theorists would object to the claim that rationality—and some account of agency—is an important element in defining personhood, O'Neill's claim that individual rational agency is the central defining feature of personhood seems to be an assumption peculiar to liberal theory. This is not to say that this idealization is false, but simply that it involves a "certain conception of the human agent," one that might not be shared by everyone.

In addition to claiming to avoid relying on any particular conception of the person, O'Neill denies employing any ideals about what human beings should be like: she suggests that one must theorize without assuming any particular conception of "the good." (This is the second sense of idealization to which O'Neill objects.) However, just as it may be impossible to avoid the first sort of idealization, it may also be impossible to theorize without the use of some particular normative ideals. A number of O'Neill's critics have suggested that the distinction that she draws between abstraction and idealization is problematic, and several have pointed to her own reliance on some sort of ideal as part of this problem. For instance, in a review of O'Neill's *Constructions of Reason*, Allen Wood notes that, as a part of her alleged abstraction, O'Neill professes to be "agnostic" about the human good and about the particular value of the person. Nonetheless, what she achieves is merely a *"selective* agnosticism about the human good": "O'Neill's Kantian constructivism affirms the value for human beings of exercising their rational agency; it seeks to protect that value at all costs, treating other components of the human good as derivable from that one." For Wood, O'Neill's analysis "threatens to involve itself in a conception of the human good that is not merely an abstraction but also an idealization."[22] Although rational agency may be important, we somehow would need to be able to measure its importance against other human goods in order to determine exactly *how* important it is. We cannot do this with O'Neill's account, however, since she requires that we abstract from all other components of the human good. Wood concludes that although O'Neill aims to criticize liberal theorists who pretend to be agnostic about the human good but nonetheless endorse particular idealizations, she herself succumbs to this very problem.[23]

Abstraction and Oppression

If it turns out that we cannot simply do away with all conceptions of the person and all use of normative ideals, we may need to focus more on the question of how to avoid employing *false* idealizations and oppressive or ideological normative ideals. On a similar note, because abstraction always involves the bracketing of certain—but not all—predicates, particular attention must be paid to the specific forms of abstraction that a theorist employs. In this section, I explore the use of abstraction in the context of circumstances of oppression.

Rather than arguing that abstraction has no role whatsoever in normative theory, some critics of abstraction object to the way that certain important features of the social structure are allegedly set aside, or bracketed, while these features nonetheless continue to influence aspects of the theory. For instance, a number of feminist legal theorists contend that many allegedly abstract theories actually assume a male norm. The context of male power is important in considering the meaning of domestic violence, rape, abortion, and numerous other feminist issues, and yet for many years, political and legal theories dealt with these issues while allegedly bracketing considerations of gender. In response, some feminists have proposed—rather than simply doing away with all abstraction (and focusing only on the concrete particularities of each and every individual) or eliminating all conceptions of the person or all use of ideals—paying attention to the *kinds* of abstractions, ideals, and conceptions of the person that the theory employs and disallowing those that are sexist and that reinforce or perpetuate women's oppression.

In contrast to those taking this feminist approach, O'Neill does not focus on which sorts of abstractions she is employing other than when it is necessary to avoid the use of idealizations and "ideals." She claims to be engaging in a method that is "merely abstract," and she does not seem to acknowledge that such abstraction necessarily includes certain features and facts, while excluding others. O'Neill's suggestion, however, that we begin theorizing with very abstract principles that all could agree to (without any use of moral ideals or conceptions of the person) could work to reinforce social power structures, and it could also end up presupposing false idealizations. The danger of this occurring seems greatest in cases where deeply entrenched hierarchies affect the sense of self that individual agents possess.[24]

To understand how employing the method of "abstraction without idealization" could end up reinforcing oppressive hierarchies, consider what happens when we apply O'Neill's method to a situation in which some of the agents possess a diminished sense of self-worth. In the context of a discussion of servility and self-respect, Thomas Hill describes the case of the "Deferential Wife," a woman who is so devoted to serving her husband that she "tends not to form her own interests, values, and ideals; and, when she does, she counts them as less important than her husband's."[25] What would happen if O'Neill's method of abstraction were employed by a plurality of agents, some of whom were like the Deferential Wife?[26] It seems that O'Neill has not ruled out this sort of agent, since her method of abstraction is meant to apply to any minimally rational agent who has an indeterminate amount of mutual independence from others. The problem is that she assumes that these agents—however characterized—would not choose principles that would undercut their own agency: "No plurality can choose to live by principles that aim to destroy, undercut or erode the agency (of whatever determinate shape) of some of its members. . . . Victims cannot share the principles on which others destroy or limit their very capacity to act on principles."[27] But what if the situation is one of systematic oppression in which some agents lack the self-respect that would motivate them to reject principles that victimize them or otherwise fail to promote their interests?

Rather than extensively discussing this sort of objection to her proposal, O'Neill mentions it only in a footnote and quickly dismisses it. She writes, "Colluding victims are not a counterexample. If collusion itself is coerced, they are not truly willing; if it is not, they are not truly victims."[28] In other words, if someone agrees to a principle that subordinates them, then they must have been coerced. There is no way that one can be a willing participant in one's own victimization. In cases such as that of the Deferential Wife, O'Neill would probably say that to the extent that this woman approves of principles that victimize her, she is being "coerced," and thus her approval is not genuine. Yet this seems a bit too quick, since it dismisses the complexity of the very identity that this woman possesses. Of course, there is something troubling about the identity of this sort of person. Her very sense of self seems to be impoverished, and she lacks the autonomous agency that O'Neill's model seems to presuppose. Rather than simply concluding that she is being coerced or that she is somehow mistaken about what she wants, one instead might argue (as Susan Babbitt has, in a commentary on Hill's essay) that it may be necessary for the Deferential Wife to undergo some sort of transformation before she will be able to form her own interests in a way that expresses a fuller sense of self.[29] However, it is precisely this sort of transformation that O'Neill's analysis prohibits. According to her method of abstraction without idealization, when a plurality of agents chooses principles, "action on the principles must leave the agency of each member of the plurality intact."[30] This is clearly problematic when some agents resemble the Deferential Wife. Preserving this sort of agency would likely reinforce what is already an oppressive situation.

Although the Deferential Wife may be an exaggerated extreme, the sorts of attitudes and the sense of self that she possesses are not entirely foreign to the situation of many women in contemporary society. Because of gender inequality, and the norms and institutions that structure and perpetuate it, many women actually do view their own interests as less important than their husbands'; thus, they might agree to principles that subordinate them in certain ways. Furthermore, similar examples could be raised concerning the situation of other oppressed groups, although the analysis of their particular forms of oppression would differ from that described here. The general problem concerns the effects of internalized oppression, which

O'Neill's theory—with its emphasis on individual agency—seems unlikely to combat successfully.

Challenging Oppression: The Role of Ideals

To address the problem of impoverished agency in situations of oppression, some feminists and other political theorists argue that specific ideals must play a role in normative theorizing, and they contend that certain features of the social context cannot be bracketed without running a high risk of reinforcing oppressive power relations. In this section, I examine the discussion of normative ideals in the work of two feminist political philosophers, Susan Babbitt and Elizabeth Anderson. While both theorists point to a variety of ways that normative ideals can be used, I focus here on Babbitt's discussion of the sorts of ideals that individuals employ when they undergo political transformation, and I describe Anderson's presentation of an ideal of democratic equality—an ideal that is posited as something for which society should strive. Both theorists pose a challenge to O'Neill by emphasizing the important role that ideals play in normative theorizing. Not only are these ideals unavoidable; they are also crucial in challenging false and ideological "idealizations."

In her 1996 book, *Impossible Dreams*, Babbitt argues that abstraction itself will not be enough to eliminate injustice. Her point is not simply that abstract principles can be misapplied, but rather that the understandings that people have of these allegedly abstract concepts are themselves skewed by injustice: "If sexism, say, is embedded in some of the concepts and terms in which information and events are understood, including conceptions of justice, it cannot simply be taken for granted that considerations of justice, in the abstract, will show us how to eliminate it."[31] In other words, the allegedly abstract definitions of *justice* and *morality* that are often central to liberal theory may take for granted sexist, racist, and classist power structures and may inadvertently support and perpetuate these structures. In a sexist context, the notion of morality or justice to which people appeal in considering an issue such as pornography or abortion is somewhat different from the way that morality or justice would be understood if it were altered or transformed by feminist analysis. Within a sexist social context, people often believe that abstract notions of morality and justice pit questions of individual privacy against the rights of the fetus in the case of abortion. Similarly, when it comes to issues of pornography within a sexist social context, people typically consider only how the pornographer's right to "free speech" is to be weighed against the rights of people who are "offended" by sexually explicit material; Ronald Dworkin's discussion of pornography in his essay "Do We Have a Right to Pornography?" which I discuss in Chapter 1, is a prime example of this.[32] Thus, the rights of women to exercise control over their own bodies and over their sexuality do not figure prominently into either side of the debate on these issues, as it is typically construed. In both these cases, sexist assumptions are embedded in the very understandings of the terms: abortion is recognized only as a privacy right and not as something that specifically affects *women's* ability to control their own bodies and lives, and pornography is recognized only as something that has the power to "offend" by depicting sex, rather than as something that has devastating consequences for women's status and equality. As a result, when people in a sexist social context think about what morality or justice requires *in the abstract*, this is the way the issues will typically be formulated. As Babbitt notes, "If sexist assumptions are embedded in the social context of meanings and values, they are not understood as sexist assumptions; rather, they are norms."[33]

In order to root out sexist assumptions and change the social understandings of what is required by "morality" and "justice," more specific work is needed. Babbitt explains, "Discrimination that is built into social norms and values requires work to be identified. Appeals to principles of justice, however defined, are not going to be enough if such discrimination is not identified as *in*justice to begin with. Changes to social structures may be required before the sexism that has always been there comes to be understood and treated as sexism."[34] In other words, it is not always evident what constitutes sexism, racism, or other forms of unjust power. To identify and uproot structures of oppression, greater attention must be paid to the operation of specific social structures. Furthermore, appealing to individual interests or choices will not be sufficient. Rather, social change must be undertaken as a necessary part of promoting the interests of individuals. Liberal theory goes wrong when it assumes that we can unproblematically know what these interests are without undertaking an analysis and critique of social power structures. By employing methods of abstraction that fail to question the interests that individuals currently express, social structures of power may be reinforced and social change may be impeded. If we wish to transform oppressive structures, Babbitt suggests, we must at least implicitly also appeal to some ideal or vision of how society could be otherwise. Because of the ways that sexism and racism (for example) are built into many of our assumptions, it may be that identifying the wrongness of these forms of oppression requires "an alternative *vision* of what society should be and how it should be divided up, one that permits judgments about how the existing society is wrong."[35] Merely abstract principles may not be sufficient to do this, and they may end up reinforcing the problematic and false idealizations of current hierarchies.

Rather than sketching an alternative vision of a society, Babbitt discusses examples drawn from fiction in which a character engages in some sort of transformative activity, or becomes a member of a community or group that changes both how she views herself and how she evaluates social institutions and practices. Babbitt describes how the protagonist in Alice Walker's *Meridian* "comes to understand her political goals primarily as a result of her experiencing what it is like to be part of the 'togetherness, communal spirit [and] righteous convergence' of the black political movement."[36] It is this involvement in the movement that affects Meridian's knowledge of herself and shapes her political ideals and visions, not the discovery of abstract principles. As Babbitt explains further, "Her actual situatedness within a network of political and emotional relationships itself provides her with epistemic standards, making interpretations possible that were not so previously."[37] In the following chapter, I make a similar point when I describe how involvement in feminist activism—and even in discussions with others about feminist issues—can empower women to view their situations in radically new ways. By engaging in various forms of activism and working to create and nurture institutions and practices that were previously marginalized or nonexistent, women come to know first-hand that the dominant institutions of society are oppressive and that they are not inevitable.

Although her writing focuses on different issues from Babbitt's, Elizabeth Anderson also argues for the importance, and the unavoidability, of ideals in normative theory. Rather than claiming that these ideals are abstract or that they can be derived from some ahistorical, acontextual, impartial starting point, Anderson suggests that they arise out of concrete circumstances, that they are subject to change as they are questioned and challenged, and that they evolve as society itself goes through transformations.

In her book *Value in Ethics and Economics*, Anderson defends a pluralist theory of value that emphasizes the importance of normative ideals. These ideals are unavoidable, she says, since we require them to make sense of ourselves: "Ideals are the self-conceptions through which we try to understand ourselves, to make sense of our emotions, attitudes, and concerns. . . .

We *make* ourselves intelligible to ourselves by cultivating attitudes that make sense to us, by determining to act in accord with ideals we accept that have survived critical scrutiny."[38] Instead of suggesting that ideals are merely subjective visions that people hold but that cannot be criticized by (or justified to) others, Anderson argues that ideals are contestable, that they require empirical support, and that they are subject to criticism and revision.[39] Thus, these ideals are neither abstract in the sense that they bracket all information about actual people, nor are they merely subjective in the sense that they pertain only to an individual's own personal vision and have no wider application.

To illustrate how an ideal that is situated in an understanding of social relations of power can be used to challenge problematic idealizations, I turn now to Anderson's discussion of the ideal of "democratic equality." In her essay "What Is the Point of Equality?" Anderson uses this ideal to challenge theorists such as Ronald Dworkin who advocate what she calls "luck egalitarianism" or "equality of fortune."[40] Many of Anderson's criticisms of these theorists are similar to those that I leveled against Dworkin's equality of resources (see Chapter 2), but she is critical not only of resource egalitarians such as Dworkin but also of those who advocate "equality of welfare." Rather than simply offering negative criticisms of these equality-of-fortune theories—by showing how such constructions fail to embody certain values that they purport to advocate—Anderson proposes an alternative ideal, democratic equality. Her strategy of employing an ideal that does not abstract from social relations of power is superior to simply attempting to abstract from all knowledge about society, rationality, and human behavior and agency. While attempting to engage in theorizing that is "merely abstract" makes it difficult to examine the problematic relations of power that serve as the background context of such theorizing, Anderson's method of employing an ideal that is situated in social analysis is more likely to succeed in identifying and challenging unjust structures of power.

As Anderson has it, luck egalitarianism encompasses both equality of resource and equality of welfare theories, and it "relies on two moral premises: that people should be compensated for undeserved misfortunes and that the compensation should come only from that part of others' good fortune that is undeserved" (290). Although she launches a thorough and convincing attack on this theory, I discuss only a few significant aspects of her critique, which focus on the problematic assumption that equality concerns the luck or fortune to which individuals are subject once they have been awarded that for which they are legitimately "responsible."

Two objections that Anderson raises against this conception of equality are that it assumes that we are in a position to assess individual responsibility and that it centers on matters of individual luck or chance, rather than on the systemic, socially and politically created forms of inequality. She notes that all luck egalitarians "place great stress on the distinction between the outcomes for which an individual is responsible—that is, those that result from her voluntary choices—and the outcomes for which she is not responsible—good or bad outcomes that occur independent of her choice or of what she could have reasonably foreseen" (291). Thus, luck egalitarians rely on this distinction—and require that we be able to make such a distinction—in order for the theory to work. In contrast to this concentration on individual luck and personal responsibility, Anderson's ideal of democratic equality focuses on the social structure and aims to create less hierarchical and more genuinely democratic relations between people. She explains: "Egalitarianism ought to reflect a generous, humane, cosmopolitan vision of a society that recognizes individuals as equals in all their diversity. It should promote institutional arrangements that enable the diversity of people's talents, aspirations, roles, and cultures to benefit everyone and to be recognized as mutually beneficial" (308). In acknowledging that social conditions are currently not reflective of this genuine human diversity, she promotes the notion that some ideal or vision of a more egalitarian society must play a role in transforming our current social order.

In addition to demonstrating the positive value of appealing to a normative ideal, Anderson illustrates the importance of examining—and refusing to abstract from—social relations of power. Whereas O'Neill attempts to begin theorizing from a starting point of "merely abstract" principles, Anderson contends that it is necessary to appeal to an understanding of the social order in challenging particular normative theories. Because democratic equality "aims to abolish socially created oppression" (313), our pursuit of this ideal requires us to examine society and to acknowledge its hierarchical structures; thus, we must attempt to construct and apply our normative theories in the context of this understanding. One problem with luck egalitarians is that they pay insufficient attention to the extent to which institutional arrangements affect people's choices and limit the options of what they can and will agree to under certain circumstances. In response to the emphasis that luck egalitarians place on the "voluntary agreements" of individuals, Anderson replies that the "suffering and subjection generated by people's voluntary agreements in free markets" should not be justified by the mere fact that these situations arose due to voluntary choices, in that "free choice within a set of options does not justify the set of options" (308–9). Examining the social structures in which individuals make their choices is a crucial part of understanding how "free" these choices really are. Simply by bracketing facts about the social structure, as O'Neill's method of abstraction advocates, we will be unlikely to uncover and challenge these problematic assumptions.

In contrast to O'Neill's unwillingness to endorse any particular values, ideals, or conceptions of the good, Anderson's theory of democratic equality would work to guarantee certain social goods for everyone.[41] Anderson points out that the luck egalitarians seek to compensate people for "undeserved losses of all kinds within the general space of equality they specify (welfare or resources)" and that they would oppose any more specific guarantees by society.[42] They rely on individual choices and preferences to such an extent that they preclude larger collectively made decisions about goods to which each person is entitled. Even if these goods would not be chosen by individuals, they may still be essential in guaranteeing the conditions of equality. Anderson notes that "egalitarian theory . . . must supply principles for collective willing—that is, for what citizens should will together, not just for what each can will individually."[43] Although O'Neill does not rely on market decisions, as the luck egalitarians all do (in various ways), she does advocate beginning with principles to which all could agree. She seems to emphasize individuals' making decisions for themselves in accordance with the decisions that other individuals make for themselves, and this differs from Anderson's attention to what could be willed *collectively*. Anderson specifically notes the possibility that some people could agree to situations that oppress them, but argues that this does not justify such arrangements: "If people find happiness in their lives despite being oppressed by others, this hardly justifies continuing the oppression."[44] To challenge the oppressiveness of such a situation, one must appeal to some normative ideal.

Conclusion

Unlike the allegedly abstract ideals of liberalism, the ideals proposed by Anderson and Babbitt do not attempt to abstract entirely from all "contextual values" or from all knowledge about the social structure. In this sense, they can be said to be more concrete than the abstract ideals of liberal theory, which purport to be value free and to have arisen from abstraction alone. As O'Neill points out, however, idealizations often appear in places where the theorist claims to be avoiding them: many allegedly abstract theories actually rely on idealizations of some sort. Unfortunately, she herself falls victim to her own criticism, since she ultimately cannot avoid all reliance on idealizations. Rather than arguing that such avoidance is possible, or even that it is desirable, I have suggested that the use of idealizations (and ideals) is problematic when these are false and when they assume the inevitability of oppressive hierarchies. As Babbitt and Anderson demonstrate, it is possible to make use of normative ideals in a way that neither reinforces oppression nor endorses false idealizations. Moreover, challenging oppressive social structures, such as race and gender hierarchy, may actually require appeals to "ideals" that explicitly suggest nonhierarchical alternative models for how society might be structured.

Thus, in examining O'Neill's work and contrasting it with that of Babbitt and Anderson, I have elaborated further on the specific issue of abstraction that I raised earlier in my analysis of the work of liberal theorists such as Dworkin and Rawls. In addition to criticizing the method of "mere abstraction," I have illustrated how an alternative method—one that employed ideals embodying norms of nondomination—could be more effective for feminist theorizing than the abstraction endorsed by most contemporary liberals. In the following chapter, I examine more carefully the issue of individualism in feminist theorizing; like attempts to restrict the debate to abstraction, efforts to focus solely on individuals may in fact end up hindering the theorist from uncovering and challenging various forms of sexism. Just as feminist political theorists must pay more careful attention to social structures of power, they must understand individuals as always situated in the context of specific relations of power and hierarchy. To challenge such structures, one often needs to take the perspective of the group or groups who are experiencing various forms of social domination. In Chapter 5, I advocate a form of theorizing that makes central the perspective of those who are suffering and resisting various forms of oppression. Along with the use of ideals of nondomination, such a perspective can provide a firmer grounding for feminist critiques of unjust power structures.

5

Feminism as an Alternative Methodology

In recent years, a number of feminist liberals have asserted that various aspects of liberalism can be adapted to feminist ends. In Chapter 3, I examined Okin's contention that, with some modification, Rawls's original position can yield feminist conclusions, and in Chapter 4 I considered O'Neill's arguments that the problems with liberal theory arise only with idealization, and not with abstraction, which she suggests is central to pursuing gender and global justice. I begin this chapter by considering the recent writings of another philosopher who is both a feminist and a liberal, Martha Nussbaum. Unlike Okin and O'Neill, Nussbaum is very explicit in her defense of liberalism as a tradition and a method that feminists should adopt (though not entirely without revision), and she explicitly advocates an individualistic methodology, with which I will take issue here. Ultimately, an alternative methodology is more fruitful for achieving feminist insight and for attempting to bring about feminist social changes.

In her essay "The Feminist Critique of Liberalism," Nussbaum raises and responds to three central feminist objections to liberalism: (1) liberalism is too abstract, (2) it is too individualistic, and (3) it focuses too heavily on reason and not sufficiently on emotion. She addresses each of these criticisms separately and argues for the more general view that liberalism can accommodate its feminist critics by appealing to its "deepest" core values and ideals, which have to do with the "protection of spheres of choice" and promoting "equal respect for personhood."[1] I focus here on the first and second criticisms raised by Nussbaum: the feminist critique of liberal abstraction and the related attack on liberal individualism. Using the resource of Catharine MacKinnon's work in responding to Nussbaum, I make the case that while liberalism can *accommodate* the critique of abstraction put forth by some feminists, it is unlikely to be an effective tool for the *discovery* and the *identification* of women's oppression. Once women's oppression has been identified, often through feminist methods that are more "radical" than "liberal," liberalism can acknowledge and even promote feminist concerns. The alternative "nonliberal" methodology proposed by feminists such as MacKinnon includes an appeal to such concepts as justice, equality, liberty, and rights, but engages in inquiry with an explicit commitment to ending women's oppression. In other words, this type of feminism is not unbiased, neutral, or individualistic; rather, it takes the perspective of "women" as a starting point for uncovering abuses and injustices. This makes it methodologically very different from liberalism, which eschews any explicit commitment to a particular perspective. In the end, I suggest, it is this alternative methodology that distinguishes some "radical" feminists from liberals, and it is the feminist critique of the liberal *methodology* of abstraction—and of focusing on individuals *as individuals*—that feminist defenses of liberalism, like Nussbaum's, fail to address.

Nussbaum's Account of the Feminist Critique of Liberalism

According to Nussbaum, the feminist critique of liberal abstraction has been made in two different ways. The first (and, according to Nussbaum, most powerful) critique is the one Nussbaum associates with MacKinnon and Alison Jaggar: "Their claim is that liberalism's disregard of differences between persons that are a product of history and social setting makes it adopt an unacceptably formal conception of equality, one that cannot in the end treat individuals as equals given the reality of social hierarchy and unequal power."[2] Conceding that this would be "an extremely serious *internal* criticism of liberalism" if it were true, Nussbaum suggests that liberals for the most part do not hold this unacceptably formal conception, and that they typically *do* pay attention to differences that result from history and social setting. She states merely that it "seems plausible that the liberal principle of formally equal treatment, equality under the law, may, if it is applied in an excessively abstract or remote manner, end up failing to show equal respect for persons" (68). Nussbaum raises a couple of examples in which this has occurred, but ultimately concludes that it "seems mistaken

. . . to think that liberalism has ever been committed to this type of unrealistic and ahistorical abstraction" (68). Furthermore, she contends that "liberal philosophers have, on the whole, seen more deeply . . . when they have rejected the purely formal notion of equality" (68). Here, as elsewhere in her article, Nussbaum appeals to what is "deep" within the liberal tradition and suggests that because the best interpretation of liberalism is one that can address these concerns, liberalism can accommodate this feminist critique. Examples of liberal theorists who, she argues, provide resources for this accommodation include Amartya Sen, whose capabilities approach Nussbaum endorses, and John Rawls, who explicitly opposes the perpetuation of advantages derived from morally irrelevant characteristics. In the work of such liberals, Nussbaum finds a rejection of the sort of abstraction criticized by these feminists.

The second feminist critique of liberal abstraction is one that Nussbaum links to communitarian critics of liberalism. This critique "cuts deeper" than the first one, and it cannot be accommodated so easily within the liberal tradition. In this communitarian view, liberalism focuses too heavily on the need to look at persons in abstraction from morally irrelevant features—such as ethnicity, gender, race, and religion—and as a result disregards the extent to which these differences shape people. Nussbaum's response is that liberalism is concerned with such differences, since it must take them into account "in order to ensure fair equality of opportunity"; nonetheless, she admits that liberalism holds that the "core of rational and moral personhood is something that all human beings share" (70). Not only is this unproblematic, according to Nussbaum, but it is also an important feminist insight; she defends liberalism's emphasis on rationality and choice as being crucial to feminism:

> What values prized by feminists are likely to be slighted by this liberal emphasis on choice? If women are understood to be, first and foremost, members of families, or members of religious traditions, or even members of ethnic groups—rather than, first and foremost, as human centers of choice and freedom—is this likely to be in any way better for women than is the "abstract individualism" of liberalism? . . . And the communitarian vision of persons, in which we are at heart and essentially what our traditions have made us, is a vision that leaves reduced scope for feminist critique. (70–71)

Clearly, she makes an important point here: the communitarian view that persons are defined by their communities and by "traditions" is hardly a feminist view. However, given the significant and widely acknowledged differences between feminism and mainstream communitarianism, it is unclear why Nussbaum includes the communitarian critique of liberalism in her discussion of the *feminist* critique of abstraction.[3] In discussing this second critique of abstraction, she does not explicitly engage the work of *any* feminists who she claims raise this objection. In a footnote, she makes reference to an essay by Onora O'Neill in which this second critique of abstraction is detailed and notes that "[t]he feminists criticized by O'Neill include Carol Gilligan, Eva Kittay, Genevieve Lloyd, Sara Ruddick, and Nel Noddings."[4] Yet in this section of her essay, Nussbaum does not explain how the works of these theorists—or of any other feminists who hold this view—differ from the communitarian position she describes and criticizes. Although there are numerous problems with the feminist view commonly referred to as "care ethics," embodied in its most extreme form in the work of Noddings, the problems with this perspective are *different* from those with the standard communitarian view that Nussbaum discusses here. Although many feminists are interested in communities (as opposed to mere individuals), feminists understand and define *community* and *group* differently from the way communitarians do. It thus seems mistaken for Nussbaum to reduce the discussion of communities to the communitarian celebration of traditional religious and cultural practices, which often marginalize and oppress women.

Liberal Abstraction and Feminist Methodology

To her credit, Nussbaum succeeds in identifying several important strands of the feminist critique of liberalism—individualism, abstraction, and the focus on reason—and she rightly points out that the critique of abstraction offered by radical feminists such as MacKinnon, Jaggar, and Carole Pateman differs from that formulated by the care/communitarian theorists (even though she fails to properly distinguish the feminist care theorists from non-feminist communitarians). Nevertheless, there are significant ways in which Nussbaum misrepresents the radical feminist critique of abstraction:

1. This critique focuses not on "differences" that are a product of "history and social setting," but on the effects of domination.
2. It posits not merely that it is plausible that liberal abstraction could function in problematic ways, but rather that many liberal thinkers—

including liberal political philosophers—have typically not paid adequate attention to actual power differentials in society.

3. Radical feminists such as MacKinnon do not argue that liberalism is "too abstract" or that it adopts an "unacceptably formal conception of equality," as Nussbaum suggests.[5] Rather, they argue that liberalism purports to theorize in ways that are "abstract" and it invokes conceptions of equality that it contends are merely "formal," while in fact the subject of these "abstractions" and the content of these allegedly "formal" conceptions is particular, concrete, and biased in favor of men.

In this section, I draw on MacKinnon's critique of liberalism to explain and defend these three points.

With respect to the first point, it is important to note that in opposing the "abstraction" of liberalism, MacKinnon is not, as Nussbaum suggests, critical of liberalism's "disregard of *differences* between persons that are a product of *history and social setting*."[6] MacKinnon's critique of abstraction is far more specific than this: she is opposed to the ways in which the effects of domination and hierarchy get labeled and understood as mere "differences." Rather than discussing "history" and "social setting," MacKinnon describes relations of power between men and women. In her view, systems of power construct male and female identities: our personalities, preferences, sexuality, and even styles of bodily movement are all shaped by conditions of male domination and female subordination. It is wrong to think of the "men" and "women" that result from these power structures as being merely "different" from one another, when these supposed "differences" are defined in part by domination: "to be on the top of a hierarchy is certainly different from being on the bottom, but that is an obfuscatingly neutralized way of putting it, as a hierarchy is a great deal more than that."[7] She aims to dispel the idea that gender is a matter of "difference," since this view justifies the denial of women's political and legal equality. Whereas the traditional debate in feminist legal theory has been over whether women are *the same as* men or *different from* men, she shifts the focus to questions of domination. In sum, although Nussbaum is clearly aware of MacKinnon's specific emphasis on the results of male domination, not on "differences," she offers a somewhat misleading characterization of MacKinnon's position.

Second, I noted that in responding to MacKinnon's critique of liberal abstraction, Nussbaum argues that although it "seems plausible" that liberalism could be "applied in an excessively abstract or remote manner," and that liberalism has "sometimes been taken to require that the law be 'sex blind,'" it nonetheless ultimately "seems mistaken . . . to think that liberalism has ever been committed to this type of unrealistic and ahistorical abstraction."[8] Clearly, MacKinnon and Nussbaum hold divergent views about the prevalence of this type of liberalism, and it is beyond the scope of this chapter to track just how entrenched liberals' commitment to abstraction is. In any case, Nussbaum seems to overlook the fact that MacKinnon is not saying simply that liberalism *could* function in the manner she describes, nor is she saying that it must always function this way. MacKinnon's point is rather that liberalism tends to work in the manner that she suggests. In legal theory and practice, in philosophy, and in social policy more generally, when theorists and policy makers attempt to be "abstract," their efforts often obscure and thereby reinforce relations of male dominance. One example of this is Rawls's initial description of the original position as involving individuals who are heads of households. While these are supposed to be "representative persons," the details of Rawls's early description of these persons reveal that they in fact resemble men. Rather than raising other similar examples from liberal political philosophy, I want to note simply that Nussbaum needs to offer more evidence for her claim that such occurrences have been rare; MacKinnon contends that they are pervasive.[9]

Finally, the third and most important element of the feminist critique of abstraction is one that Nussbaum seems entirely to overlook: the problem with liberalism is not that it is too abstract, or that it employs a conception of equality that is too formal, but that it embodies the interests of those who actually already hold unjust power over others. To further explain this important critique of liberalism and to demonstrate the inadequacy of Nussbaum's response, I provide a brief overview of MacKinnon's theory of equality, difference, and dominance under liberalism.

Much of MacKinnon's work in legal theory focuses on analyzing and criticizing the way that mainstream (liberal) legal theory treats equality as a matter of "sameness" and gender as a matter of "difference." MacKinnon argues that women and men are not merely "different"; they are "different" primarily in the sense that men have more power than women. Because the liberal approach to sex equality requires that people already be the same before they can be seen as deserving of equal treatment, women who suffer the effects of sex discrimination encounter difficulty achieving equality. As an alternative to this sameness/difference approach, MacKinnon proposes her own "dominance" approach, according to which both equality and gender are understood as matters of power and domination. She views the gender or sex division as one of domination/subordination, and she understands the goal of "equality" to be the elimination of unjust hierarchies of power. Thus, for MacKinnon, equality is not a matter of abstract comparisons between "persons" who must be similarly situated as individuals. Instead, questions of equality are about social power: political, economic, sexual, and other forms of domination. To achieve equality, one must consider substantive, concrete questions about who has power over whom in society.

According to Nussbaum's interpretation, MacKinnon is essentially stating that whereas the dominance approach to the law is substantive, since it mandates an examination into actual relations of power, the sameness/difference approach of mainstream liberal theory is formal and overly abstract. Upon closer examination, however, it becomes clear that this is *not* MacKinnon's view. Although MacKinnon sometimes uses the terms *abstract* and *concrete* to contrast liberalism to her own approach, her more detailed discussion of liberal abstraction reveals that she does not believe that the liberal approach actually is as abstract as it claims to be. Rather, she argues, this approach is already "substantive" in that men are the ones who set the standard to which women need to be "similar" in order to deserve equal treatment. The reason that liberalism is not seen as being substantive, or as embodying any particular viewpoint, is that the male perspective already defines so many aspects of our society.[10] The substance and content of the categories are already defined, yet the approach appears to be merely abstract: "It is testimony to how substance becomes form in law that this rule is considered formal equality. Because it mirrors the values of the social world, it is considered abstract, meaning transparent to the world and lacking in substance."[11] Yet as MacKinnon explains elsewhere, "From women's point of view, adjudications are already substantive; the view from nowhere already has content."[12] Although liberal legal theorists *claim* to be engaging in mere "abstraction," they actually employ a male standard.

MacKinnon makes a similar point about abstraction and male domination when she addresses the liberal state and its invocation of the rights of abstract persons, such as the rights to free speech and privacy, and its advocacy of state "neutrality" between individuals' conceptions of the good. Just as liberal equality law employs a male (not to mention white, upper-middle-class, and heterosexual) conception of the person as its implicit standard, so too does liberal political theory implicitly assume a male subject as the bearer of rights: "To be a person, an abstract individual with abstract rights, may be a bourgeois concept, but its content is male. . . . Human rights, including 'women's rights,' have implicitly been limited to those rights that men have to lose. This may be in part why men persistently confuse procedural and abstract equality with substantive equality: for them, they are the same. Abstract equality has never included those rights that women as women most need and never have had."[13] Examples in which rights have functioned this way include the invocation of privacy rights in cases of marital rape and domestic violence and appeals to the right to free speech in debates about restricting pornography that is harmful to women. MacKinnon's position is not that the rights to free speech and privacy are unimportant, nor does she argue that such rights are defined in a way that is too abstract. Her point is that specific rights are invoked according to the perspectives and interests of men, and more generally, they are defined to protect the interests that men already have and do not want to give up.

Offering an alternative to the problematic manner in which liberal rights are defined and applied, MacKinnon encourages women to redefine rights in ways that enable us to argue for what we, as women, most need: for instance, the right to be free from rape, from sexual harassment, abuse, and violence and—more generally—the right to define ourselves as persons, and as individuals, in a context free from male domination. Because MacKinnon seeks to redefine these rights and liberties so that they embody women's perspectives and interests, it seems that Nussbaum is incorrect to accuse her, and other radical feminists, of entirely abandoning the "language of liberalism." Nussbaum begins her essay with the statement "Women around the world are using the language of liberalism."[14] She then offers several examples of women in different cultural contexts who are using terms such as *rights, personhood, autonomy,* and *self-respect* in order to better their positions in society and to challenge male domination. She explains: "It is obvious that the activists from whom I have quoted have gone about their business undaunted by the feminist critique, and they will not be daunted now, if feminists once again tell them that autonomy and personhood are bad notions for feminists to use" (56). Insofar as Nussbaum has feminists like MacKinnon in mind here, this is a misrepresentation of the feminist critique. Few feminists state that women should not invoke any notion of autonomy or personhood in their arguments. The debates and questions are over what exact role these concepts should play in a feminist critique of society and about precisely *how* these terms should be understood. In this, there is a sense in which Nussbaum's attempt to defend the "language of liberalism" is too simplistic.

To the contention that allegedly abstract rights and supposedly formal conceptions of equality are not actually abstract, but in fact embody the particular interests and perspectives of men, liberal theorists such as

Nussbaum might respond that the solution to this problem lies in a more "consistent" appeal to the "deepest" principles and commitments of liberalism. This is in fact the response that Nussbaum offers to many of liberalism's feminist critics, and she makes this point numerous times throughout her essay:

> The deepest and most central ideas of the liberal tradition are ideas of radical force and great theoretical and practical value. These ideas can be formulated in ways that incorporate what is most valuable in the feminist critique—although liberalism needs to learn from feminism if it is to formulate its own central insights in a fully adequate manner. Taking on board the insights of feminism will not leave liberalism unchanged, and liberalism needs to change to respond adequately to those insights: But it will be changed in ways that make it more deeply consistent with its own most foundational ideas. (56–57)

For Nussbaum, liberalism involves a commitment to the view that individuals each possess "equal dignity and worth" and that the "primary source of this worth is a power of moral choice . . . that consists in the ability to plan a life in accordance with one's own evaluations of ends" (57). To the extent that liberal legal theorists and political philosophers have taken male lives as the norm, marginalizing and suppressing women's interests and needs, the problem has not been one within liberalism itself. According to Nussbaum, we can appeal to the very principles of liberalism—its emphasis on equal dignity and individual moral choice—to remedy the problems of male bias, which involves rather than too much abstraction, a *failure* of abstraction, an unjust form of particularity and favoritism. The solution to these problems can thus be found within liberalism, by appealing to its deepest principles.

Feminist Alternative to Liberal Individualism

While Nussbaum is correct to suggest that there is room within liberal principles to accommodate feminist concerns, the methodology to which liberalism is committed is not the most effective route toward achieving feminist insights and bringing about feminist changes in society. MacKinnon suggests a fruitful methodology, one that does not dismiss the liberal concepts of freedom, rights, liberty, and equal concern and respect, but offers a different (and in a sense nonliberal) method of attempting to achieve them. In contrast to Nussbaum's emphasis on the "deepest" insights of liberal principles and on liberalism's concentration on individuals, MacKinnon's view holds that we must pay particular attention to the interests of oppressed groups, such as women, and formulate laws—as well as devise theories about rights, liberty, and equality—with the specific interests of women in mind.

According to Nussbaum, feminist concerns are best addressed within liberalism not only because liberal principles are able to accommodate feminist concerns, but also because the liberal method of paying specific attention to each and every individual is a promising strategy for discovering women's problems and for achieving feminist aims:

> Liberalism holds that the flourishing of human beings taken one by one is both analytically and normatively prior to the flourishing of the state or the nation or the religious group. . . . The central question of politics should not be, How is the organic whole doing?, but rather, How are X and Y and Z and Q doing? . . . Putting things this way . . . just asks us to concern ourselves with . . . how well *each and every one of them* is doing, seeing each and every one as an end, worthy of concern. Put this way, liberal individualism seems to be a good view for feminists to embrace. (62–63)

In other words, Nussbaum advocates an individualistic methodology for identifying and attacking women's difficulties; rather than women's interests being lumped together with that of their communities, religions, or even families, women should be seen first and foremost as individuals with interests of their own. This is particularly important in cases of family violence, since "women and girls are overwhelmingly likely to be its victims" (63). Mentioning problems such as sexual abuse, domestic violence, marital rape, and genital mutilation, Nussbaum writes: "To people who live in the midst of such facts, it is important to say, I am a separate person and an individual. I count for something as such" (63). For Nussbaum, the problem is not that liberalism has been focused too exclusively on abstract individuals, but instead that "where women and the family are concerned, liberal political thought has not been nearly individualist enough" (63).

In one sense, she is correct: examining each and every individual, *as an individual*, should lead to feminist insights. In a context in which the terms *domestic violence*, *sexual harassment*, and *rape* have become fairly common words in our vocabulary, this indeed does occur. Her own writing on the situation of women in India reflects an awareness of many forms of oppression that affect women and a concern for uncovering the empirical facts of women's oppression.[15] Nonetheless, before feminists began openly discussing these problems, individual women—and those investigating the lives of individual women—were unlikely to label their experiences in these ways and, in fact, often regarded such problems as merely "personal." It was (and to some extent still is) common for individual women to blame themselves for having provoked an unwanted sexual encounter or to consider themselves deserving of verbal or physical abuse by their partners. Now that feminists have uncovered and articulated the social and political nature of these events, it is relatively easy to look at the lives of individual women and see that such phenomena are not unusual and to think that focusing on each and every individual would be sufficient to detect them. But before a critical understanding of such circumstances was articulated, looking at the lives of individual women was unlikely to lead to feminist insights.

In another recent book, *Women and Human Development,* Nussbaum offers an extended discussion of the ways in which women's preferences may be "adaptive" to circumstances of deprivation and oppression, and her treatment of this problem sheds light on her analysis of liberalism.[16] Reflecting on the situation of Indian women in Andhra Pradesh and the effects of a government-sponsored consciousness-raising program, Nussbaum writes of the women: "All to some extent undervalue basic human capabilities that they later come to value, because of social habituation and social pressure."[17] Offering one example of an Indian woman who was unhappy with her abusive marriage and her lack of control over her economic well-being, Nussbaum explains that although this woman was unhappy, "she did not yet have the conception of herself as someone who has *been wronged,* who *has a right* not be abused. . . . Over the years she learned those concepts, and now she teaches other women to see themselves as rights-bearers."[18] Although Nussbaum's main argument in this essay is different— she is positing that her capabilities approach (roughly based on Sen's work) is superior to that of other liberal approaches, and specifically to welfare-based theories—her argument has implications for her discussion of the feminist critique of liberalism. On the one hand, she clearly is aware that people can make "choices" and hold "preferences" that do not reflect their best interests and that situations of oppression can obscure this fact. Nonetheless, although she credits a consciousness-raising program for prompting these women's changed awareness, she writes as if it were the possession of certain "concepts" that these women were lacking. In her example, after a woman has "learned these concepts," that woman "teaches them" to others, so that they too can know that they are "rights-bearers." While this may be one way to describe the process, it fails to capture the transformation that occurs when a woman begins to think of herself in a radically new way. One does not suddenly "learn" that one is worthy of not being abused, as one might learn the basic principles of geometry. Rather, through involvement in various educational and economic programs, and through interaction with other women who are also politically engaged, a woman may come to view herself and her life possibilities differently. It is not simply that the liberal concepts of "rights" and "personhood" are out there to be grasped intellectually and that once one understands them, one's choices and preferences change. Rather, the process is far more complex than Nussbaum suggests. It involves a political awareness of women's collective oppression that is not mentioned in her account, which makes it seem as though an individual's knowledge of liberal concepts is sufficient for social change.

Nussbaum fails to appreciate the significance of this epistemological point: knowledge about women's problems in the context of male dominance is not uncovered simply by focusing on individuals *as individuals* who gain an awareness that they are in fact rights-bearing persons. In a context in which ideologies of male superiority are entrenched, liberalism's focus on individuals will be insufficient for the discovery and development of critical feminist perspectives. What is needed is an analysis of social structures of power. Although Nussbaum suggests that the alternative to individualism is a focus on the "organic whole," or on the "flourishing of the state or the nation or the religious group," this is not the only—nor is it the best—alternative.[19] Feminists differ from communitarians *and* from liberals in that it is neither the entire community/religion/nation upon which we focus, nor is it simply the individual. What makes feminism unique is its focus on the group *women*.

As an alternative to liberalism's method of focusing on each and every individual *as an individual*, MacKinnon and other feminists propose a different methodology, one that begins with the perspective of women living under male dominance (while acknowledging that the group *women* is made up of women who have a variety of different experiences, based in part on the prevalence of other forms of social and political hierarchies—such as race, class, sexual orientation, disability, and nationality). Rather than advocating the strategy of "abstracting" to an aperspectival point of view that would value the perspective of each agent only as an individual, MacKinnon proposes another method: taking the point of view of women's experience of male domination. As she outlines it, "Feminist method adopts the point of view of women's inequality to men. Grasping women's reality from the inside, developing its specificities, facing the intractability and pervasiveness of male power, relentlessly criticizing women's condition as it identifies with all women, it has created strategies for change, beginning with consciousness raising."[20] Advocating consciousness-raising, MacKinnon makes reference to the "CR" groups formed in the early 1970s women's liberation movement, but she does not mean to limit her discussion to these specific groups.[21] More generally, she urges that women collectively examine their lives and come to new understandings of the structures of social, economic, political, and sexual relations. Through discussions that engender this, individual women become conscious of the fact that they are not the only ones who have had to endure experiences of abuse; low-paying and sexually exploitative jobs; or sexual harassment, rape, and other forms of violation. Discussing their concrete experiences with one another, women see patterns and similarities emerge; problems that formerly seemed to be rooted in women's "nature" or in their own personal failures become recognizable as products and manifestations of male dominance and female subordination. As MacKinnon puts it, "The discovery that these apparently unchangeable dictates of the natural order are powerful social conventions often makes women feel unburdened, since individual failures no longer appear so individualized."[22] In fact, as she points out, the realizations that "the personal is political" arose from consciousness-raising, and this consists of a number of interconnected facets: First, women are dominated by men as individuals because they are dominated by men *as a group*. Next, they are subordinated *in society*, not by personal nature or biology. Third, the gender division, including the sexual division of labor, pervades women's personal feelings in relationships. And fourth, women's problems must be addressed as a whole, not merely as if they were the problems of individual women.[23] In other words, by offering consciousness-raising as the method of feminism, MacKinnon poses a challenge to both the focus on individuals and the methods of attempted abstraction common to traditional liberal theorizing. It is only by taking the perspective of "women"—or by working to somehow develop a "women's perspective"—that the powerful ideology of male dominance can be understood and undone.

In response to suggestions that feminism must concern itself with the interests of women as a group, some feminists have rightly noted that calls for attention to the interests of women as a group can—and often do—

work in ways that reinforce other structures of political and social hierarchy, including racism, classism, and heterosexism. Feminists of color, for example, have declared that when differences between women are eclipsed, it is usually the most privileged women who define the meaning of the larger category *women*.[24] Offering similar arguments, other feminists problematize the feminist strategy of taking the perspective of "women," since women are a diverse group about whom broad generalizations cannot be made.[25] While it may be true that MacKinnon, in certain instances, pays insufficient attention to the experiences of women of color, working-class women, or women living in third world countries, I would argue that these claims are best understood as objections to specific generalizations that she makes, not to her desire to come up with some kind of an analysis of the situation of "women."[26] For an analysis of the situation of women to be acceptable, it would have to adequately take into account a variety of other forms of oppression and incorporate the perspectives of women of color, lesbians, working-class women, and many other women who are caught in the interstices of various intersecting forms of oppression. Although MacKinnon's treatment of interlocking systems of oppression in her 1987 and 1989 books lacks the complexity of more recent work on these issues, I believe that her formulation could be extended and employed in ways that do not assume or endorse racist, sexist, classist, or other oppressive hierarchies.

In emphasizing the importance of women's experience of oppression, MacKinnon distances herself from methods of abstraction, as well as from attempts to be "neutral," "impartial," and "universal." What she criticizes is not abstraction or aperspectivity per se, but rather the *strategy* of abstraction: "Feminism does not see itself as subjective, partial, or undetermined but as a critique of the purported generality, disinterestedness, and universality of previous accounts. These have not so much been half right as they have invoked a wrong because partial whole. Feminism not only challenges masculine partiality but questions the universality imperative itself. Aperspectivity is revealed as a strategy of male hegemony."[27] Although she fails to adequately distinguish a number of terms that are interrelated but nonetheless distinct—impartiality, aperspectivity, universality, neutrality, and abstraction—the point that she makes here about the "universality imperative" and the "strategy" of aperspectivity is one that seems also to apply to abstraction. Methods of abstraction applied in the context of unequal relations of power function to obscure these relations of power. Because abstraction always involves the bracketing of certain features and the retention of others, this method is itself not apolitical and can never be fully impartial or neutral.[28]

In taking up the viewpoint of "women," and more specifically the perspective of women's subordination under a system of male dominance, MacKinnon suggests that all laws, and all theories, embody *some perspective* or other. Likewise, all attempts to "abstract" remain concrete in some way, since one cannot abstract from absolutely everything. In a sense, then, a theory cannot be problematic simply because it is "partial" or because it embodies some particular perspective. But insofar as liberalism is committed to equality and justice, it seems that it has a commitment to represent the perspectives of everyone equally, and the fact that the perspectives of some are left out, misrepresented, and—worse—often prevented from being developed and cultivated in the first place, is a serious shortcoming.

Conclusion

In this chapter, I have argued that Nussbaum fails to address and respond to important feminist criticisms of liberal abstraction and individualism. Although she distinguishes the more radical feminism of MacKinnon, Pateman, and Jaggar from communitarianism and from feminist care ethics, she does not acknowledge the extent to which this radical critique is an attack on the *methodology* of abstraction. I have argued that the attempt to be very abstract, and to bracket much of our knowledge about the social world, can be damaging to social and political theorizing. Efforts to eschew any particular perspective often fail to achieve the neutral impartiality for which they strive, and as a result, social power structures and ideologies of domination can be implicitly endorsed and perpetuated.

The solution liberals offer to this problem is an appeal to liberalism's own "deepest" principles, which leads it to focus on individuals and to attempt to eschew any particular biased perspective. I have set out to prove, however, that this approach is problematic, since it is not possible to avoid taking *any* particular perspective. Theorizing is always influenced by one's perspective, and attempts to eschew perspectives can easily backfire. Although taking the perspective of "women" is not unproblematic, attempting to examine social phenomena with an eye toward the collective situation of women in some particular context will be more likely to unearth the sources, causes, and effects of oppression than will attempts to appeal to liberal concepts as if these existed in a vacuum.

PART THREE

Feminist Postmodernism:
An Alternative to Liberalism?

6

Politicized Identity, Women's Experience, and the Law

In previous chapters, I drew on the work of Catharine MacKinnon, Susan Babbitt, Elizabeth Anderson, and Iris Marion Young to argue that certain forms of feminist theory and practice offer an alternative to both the abstraction and the individualism of liberalism. I suggested that without entirely dismissing the concepts of rights, equality, and justice, feminists can recognize that such concepts reinforce male power but that they must be redefined from a feminist perspective. Through projects of redefining these concepts and working to implement them through feminist theory and activism, women can bring about changes in social institutions and practices.

In Chapters 6 and 7, I examine the recent work of two feminist theorists who are rooted in the postmodern tradition, Wendy Brown and Judith Butler.[1] Echoing the concerns of other postmodern feminists, Brown and Butler offer a number of arguments against the analysis I have defended, and they raise important questions about the nature of political, linguistic, and legal structures in the context of oppression. Employing a Foucaultian conception of power, in which power circulates and cannot be seen as originating in one specific locale, postmodern feminists resist efforts to devise structural or systemic analyses of the experience of oppression. Although one reason for such resistance is the worry that a structural account of women's oppression could reify women's status as "victim," postmodern feminists also call attention to the very real danger that radical feminist attempts to formulate laws based on a feminist understanding of women's equality might in fact lead to legislation that will be co-opted and used to reinforce the status quo. Focusing on different aspects of how the law works, both Brown and Butler suggest that one cannot make the law embody feminist understandings of oppression without taking part in highly restrictive and problematic forms of regulation. In fact, both suggest that if the law were to acknowledge certain forms of male dominance as oppressive, this might preclude the possibility that such practices could be given a different meaning at some point in the future.

I examine these arguments because I think it is important to distinguish my project from feminist postmodern critiques of liberalism. Like Brown, Butler, and other postmodernists, I am critical of liberalism's abstraction from actual power relations and of its narrow focus on individuals. Nonetheless, I suggest that the concepts typically employed in liberal discourse— such as rights and equality—can be radically reformulated to embody feminist perspectives. In previous chapters, I have argued that dominant conceptions of rights and equality are not in fact abstract, as liberal political and legal theorists purport, but actually embody hierarchical and oppressive understandings of power. By introducing an analysis of male dominance that takes women's lived experience as central, feminists can use these allegedly universal concepts to promote the interests of people who are marginalized and oppressed.

While Brown and Butler share some of my objections to liberalism, they oppose efforts to devise structural or systemic analyses of the experience of oppression. Whereas Brown focuses on the issue of identity, Butler highlights the linguistic aspect of experience, noting that because speech acts must be repeated in order to be part of a structure or system of oppression, there is always the chance that such repetition could fail. The risk of failure, and the possibility that speech could be "restaged" or "resignified," undermines attempts to describe the situation of women, people of color, or gays and lesbians in any systemic manner. Both Brown and Butler contend that structural analyses of group-based oppression become particularly dangerous when articulated in the universalistic language of the law. They warn that feminist and antiracist attempts to regulate pornography or restrict racist hate speech could solidify the oppression and the victim-based identities of those who seek liberation.

In addition, Brown and Butler treat MacKinnon's arguments against pornography, each objecting to the way that her analysis focuses on sexual subordination and not on other aspects of women's experience. Rather than specifying what these other experiences are, however, and rather than attempting to correct MacKinnon's analysis so that it more adequately takes the interests of women into account, they ultimately decide that a structural analysis of women's oppression is simply not possible and that any attempt to devise such an analysis runs the risk of being politically repressive and counterproductive. Thus, unlike theorists who fault MacKinnon for paying insufficient attention to the experiences of women of color, working-class women, or other nonprivileged women, and unlike those who claim that MacKinnon must devise a more adequate account of women's experiences of sexual pleasure, of lesbian experience, of caring, or of any one of a number of issues on which feminists focus, Brown and Butler both seem to reject the very idea that one could devise an analysis that would apply beyond very specific groups of women.[2] For example, Brown suggests that women give up the reliance on "established rights and identities" in favor of "unwieldy and shifting pluralities adjudicating for themselves and their future on the basis of nothing more than their own habits and arguments."[3] She explains that this does not mean that women cannot speak about their experience, only that their speech cannot be used to draw any general conclusions that would apply beyond their own particular situations. This suggestion— made in different ways by Brown and Butler—is extremely problematic, both for feminists and for others who seek to challenge social hierarchy and to change structures of power. While one can raise specific problems with any particular analysis of women's experience, or of women's oppression, denying that any such analysis is possible is a different—and far more vexed—claim.

In this chapter, I carefully examine Brown's objections to feminist refor-mulations of the right to equality. Although I touch upon her general analysis of the liberal interpretation of rights, my central concern is her more interesting contention that feminists cannot and should not attempt to reformulate moral concepts such as *rights* and *equality*, nor should they analyze women's oppression by means of these categories. I begin by con-trasting Brown's view of rights with the position of the theorists she attacks, investigating her response to MacKinnon, in particular. While MacKinnon criticizes liberal theories of rights and equality, she reformulates and rein-terprets these universal concepts in ways that work to challenge women's oppression. Brown's attack on this feminist reformulation is misguided for several reasons. First, she collapses the feminist contention that women are victimized by male dominance into the claim that women are inherently and necessarily victims. Second, she reduces feminist discussion of rape, sexual abuse, and sexual harassment to a "confessional discourse" limited to the individual victim's personal suffering. Finally, linking the notions of

rights, equality, and justice to the law, Brown dismisses attempts to reformulate these concepts but does not offer adequate feminist alternatives. In
the final section of this chapter, I examine Brown's general rejection of
legal approaches, as well as her claim that feminists should neither engage in
"moral critique" nor facilitate the establishment of "new norms." Contra
Brown, I argue that not all uses of the law are problematic: radical legal
strategies can sometimes function as part of a larger struggle against oppression. Moreover, I suggest that in dismissing any arguments she associates
with "moral critique," Brown leaves women with few tools for constructing
critical analyses of oppression. I conclude by stressing the importance of
collective and critical analyses of social systems of oppression, analyses that
are open to revision but that nonetheless can describe, critique, and alter
unjust systems of power.

Brown's Objection to "Identity-Based" Political Critique

In "Rights and Losses," a chapter from her 1995 book, *States of Injury*,
Brown acknowledges that radical feminist formulations of rights and equality
depart from the liberal understanding of these concepts. Whereas liberals
support granting abstract rights to individuated rational agents, some feminists and critical race theorists advocate granting women, people of color,
and other members of oppressed groups certain rights, and certain claims
to equality, based on a critical analysis of male dominance, racism, and
other forms of oppression. For instance, on the basis of evidence that racist
hate speech harms people of color, Kimberlè Crenshaw and Mari Matsuda
maintain that such speech is a violation of their right to equal treatment.
MacKinnon, Rae Langton, and other feminists make similar arguments
about certain forms of pornography: because it is harmful to women, this
material violates women's right to equality and cannot be defended by any
simplistic appeal to the right to free speech.[4] Without dismissing the idea of
free speech, they assert that questions must always be asked about *whose* speech
is being protected; if free speech is to be contextualized in an analysis of
social power, questions of social hierarchy and oppression cannot be ignored.

Brown objects to the arguments of activists, legal scholars, and theorists
who attempt to make "concrete" the allegedly abstract content of such
categories as rights and equality, because of her concern that their efforts
are more likely to lead to further oppression. She worries that "rights for
the systematically subordinated tend to re-write injuries, inequalities, and

impediments to freedom that are consequent to social stratification as matters of individual violations and rarely articulate or address the conditions producing or fomenting that violation."[5] She raises a number of questions: What happens when rights are articulated not on the basis of one's generalized humanity or abstract personhood, but on the basis of one's being a woman, a gay person, or a Native American? How can a person have specific rights based on an identity that is particular if the very discourse of rights itself is abstract and universal? In answering these questions, Brown suggests that the universal discourse of rights simply cannot accommodate these specific and "historically contingent" identities that feminists and antiracist activists attempt to insert into the discourse, for "the more highly specified rights are as rights for women, the more likely they are . . . to encode a definition of women premised upon our subordination in the transhistorical discourse of liberal jurisprudence."[6] In other words, because identities have developed in the context of oppression and subordination, they carry the marks of that oppression and should not be reified through being inserted into the universalistic categories of the law.

One factor in Brown's opposition to feminist attempts to analyze women's oppression with the categories of rights and equality is her objection to the development of a structural or systemic analysis of the experience of any particular oppressed group. According to Brown, women should not attempt to describe their experiences in terms of structures of oppression that go beyond very specific historical circumstances. Although we can speak about our experiences as women, "our words cannot be legitimately deployed or construed as larger or longer than the moments of the lives they speak from; they cannot be anointed as 'authentic' or 'true' since the experience they announce is linguistically contained, socially constructed, discursively mediated."[7] Thus, she warns of the dangerous consequences of formulating analyses of group-based oppression in the universalistic language of rights.

Although Brown objects to carrying out these particular types of analyses with the universalistic language of rights, her view about the value of rights in general is far more difficult to decipher. At the beginning of "Rights and Losses," she announces that she is "not asking whether rights as such are emancipatory" and that she does "not want to participate in an argument for or against rights as such."[8] Most of the essay centers on the dilemmas of articulating an analysis of oppression using the abstract concepts of rights and not on assessing the value of rights in general.[9] In a subsequent essay, Brown reiterates her objections to these feminist reformulations of rights and also offers her own general assessment of rights, concluding only that they are "deeply paradoxical."[10] Rather than directly assessing the value of rights in general, she asks whether their paradoxical nature *might* give rights the capacity to raise certain questions that could lead to political change:

> Might the political potential of paradox appear greater when it is situated in a non-progressive historiography, one in which, rather than linear or even dialectical transformation, strategies of displacement, confoundment, and disruption are operative? How might paradox gain political richness when it is understood as affirming the impossibility of justice in the present, and as articulating the conditions and contours of justice in the future? How might attention to paradox help formulate a political struggle for rights in which they are conceived neither as instruments nor as ends, but as articulating through their instantiation what equality and freedom might consist in that exceeds them?[11]

It is difficult to make sense of Brown's suggestion that rights could "articulate through their instantiation" something that "exceeds them." If equality and freedom are understood as somehow "exceeding" rights—if rights do not yet fully embody the ideals of equality and freedom—how can it be that through their instantiation, rights articulate what equality and freedom might consist in? Unfortunately, Brown never directly answers many of the questions she raises.[12] Thus, rather than attempting to make her overall assessment of the value of rights-talk coherent, I turn instead to her attack on the attempts by feminists and antiracist activists to reformulate rights based on an analysis and critique of structures of oppression.

Women's Status as "Victims"

In recent years, a number of feminists (as well as some nonfeminists) have objected to the feminist emphasis on women's status as "victims" of male domination. While nonfeminists raise this concern because they deny the existence of male dominance (in other words, they deny that women are victimized by an oppressive sex/gender system), some feminists also object to this emphasis on women's victimization because it seems to discourage women's resistance and to suggest that women are incapable of challenging their oppression. Brown is one feminist who raises this concern, and she specifically suggests that the feminist reformulation of rights perpetuates victimhood as the essential and unchanging characteristic of the oppressed.

In her critique of feminist attempts to reformulate rights, she argues that it is problematic for an oppressed group to focus on harm, suffering, or victim status as a basis for political claims. According to Brown, by discussing women as the victims of male dominance, feminists such as MacKinnon reinforce and perpetuate this as the defining element of "women's experience." In her attack on MacKinnon, Brown fails to distinguish feminist analyses of women's victimization in the context of male dominance from claims that women are inherently or essentially victims regardless of social structures. Moreover, although she alleges that focusing political attention on harms tends to backfire and "reinscribe" these harms, she fails to offer a coherent defense of this claim.

In Brown's view, MacKinnon "equates women's equality with women's rights against the incursions of male sexuality" and thereby reinforces the view that women are inherently sexually violable and in need of state protection.[13] She claims that, for MacKinnon, the truth of "women" is reducible to the experience of sexual violation. She accuses MacKinnon of encoding "the pornographic age as the truth rather than the hyperbole of gender production," claiming that MacKinnon's theory can posit nothing beyond the identity women have as the objects of sexual domination by men, in that "this evacuation of female subjectivity of any element not transparent on the pornographic page renders any emancipatory project nearly impossible."[14] MacKinnon's position thus resembles the traditional, conservative view that women need to be protected from the violence of male desire, and her work "closely echoes the universalizing, transcultural, and transhistorical arguments about the sexual order of things proffered by orthodox political conservatives."[15]

Despite Brown's attempt to paint MacKinnon as one who holds an unchanging conception of sexuality, MacKinnon's position actually rests on the claim that sexuality itself is socially constructed and therefore historically contingent. In fact, an important aspect of MacKinnon's argument is her claim that the social practices of sexual harassment, rape, pornography, and prostitution result from the way that "sex" is constructed under conditions of male dominance: "If women have been substantially deprived not only of their own experience but of terms of their own in which to view it, then a feminist theory of sexuality which seeks to understand women's situation in order to change it must first identify and criticize the construct 'sexuality' as a construct that has circumscribed and defined experience as well as theory."[16] When Brown states that MacKinnon thinks women are subordinated through the "appropriation, commodification, and violation of female sexuality," she makes it sound as if MacKinnon actually endorses this as the meaning of "female sexuality."[17] As the quotation from MacKinnon above illustrates, however, she focuses critically on the way in which women's sexuality is itself constructed by relations of male power. In arguing against pornography, she is not aiming for the "containment" or "suppression" of female sexuality, as Brown suggests, but for "an end to the demand for eroticizing women's degradation" and for "a world in which men are no longer turned on by putting women down."[18] In this, MacKinnon challenges the very meaning of "sexuality" in the context of male dominance and seeks to open up space to change this construction.

On a more general note, Brown also claims that it is problematic for an oppressed group to focus on harm, suffering, or victim status as a basis for political claims. According to Brown, by discussing women as the victims of male dominance, MacKinnon and other feminists reinforce and perpetuate this as women's identity. Furthermore, Brown suggests that any attempt to focus on the particular suffering of a group of people as a basis for "politicized identity" is likely to backfire. Making a comparison to the "slave morality" described by Nietzsche, Brown warns that constructing one's subjectivity in this way "produces identity in reaction to power" and creates a subject that is "deeply invested in its own impotence."[19] As she frames it, "Politicized identity, premised on exclusion and fueled by the humiliation and suffering imposed by its historically structured impotence in the context of a discourse of sovereign individuals, is as likely to seek generalized political paralysis, to feast on generalized political impotence, as it is to seek its own or collective liberation through empowerment. Indeed, it is more likely to punish and reproach . . . than to find venues of self-affirming action."[20] If she is right, feminist discussions of the harms of oppression will lead to a confessional discourse that is more likely to celebrate victimization than it is to promote power. I now turn to Brown's claims, which—if true—could be very serious.

Politicized Speech and Confessional Discourse

In her essay "Freedom's Silences," Brown criticizes the feminist practice of speaking out about experiences of oppression. Although she acknowledges that such speech is "intended as a practice of freedom," she warns that it may have the opposite effect of solidifying victim-based identities and attachments.[21] Likening such speech to confessional discourse, Brown admonishes that any form of speech about one's injury or abuse runs a serious risk, as "confessing injury can become the act that attaches us to the injury, paralyzes us within it, and prevents us from seeking or even desiring a status other than that of injured."[22] This works by producing a group identity based on the sum total of the litany of abuses that individual women speak about as the "truth" of their womanhood. Thus, "even as feminism aims to affirm diversity among women and women's experiences, confession as the site of production of truth . . . tends to reinstate a unified discourse in which the story of greatest suffering becomes the true story of woman."[23] That is, by speaking too frequently of one's abuse, one may become engulfed in this identity, defining oneself as an individual solely in terms of one's victimization, and defining all members of one's social group according to a shared victim-identity. Brown demonstrates how this might occur: "Certain experiences—concentration camp existence or childhood abuse—may conservatively claim their subjects when those experiences are incessantly remembered in speech, when survivors can only and always speak of what they almost did not survive and thus cannot break with that threat to live in a present not dominated by it."[24] According to Brown, people often speak about their victimization in an attempt to relieve themselves of guilt that they feel about the experience. She asks (again in the form of a question, but with the suggestion that this is a serious potential problem), "What if, too, this endless speaking about one's past of suffering is an attempt to excoriate guilt about what one did not do to prevent the suffering, an attempt that is doomed insofar as the speaking actually perpetuates by disavowing the guilt?"[25] In other words, speaking about one's pain and suffering is not much different from confessing that one has done something wrong and thus must speak about it publicly in order to relieve the burden of guilt.[26] If this is so, "it is . . . possible to make a fetish of breaking silence. It is possible as well that this ostensible tool of emancipation carries its own techniques of subjugation—that it converges with unemancipatory tendencies in contemporary culture, establishes regulatory norms, coincides with the disciplinary power of ubiquitous confessional practices; in short, feeds the powers it meant to starve."[27] Put another way, the breaking of silence about women's oppression could serve to reinforce it. Although Brown comes to no definitive conclusions about this possibility—in fact, she characteristically avoids direct assertions—it is clear that she thinks this possibility must be taken seriously by feminists, gays and lesbians, people of color, and others who write and speak about their need for liberation.

Clearly, she has raised an important concern. In order to assess it, however, we must explore whether feminist accounts of victimization are no more than the confessional narratives to which she rightly objects. We must also consider empirical questions about the actual effects of speaking out about one's victimization by oppressive structures. According to feminist accounts of consciousness-raising, the awareness that one has been injured or harmed is in no sense sufficient for feminist consciousness. For years women have been aware of the many ways in which they are harmed by men through such practices as rape and domestic violence. But these injuries were often experienced as individual harms that brought about personal humiliation, a feeling that was not feminist or political. Without their having access to other women's experience, it would be extremely difficult for individual women to begin to see that male dominance is a *system* of abuse. By discussing their experiences with one another in a feminist context, however, women are often able to develop new, politicized understandings of them.[28] Through such discussion, women may begin to understand what has happened to them in terms that focus not on personal feelings of hurt and humiliation but rather on relations of power between social groups. This sort of understanding of one's abuse is political, analytic, and critical and thus differs importantly from the resentful confessional discourse Brown describes.

Even if Brown were to acknowledge that a political critique based on an analysis of injury need not be a confessional discourse, she still might worry about the possibility that such a political analysis could backfire. In the following section, I explore the question of why this possibility is so ominous for Brown. I argue that her real worry is that discussions of harm will provoke the enactment of legislation and the development of "regulatory norms," which she suggests are antithetical to freedom.[29] I also briefly consider empirical questions about the effects of women's speaking out about the abuses suffered under male domination and about the effects of adopting various strategies of resistance.

"Sheerly Political Battles": Brown's Alternative to "Regulatory Norms"

In addition to contending that rights should not be defined on the basis of experiences of abuse and victimization, Brown seems to oppose feminist attempts to reformulate concepts such as rights because such efforts rely on the use of legal methods and because they appeal to universal norms of what is right and wrong, just and unjust. In this section, I explain and critique her rejection of legal methods and her refusal to endorse feminist projects that seek to develop "new norms." I also explore alternatives open to her, attending particularly to her claim that feminists must engage in "sheerly political battles."[30] Ultimately, I find that Brown's arguments preclude the development of feminist analyses and critiques of power, and thus leave little room for feminist resistance.

According to Brown, feminists should neither work to provide concrete content to abstract categories and concepts nor attempt to articulate or define new norms. She contends that efforts to write "women's experience" into law are problematic because it is impossible to make generalizations that apply to all women across the lines of culture, race, and class; that is, specific historical analyses become problematic when inserted into the "universalist" legal discourse: "What does it mean to install in the universalist discourse of law an analysis of women's subordination that may be quite historically and culturally circumscribed?"[31] In other words, any specific claims that we could make about women would be too limited to accurately describe the entire category.[32] Therefore, such claims should not be the basis of a law that would hold for an indefinite amount of time and be applied beyond the specific group of women whose experience was used to shape and define it. By inscribing a particular set of experiences within the law, feminists will define and restrict the possibilities for what women can be; legal definitions reify what are actually only particular moments in history and culture.

While Brown never offers a straightforward defense of her view that legal approaches are inherently problematic, her work suggests two related reasons. First, from Brown's perspective, because the law is a universalist discourse, legal rights "necessarily operate in and as an ahistorical, acultural, acontextual idiom."[33] Given this, it does not make sense to attempt to inscribe specific identities into these abstract concepts. Unfortunately, Brown's remarks here fail to capture the complexity of the relationship between concepts and their embodiment in social and legal institutions and practices. Just because the *discourse* of the law is abstract, this does not mean that the law actually *operates* in an abstract or ahistorical manner, oblivious to any particular social meanings. People of color, feminists, gays and lesbians, labor rights activists, among many others, have argued that the way that these supposedly abstract concepts actually function reveals that they always make some use of sociopolitical, historical understandings. Specifically, it is the interests of the most privileged that typically define the particular content given to legal concepts, such as rights, equality, freedom, and privacy.

In order to challenge the problematic meanings that these allegedly abstract concepts come to embody in any particular context, these assumptions must be acknowledged and altered. This is, however, just the sort of analysis and critique that Brown discourages:

> [W]hen these material constraints *are* articulated and specified as part of the content of rights, when they are "brought into discourse," rights are more likely to become sites of the production and regulation of identity as injury than vehicles of emancipation. In entrenching rather than loosening identities' attachments to their current constitutive injuries, rights with strong and specified content may draw upon our least expansive, least public, and hence least democratic sentiments.[34]

That is, it is best *not* to articulate the concrete power relations in which rights are always actually involved.

Brown's reluctance to redefine these ideals may be rooted in her tendency to focus on the discourse in which claims are formulated rather than on the concrete content the ideals embody in any specific context. Her description of these abstract concepts as being timeless and ahistorical implies that she accepts the liberal understanding of "rights" and of legal concepts generally: like liberals, she thinks that these concepts actually are—and must necessarily be—abstract and ahistorical. While some liberal theorists think that this is a virtue, she suggests that it is problematic. For Brown, abstraction is bad because it fails to account for the particularities of specific historical situations. According to the feminists and critical race theorists I have cited, however, the problem with abstract concepts is not that they fail to account for all particularity, but rather that they rely upon certain particular, and politically problematic, assumptions when they are defined and employed in contexts of social and political hierarchies. In order to identify and confront these assumptions, one must engage in analysis of social and political reality, challenging problematic norms and concepts and replacing them with more adequate, less oppressive ones.

In fact, Brown is not entirely consistent in her objection to the abstract nature of liberal ideals and concepts. While she tends to take issue with the abstract, "universalizing" nature of these concepts, she does lapse into moments when she finds hope and inspiration in the possibility that these purely abstract ideals seem to offer. In an uncharacteristic passage at the end of her chapter on rights she claims that it is "in their abstraction from the particulars of our lives—and in their figuration of an egalitarian political community—that they [rights] may be most valuable in the democratic transformation of these particulars."[35] This passage is confusing because it seems to contradict her own opposition to abstraction, and it goes against her claim that we need to focus on the particularities of people's lives. The statement is also troubling, because it intimates that rights are most likely to contain visions of "egalitarian political communit[ies]" when they simply abstract from all discussion of social power. And yet, in her earlier remarks on Marx's analysis of rights, Brown herself acknowledges that this is false.[36]

The second reason that Brown seems to have for rejecting feminist attempts to insert an analysis of women's oppression into the law is that she opposes the development of "new norms" and of laws that would increase the degree of "regulation" in people's lives: "Freedom requires the capacity for a kind of public speaking that neither demands concurrence from others nor entails the establishment of new norms by which to live."[37] Unfortunately, she never specifies exactly what is wrong with establishing new norms when the ones by which people live are problematic. Although she would surely agree that a number of contemporary norms are oppressive, she does not advocate replacing the problematic norms with ones that are more liberatory. Rather, we should simply engage in "politics" as opposed to attempting to discuss and define new norms or moral "truths." On Brown's view—one that worries feminists opposed to postmodernism—politics is "a terrain of struggle without fixed or metaphysical referents."[38]

> Contrary to its insistence that it speaks in the name of the political, much feminist anti-postmodernism betrays a preference for extra-political terms and practices: for Truth (unchanging, incontestable) over politics (flux, contest, instability); for certainty and security (safety, immutability, privacy) over freedom (vulnerability, publicity); ... for separable subjects armed with established rights and identities over unwieldy and shifting pluralities adjudicating for themselves and their future on the basis of nothing more than their own habits and arguments.[39]

Brown's descriptions of "politics" and "truth" raise important questions of their own.[40] For one, Brown holds that truth is that which is "unchanging" and "incontestable"; this, however, is not the only way that truth can be understood. Many feminists describe the truth of women's condition without suggesting that this is a necessary truth that would remain unchanged if social structures were to alter. Furthermore, politics need not be opposed to issues of "truth, safety, and security" in the manner that Brown suggests. In political movements against oppression, members of subjugated groups often seek some degree of security; they attempt to bring about a situation in which they are less vulnerable. For instance, feminist opposition to sexual harassment is "political" (in Brown's sense) in that it involves challenging and contesting entrenched norms and practices. However, this political struggle also includes demands that women should be entitled to a greater level of security: specifically, women should not be vulnerable to the harms of sexual harassment. Thus, contrary to Brown's suggestion, the political struggle for freedom may include an attempt to achieve a degree of safety and security.

Not only does Brown fail to provide an argument for why she defines politics as she does, she also neglects to consider practical questions of current social power relations. Just because she wants to avoid all discussions of moral norms and truths, this does not mean other members of society will follow suit. The way that the current moral norms are defined is influenced by social power structures. If one decides to ignore these discussions, suggesting that morality and truth simply do not matter, this will not lessen the impact that the dominant (and often oppressive) moral norms have over people's lives. Thus, questions about which norms and regulations are best—which are most in line with Brown's view of radical democracy and freedom, or with some other view of what society should be like—are unavoidable. Given that the current moral norms and laws suffer from certain problems, and given that no society can function without any norms, laws, or regulations, it is in the interest of feminists to collectively define better, less oppressive norms and laws, even while acknowledging that these might require modification in the future.

On a similar note, the fact that not everyone possesses an equal amount of social power means that it may be impossibly utopian to suggest that we can simply engage in the sorts of contests that Brown describes, where there are "unwieldy and shifting pluralities adjudicating for themselves and their future on the basis of nothing more than their own habits and arguments."[41] Even were such political contests desirable, how would they be enacted in the context of contemporary institutions and arrangements of power? Because some people do have a lot more power than others, the former have a greater ability to succeed in the battles and contests that Brown wishes to see enacted. That being so, such contests would not be equal, nor would they take place in the absence of assumptions about truth, morality, or social norms. Without these problems being addressed, and absent some critical analysis of social relations of power, the battles that Brown advocates as "sheerly political" would amount to libertarian struggles in which anything is acceptable and in which those who have power from the start would be most likely to prevail.

All told, Brown fails to offer an alternative feminist approach to the problems of liberal rights theory. Her suggestion that women's experience cannot be made the subject of universal categories such as *rights* or *justice* implies that she views the content of these categories as necessarily abstract and not subject to historical change and revision. Such a view of rights and justice may actually align her with a very traditional view that sees these categories as abstract and unchanging. What many feminists maintain, however, is that such concepts always embody some particular social content, and the content that they currently embody is skewed by the impact of male dominance. In order to challenge and change the problematic content of these allegedly abstract norms, a feminist critique of male power is needed. While one might raise legitimate objections to any given feminist analysis, Brown's work goes beyond this to reject the very notion that there could be such an analysis.

Finally, Brown seems to pay insufficient attention to actual empirical questions about whether speaking out about various forms of sexism—and formulating feminist demands in terms of revised conceptions of rights and equality—has been successful. She raises concerns about such efforts, suggesting that they will fail and likening them to mere "confessional" discourse. Going beyond the philosophical matters raised by Brown, it is important to challenge her contention that speaking out against oppression is likely to backfire. In fact, since the start of the second wave of the women's movement, women have engaged in various forms of consciousness-raising, organizing "speak-outs" against rape, sexual harassment, and domestic violence and taking other forms of collective action to stimulate awareness and instigate social change. Such actions have not led to a worsening of these problems, but rather have worked to educate the communities in which they were undertaken and to empower the women who participated in and organized them. Given the widespread acknowledgment that rape, domestic violence, sexual harassment, and other similar problems can be eliminated only through collective awareness of how these practices violate and oppress women, Brown must offer at least some reason to persuade her readers that speaking out against these practices is likely to backfire.

Law, Activism, and Social Change

At a number of points in her work, Brown writes as if legal reform and other forms of social change were mutually exclusive, as if one either appeals to the law or one does something else. For instance, she suggests that engaging in legal argumentation involves giving up the more democratic sphere of "popular contestation": "Perhaps the warning here concerns the profoundly antidemocratic elements implicit in transferring from the *relatively accessible sphere of popular contestation* to the *highly restricted sphere of juridical authority* the project of representing politicized identity."[42] Contrary to Brown's suggestions, engaging in discussions about how to best interpret the concepts of rights and equality, and offering legal arguments that employ these concepts, does not necessarily preclude other forms of political change. It is certainly possible to work for legal change while at the same time engaging in other forms of social, cultural, and political activism.

On a similar note, it is naive to assume that the law has no power to shape and define the cultural, political, and economic institutions that Brown seeks to change. At times she writes as if the law only has the power to hold individual agents accountable for harms committed against identifiable victims. For instance, she claims: "When social 'hurt' is conveyed to the law for resolution, political ground is ceded to moral and juridical ground. Social injury such as that conveyed through derogatory speech becomes that which is 'unacceptable' and 'individually culpable' rather than that which symptomizes deep political distress in a culture."[43] While the law may impose its immediate effects on individual agents and victims, it also has serious implications for the status of larger social groups. Making illegal certain forms of racism, sexism, and homophobia—and creating laws that are actually effective in preventing these harms—certainly can affect the level of racism, sexism, and homophobia present in the larger society and culture.

According to MacKinnon, the law does not exist in a vacuum; it has effects on the ways that people view themselves, both as individuals and as members of various social groups. The law does not only come into play after the fact of abuse, as a means of regulating or punishing the individual perpetrator; rather, it also gives people a different sense of what is occurring to them as it is happening. MacKinnon explains: "Especially when you are part of a subordinated group, your own definition of your injuries is powerfully shaped by your assessment of whether you could get anyone to do anything about it, including anything official. . . . When the design of a legal wrong does not fit the wrong of what happens to you . . . that law can undermine your social and political as well as legal legitimacy in saying that what happened to you was an injury at all."[44] She notes, for example, that having the legal right not to be subjected to sexual harassment gives women a different sense of what is going on when such harassment occurs. Whereas before, the experience might have been thought of as just an annoying but inevitable part of life in the male-dominated workplace—and if a woman was bothered by it, she was "overly sensitive"—it is now something that many women see as an issue of women's equality. Sexual harassment has become something that many women now experience differently, and this is in part a result of the fact that women's experience has finally been incorporated into the way the law defines this harm.[45]

Not only are women's experiences affected by the law, and by what is defined as legal and illegal, but so too is the law affected by women's experience and by the sociopolitical movements in which feminist activists are engaged. As I have noted, at a number of points in her work, Brown pits the "relatively accessible sphere of popular contestation" against the "highly restricted sphere of juridical authority" as if these two spheres were unrelated.[46] But why portray the realm of feminist activism and popular contestation as if it had no impact on the realm of the law? Even when feminists are not directly engaged in legal debates, their arguments and actions affect the context in which the law is practiced, and sometimes also directly influence laws and judicial decisions. Furthermore, debates about legislation and court decisions clearly play some role in shaping public consciousness and in shifting people's ideas about different issues. For example, MacKinnon and Andrea Dworkin crafted an antipornography ordinance that defines pornography as "graphic sexually explicit discrimination" and makes the following four practices legally actionable: "coercion into pornography, forcing pornography on a person, assault due to specific pornography, and trafficking in pornography."[47] Although the ordinance was certainly controversial, even among feminists who oppose the objectification of women in pornography, one effect of this proposed legislation was to introduce a view about pornography that many had not before considered. While their attempts to pass the legislation were unsuccessful and short-lived, MacKinnon and Dworkin at least succeeded in introducing a novel perspective on what had been a debate about the interests of free speech verses the censorship of "obscenity." Indeed, prior to the introduction of the ordinance (in Minneapolis; Indianapolis; and Cambridge, Massachusetts), the legal discussion of pornography centered not on whether it was harmful to women, but on whether it passed the obscenity standard. The obscenity standard targets any material that is "offensive" to community standards and has no scientific, artistic, literary, or political value. Although the discussion of the ordinance did not entirely eclipse the debate about obscenity and community standards, it added a new element—concern for women's equality—to the legal debates about this issue. While feminists already had been discussing pornography as a feminist issue, the introduction of the ordinance brought these feminist arguments into the legal arena for the first time. Thus, as this example illustrates, legal debates should not be understood as irrelevant to the realm of popular opinion and public discourse.

Conclusion

In conclusion, Brown's argument seems to rely on a misunderstanding of several features of the position she attacks. First, she overlooks the importance of social construction in feminist accounts of women's oppression and thereby suggests that statements about women's experience of male dominance must be linked to the view that women are inherently and eternally victims. As a result, Brown fails to distinguish critical descriptions of the conditions of women's lives under patriarchy from antifeminist assertions that women's status as victims reflects their inherent nature. Second, she confuses criticisms of oppression and abuse with "confessional" discourse, which concerns only personal issues understood apart from their political context. She fails to offer any evidence that feminist criticisms of systematic abuse would lead to further repression and control of women's lives, rather than liberation. And finally, Brown dismisses feminist attempts to generalize about such matters as oppression, injustice, rights, and equality, claiming that we cannot make statements that go beyond our own specific circumstances without falling into the problematic aspects of universalism.

The one solution that Brown does offer—that women engage in political battles that proceed without making any reference to "established rights and identities"—fails to account for the collective and critical nature of social change. To succeed in the feminist battles that she advocates, women need both an analysis of the problems that must be addressed and a vision of what a better society might look like. Feminists have been engaged in political struggles for years, and most of these struggles have involved a collective understanding of women's experience, as well as a general description of the problem of male dominance. To the extent that these feminist analyses themselves reflect unequal relations of power between women, they should be altered and replaced with more accurate, less oppressive analyses. However, feminism simply cannot succeed without some understanding of systems of oppression. By employing an analysis of male dominance that is open to criticism and revision, feminists can increase consciousness of oppression; develop creative ways of challenging structural inequalities; and construct less oppressive, more egalitarian norms, practices, and institutions.

7

Speech, Authority, and Social Context

In Chapter 6, in examining Wendy Brown's postmodern critique of liberal rights, I argued that Brown does not offer any real alternative to liberalism's abstraction. Like the liberal theorists whom she criticizes, Brown fails to engage in concrete analyses of social relations of power. In this chapter, I treat the work of another postmodern feminist, Judith Butler, whose views are in many ways similar to Brown's, and whose work suffers from a number of similar problems.

Before delving into a careful analysis of how Butler's writings on hate speech relate to my critique of liberalism, I want to note the enormous impact Butler's work has had on feminist theory. Beginning in her groundbreaking *Gender Trouble: Feminism and the Subversion of Identity*, Butler has developed a Foucaultian theory of power that calls into question the traditional distinction between *sex* and *gender* (where *sex* refers to the biological categories of female and male, and *gender* to the social categories of woman and man). Rather than viewing subjects as having already formed identities, she asserts that identities are produced by power and specifically that our identities as women and men are largely the result of social forces of heteronormativity. Finally, she offers an account of subversion focused on "performativity," which involves challenging linguistic norms through acts of resignification. Since *Gender Trouble*, Butler has expanded her theory in a variety of ways, and in her 1997 book, *Excitable Speech*, she applies her analysis to the issue of hate speech, confronting important questions of speech, authority, and social context.

In *Excitable Speech*, Butler criticizes several feminist and antiracist theorists who advocate that pornography and racist hate speech be subject to some form of legal regulation. The theorists she cites—Rae Langton, Catharine MacKinnon, and Mari Matsuda—all put forward some version of an "equality" argument for regulating speech: speech should be subject to restriction if it subordinates, marginalizes, or harms members of an oppressed group. Employing J. L. Austin's speech act theory and emphasizing the open-ended nature of speech, Butler rejects these arguments. Ultimately, she advises against enacting any restrictions on hate speech because they could work to silence those who otherwise would be roused to challenge this speech by "resignifying" and "restaging" it.

I begin by summarizing Butler's view of speech acts and by explaining the important role that the "gap" between speech and its effects plays in her theory. In the following section, I argue that Butler gives an inaccurate and problematic portrayal of what it means for a speech act to be an illocution; I take issue with her interpretation of Austin's account as well as with her understanding of how Langton, MacKinnon, and Matsuda apply this account. Next, I emphasize the necessity of examining relations of power in the social context in which speech acts occur. I turn to Langton's discussion of "authority" and argue, with Langton, that the question of whether pornography or hate speech is efficacious cannot be answered without examining empirical questions about whether such speech has the authority to effect the subordination of the group it targets. I contend that Butler avoids examining this kind of evidence, and I link this avoidance to her belief that the social structure cannot be "pinned down," since it is always changing. Finally, I critically examine Butler's proposal for change, namely her suggestion that speech must be restaged and resignified, and her assertion that the "agency" to bring about such change is "derived from injury."[1] I claim that Butler's analysis of how change arises lacks a crucial element: an account of the social structures of power. I conclude by suggesting that it is movements against oppression that alter the social context and make possible the "resignification" that Butler celebrates; it is not the hate speech itself—or the "gap" between speech and its effects—that incites change.

Butler's Account: Gap Between Speech and Its Effects

Throughout *Excitable Speech*, Butler emphasizes the importance of acknowledging that there is (what she calls) a gap between speech and its effects.

When someone utters words, the exact effects that these words will have cannot be fully determined in advance; there is a gap between the intention of the speaker and the effect that the words have on the recipient. For instance, I may use words to formulate a statement that I intend to mean one thing, only to have my words misinterpreted or understood in a way that I did not intend. According to Butler, the possibility that a speech act can have a meaning other than the one intended by the speaker is what makes social and political change possible. She repeatedly reminds us that language has the ability to be restaged and resignified, and she argues that this possibility depends on understanding all speech acts to involve a gap between the originating context or intention and the effects the speech act produces.[2] Explaining the significance of this gap, Butler writes:

> That no speech act *has* to perform injury as its effect means that no simple elaboration of speech acts will provide a standard by which the injuries of speech might be effectively adjudicated. . . . [T]he gap that separates the speech act from its future effects has its auspicious implications. . . . The interval between instances of utterance not only makes the repetition and resignification of the utterance possible, but shows how words might, through time, become disjoined from their power to injure and recontextualized in more affirmative modes.[3]

In Butler's view, those who advocate legal remedies to hate speech fail to acknowledge the existence of this gap and wrongly suggest that words have the power to inflict injury in a way that is immediate and fully predictable. This "presumption that hate speech always works" is, for her, politically problematic because it does not allow for the possibility of a "critical response"—the possibility that the injurious words could be repeated in a way that they would come to mean something else, something liberatory.[4]

Although Butler contends that the importance of this gap has been overlooked in recent discussions of injurious speech, she does not think that the existence of a gap between the intention of a speech act and its effects generally is a novel discovery. On this general point, she cites J. L. Austin's discussion of "felicitous" and "infelicitous" speech acts. In *How to Do Things with Words*, Austin explores the "performative" quality of language, proposing that there are numerous uses of language in which "to *say* something is to *do* something"; he refers to these speech acts as "performatives."[5] Unlike mere statements of fact, which are either true or false, performatives can be either felicitous or infelicitous, depending on whether they are successful speech acts. Thus, if someone utters a performative, it may or may not be felicitous; in this sense there is a gap (in Butler's terms) between the intention of the speaker and the effect the speech has on the recipient.

According to Austin, there are two types of performatives. The first is a *perlocutionary* act, which is "what we bring about or achieve *by* saying something" and which is thus linked to the consequences brought about by a speech act.[6] One example would be *"By* saying, 'I'll be home by dark,' Samantha calmed her worried mother." One effect of Samantha's utterance is to calm her mother. The same utterance, however, could have additional consequences; for instance, it also could upset Samantha's best friend, Jill, who was hoping they would spend the evening together. Thus, one utterance can have numerous perlocutionary effects. The second type, an *illocutionary* act, is that which we perform *"in* saying something"; illocutionary acts are tied to the conventions of a society, since they will not be felicitous unless certain conventions hold.[7] Returning to the same example, *"In* saying, 'I'll be home by dark,' Samantha promised that she would return." Given the social norms about promising, and assuming that her mother believes that Samantha is not simply joking or being sarcastic, in uttering this statement Samantha has promised her mother that she will return by dark. Other commonly cited examples of illocutionary acts include statements made as part of an official ceremony or legal action; for instance, in saying, "I do," in the context of a marriage ceremony, one marries. Getting married is not merely a consequence or an effect of uttering these words. Rather, provided that one is in the right circumstances (defined by law and social convention), uttering the phrase "I do" constitutes the act of marrying.

Discussing these two types of speech acts, Butler considers the question of when a speech act can "fail," that is, when it is "infelicitous." Despite her occasional suggestion that both illocutionary and perlocutionary speech acts can be infelicitous, Butler seems to link the notion of infelicity to speech acts that are perlocutionary. Initially, she acknowledges that both types of speech act are subject to failure: "Not all utterances that have the form of the performative, whether illocutionary or perlocutionary, actually work"; and she points out that this has "important consequences for the consideration of the putative efficacy of hate speech."[8] Even though illocutionary speech acts aim at accomplishing something in the very action of uttering the words, these acts can still fail. For instance, the act of performing a marriage involves speaking certain words. But speaking the words "I do" and the words "You are now husband and wife" only constitutes marriage under certain conditions: the person performing the ceremony must be authorized to do so, the act must be done in a society that recognizes this particular law of marriage, and (in most states) the couple intending to marry must be a man and a woman. It thus seems that illocutionary acts are also subject to failure, even though they are not the sorts of acts that initiate—or bring about—certain consequences, as perlocutionary acts do.

When describing the way that illocutions and perlocutions work, however, Butler suggests that illocutionary acts are much less likely to fail, since all that is required is that certain conventional structures be in place. In the preceding example, as long as the person performing a marriage ceremony really does have the proper authority to do so, and as long as the participants really do intend to marry (and all other conditions are met), the very action of their uttering these words will successfully constitute the act they intend. Thus, while perlocutionary acts can fail to produce the intended consequences for a number of reasons—since the "consequences are not the same as the act of speech" but instead are "temporally distinct" (17)—illocutionary acts can fail only if the social context is somehow not what one thought, that is, if the necessary conventions are not in place. This leads Butler to claim. "Implicit in this distinction [between perlocutionary and illocutionary acts] is the notion that illocutionary speech acts produce effects without any lapse of time, that the saying is itself the doing, and that they are one another simultaneously" (17).

Butler remarks that Langton, MacKinnon, Matsuda, and others have relied to some extent on Austin's account of illocution in their assertion that pornography and racist hate speech are injurious. Although Butler does not state it directly, she implies that the attempt to view hate speech as illocutionary—and not perlocutionary—is misguided. Indeed, she claims that Austin himself would not have located hate speech in the realm of illocution: "Austin remarks . . . that some consequences of a perlocution may be unintentional, and the example he offers is the unintentional insult, thus locating verbal injury within the orbit of perlocution. Thus, Austin suggests that injury does not inhere in the conventions that a given speech act invokes, but in the specific consequences that a speech act produces" (17). She goes on to criticize the way in which feminists and antiracist activists have proposed that speech can injure in a more direct manner: pornography and racist hate speech are construed as inflicting injury not because they tend to produce injurious *consequences,* but because they are— in and of themselves—injurious *actions.* Thus, Butler suggests that, according to MacKinnon, it is the "pornographic text" itself that has the power to "effect the subordinated status of women" (73); more generally, Butler points out that those who advocate the legal regulation of pornography and racist hate speech hold the view that speech acts *act* in a way that is "efficacious," "unilateral," and "transitive" (74). She takes issue with this conception of how hate speech works, emphasizing the many different possibilities that such speech can fail to be efficacious. Speech, even injurious speech, does not always work as intended, nor does it always constitute the intended act. As I will explain shortly, the importance that Butler attributes to this possibility that speech acts can fail (or that they can "misfire") is linked to her view that language is always to some extent unpredictable, and she notes that "the question of mechanical breakdown or 'misfire' and of the unpredictability of speech is precisely what Austin repeatedly emphasizes when he focuses on the various ways in which a speech act can go wrong" (19).

As I will show, Butler misconstrues both Austin's own account of illocution as well as the accounts provided by Langton, MacKinnon, and Matsuda. She wrongly suggests that illocution is a matter of focusing on the *words* that are spoken, rather than on the broader *speech act* itself. In failing to heed this distinction, she finds that the illocutionary view of speech locates harm in the words themselves rather than in the *act* of speaking those words in a particular social context.

Words, Speech Acts, and Conventions

For Butler, the view that hate speech is illocutionary is the view that "speech is the immediate and necessary exercise of injurious effects" (39); and this view is problematic because it collapses speech into conduct (23) and it holds that the speech immediately does what it says. At a number of points in her work, Butler claims that the illocutionary model of speech offered by Austin and employed by Langton, MacKinnon, and Matsuda focuses on the *words* that are spoken, rather than on the *act* that is constituted by any particular uttering of those words. She notes that the very title of Austin's book, *How to Do Things with Words*, raises the question of how it is that things might be done with words, which she suggests involves a "question of transitivity." She asks, "What does it mean for a word not only to name, but also in some sense to perform and in particular, to perform what it names?" (43). To this question, she provides one answer in the case of perlocutionary speech and another—far more problematic—in the case of illocution: "According to the perlocutionary view, words are instrumental to the accomplishment of actions, but they are not themselves the actions which they seek to accomplish. . . . [T]he words and the things done are in no sense the same. But according to [Austin's] view of the illocutionary speech act, the name performs *itself*, and in the course of that performing becomes a thing done" (44). The distinction that Austin draws between perlocution and illocution is "tricky and not always stable" (44), and it makes more sense to understand words as accomplishing things in the manner of perlocution than in the manner of illocution. She believes that a dangerous view of speech—and the power of speech—arises out of the view that words themselves have the power to do things. According to this view, "the doing is less instrumental than it is transitive. Indeed what would it mean for a thing to be 'done by' a word . . . ? When and where, in such a case, would such a thing become disentangled from the word by which it is done . . . ?" (44). Thus, Butler worries that viewing hate speech—or any speech for that matter—as illocutionary entails the problematic view that words themselves have the power to "do things" and that this occurs in a way that is immediate and transitive.

Although there is a sense in which illocutionary speech is immediate, Butler mischaracterizes Austin's account when she suggests that it is the word or the speech itself—and not the speech act—that constitutes the injury. In discussing how to do things with words, Austin takes care to distinguish the *words* that are spoken from the *speech act* that is constituted by any particular use of these words. In a performative, "the uttering of the sentence is, or is a part of, the doing of an action."[9] It is significant that Austin claims that it is the "uttering" of the statement, and not the words themselves, that constitutes the performative. The speech act is not merely the words that are spoken but is instead the act, or "action," in Austin's terms, that the speaking of the words constitutes. While a speech act may be illocutionary—and may be injurious (following Langton, MacKinnon, and Matsuda)—words themselves do not have the power to cause injury.

To clarify Austin on the ways in which performative speech can constitute particular acts, Jennifer Hornsby draws a useful distinction between actions and acts, which she suggests is compatible with Austin's speech act theory, even though he does not make this distinction himself. According to Hornsby, speech acts are the *"things* done with words," whereas actions are "events."[10] As she puts it, "When there is an utterance, there is an action of someone's. But in the case of any one such action, there will be many things the speaker has done—many acts that she has performed."[11] In other words, Hornsby contends that there is an important distinction between the utterance of certain words—a single action—and the multiple speech acts that can be accomplished with this utterance. Not only does the uttering of the same words—taking the same "action"—in a different context often constitute a different speech act, but any single action of uttering certain words might also constitute several different speech acts even within one particular context.[12]

Contrary to Butler's suggestion, on Austin's account a performative utterance is never reducible to the words themselves; the words must be said in a particular context, or accompanied by other actions, and it is essential that they secure "uptake":

> The uttering of the words . . . is far from being usually, even if it is ever, the *sole* thing necessary if the act is to be deemed to have been performed. Speaking generally, it is always necessary that the *circumstances* in which the words are uttered should be in some way, or ways, *appropriate*, and it is very commonly necessary that either the speaker himself or other persons should also perform certain other actions, whether 'physical' or 'mental' actions or even acts of uttering further words.[13]

Austin thus emphasizes the importance of circumstances and other actions—even subsequent actions—in successfully accomplishing a performative. This seems to call into question Butler's focus on the "immediacy" and "transitive" nature of illocution. An illocution is a performative, and it is thus subject to the conditions described above by Austin. It cannot be the case that illocutionary performatives always work, or that they are transitive or immediate in any *simple* sense, because it is necessary that they succeed in securing uptake—that is, in bringing about the "understanding of the meaning and the force of the locution."[14] Austin is very clear about the importance of this: "Unless a certain effect is achieved, the illocutionary act will not have been happily, successfully performed. . . . [T]he performance of an illocutionary act involves the securing of *uptake*."[15] How can one know whether such uptake will be secured? On what is uptake dependent? Austin answers this by making reference to the context and to conventions. Although, at one point, Butler does note that illocutionary acts are considered by Austin to be a matter of convention, she does not discuss extensively what Austin might mean by this, or why the conventional nature of illocution is important to him.[16] And yet this is crucial to understanding how illocutionary speech acts work. An illocutionary act is a "conventional act: an act done as conforming to a convention."[17] Thus, if a person is mistaken about the conventions of her society, or if the conventions have somehow changed without her having realized it, her attempt to "do" something through an illocutionary speech act likely will fail.

One reason Butler might have for avoiding questions of convention is that she sees these as being a simple matter of authority and "sovereignty." She suggests at several points that the sort of authority or power that exists in Austin's examples is the type that is granted formally by the state or by some other official—for example, the power vested in someone to perform a marriage ceremony or the power of a recognized official to name a ship. The question of whether the person uttering the words involved in these illocutions has the relevant kind of authority is usually a fairly simple matter. Butler explains, "The subject as sovereign is presumed in the Austinian account of performativity: the figure for the one who speaks and, in speaking performs what she/he speaks, as the judge or some other representative of the law."[18] The speech of a judge, for instance, is binding as long as "the judge is a legitimate judge and the conditions of felicity are properly met."[19] While this may seem to be a simple question in the examples described by Austin, it is much less simple when one applies Austin's account of illocutionary speech acts to questions of sexist and racist hate speech. It is also much less simple when one acknowledges that meeting other felicity conditions is essential to securing uptake. Determining whether or not the context is such that a particular speech act will succeed in securing uptake is not the simple matter that Butler describes it to be if one acknowledges that it is not the words themselves, but the words *in the context of social conventions*, that constitute the speech act. Furthermore, it is not clear that the authority granted to the subjects in the examples of marriage and ship-naming is the exact same sort that would be required in any situation. The important factor seems to be that the social conventions support the relevant utterance in a way that makes it felicitous. The question of whether the conventions lend this kind of support (or "authority") may be a tricky one.

Before focusing particular attention on the issues of authority and convention, I first turn to a brief consideration of the specific arguments that Matsuda, MacKinnon, and Langton make using Austin's model. In the following section, I argue that in addition to mischaracterizing Austin's account of illocution, Butler distorts the account provided by these three theorists.

Hate Speech as Illocution: Matsuda, Langton, and MacKinnon

Contrary to Butler's contention, Matsuda, Langton, and MacKinnon do not claim that the words that are uttered—or the images that are depicted in pornography—are "efficacious" or "transitive" in the sense that they necessarily succeed. For instance, in her discussion of racist hate speech, Matsuda explicitly notes that it is not the words themselves that constitute racist hate speech, but their being *used* in a particular way, or spoken in a particular *context*, that makes them racist. As an example of speech that is not racist hate speech—but that certainly could be if it were spoken in a different context—Matsuda discusses Spike Lee's film *Do the Right Thing*. The film "contains a rapid-fire sequence of racial epithets spoken by characters from different racial groups in a Brooklyn neighborhood" but because of the "hyperrealism of the sequence" it serves as an "incisive antiracist critique of racist speech."[20]

According to Matsuda, racist hate speech, which should be subject to legal regulation, must be defined according to three characteristics: (1) it contains a message of racial inferiority; (2) it is directed against a historically oppressed group; and (3) it is persecutory, hateful, and degrading.[21] As defined by these criteria, racist speech is harmful not because the words *all by themselves* cause harm and pain, but because of the social, historical, and political context in which they are uttered. Racist hate speech is harmful "because it is a mechanism of subordination, reinforcing a historical vertical relationship," not because the words have some special power to magically cause injury.[22] There are a number of situations in which words that might be racist, or that would clearly constitute racist hate speech in a different context, would fail to meet Matsuda's standard. For example, "arguing that particular groups are genetically superior in a context free of hatefulness and without the endorsement of persecution is permissible," as is "[s]atire and stereotyping that avoids persecutory language."[23] Furthermore, determining whether certain words constitute hate speech may require examining the standards of the recipient's community. Describing cases that involve anti-Semitism and racism within subordinated communities, Matsuda explains that history and context are important in such cases "because the custom in a particular subordinated community may tolerate racial insults as a form of wordplay. Where this is the case, community members tend to have a clear sense of what is racially degrading and what is not. The appropriate standard in determining whether language is persecutory, hateful, and degrading is the recipient's community standard."[24]

A similar analysis can be offered regarding the sexist nature of pornographic depictions and the link that pornography has to women's subordination. Neither Langton nor MacKinnon thinks that all depictions of sexual abuse *necessarily* subordinate women. MacKinnon clearly states that her definition of pornography "does not include all sexually explicit depictions *of* the subordination of women."[25] For instance, depictions of rape or domestic violence could be said not to be pornographic if they were done in such a way that the abuse was not eroticized and if it were clear that it was not being endorsed. Likewise, Langton argues that the claim that pornography "subordinates" is not a statement about what the pornographic text accomplishes all by itself. She notes that the courts sometimes view the claim that pornography subordinates "as a description of pornography's content"; this view is mistaken, however, since it is not the content of the material itself that is capable of subordinating.[26] She explains: "Utterances whose locutions depict subordination do not always subordinate. Locutions that depict subordination could in principle be used to perform speech acts that are a far cry from pornography: documentaries, for example, or police reports, or government studies, or books that protest against sexual violence, or perhaps even legal definitions of pornography. It all depends, as Austin might have said, on the *use* to which the locution is put."[27] Furthermore, Langton points out that even if we follow MacKinnon in using the term *pornography* to refer only to sexually explicit materials that *do* subordinate, this still does not dictate that any particular text or image *is* pornography: "If, however, one follows MacKinnon in saying that as a matter of definition pornography subordinates, then it will no longer be a contingent matter whether *pornography* subordinates: it then becomes part of the meaning of the word that pornography subordinates. However, the question about illocutionary force will return as an empirical question, not this time in the form 'Does pornography subordinate?' but in the form '*Is* there any pornography, so defined?'"[28] In other words, the fact that MacKinnon *defines* pornography as that which subordinates does not mean that any particular text or image necessarily does this. For Matsuda, Langton, and MacKinnon, therefore, in order to tell what the particular locution is doing—in order to tell what its illocutionary force is—one must look beyond the mere text itself. Questions about the social context and about the power of the speech (and the speaker) within that context must be examined.

The Question of Authority and the Power of Social Context

In order to determine whether hate speech *injures* and whether graphic depictions of sexuality *subordinate*, attention must be turned to the context itself. Nevertheless, Butler does not think that examining the social context or conventions will be fruitful. As noted earlier, she points out that pornography and racist hate speech lack the sort of authority that "official" speech possesses (speech of state officials or other easily recognized authority figures). While it is true that the type of authority these injurious forms of speech have *differs* from the type of authority invested in the proclamations of government officials, this does not prove that such speech has no authority.

Butler takes note of Austin's point that in order "to know what makes the force of an utterance effective, what establishes its performative character, one must first locate the utterance within a 'total speech situation.'"[29] This presents a problem, however, according to Butler. To characterize the total situation of the speech act, one would need to provide an account of exactly what conventions were invoked at the moment of utterance, as well as of the "rituals" that were at work. Because conventions and rituals are not fixed, but must be repeated in time, Butler suggests that attempts to delineate the "total speech situation" will always, in some ways, fail. She explains that there is simply "no easy way to decide on how best to delimit that totality" (3). Thus, she concludes that Austin's demand that we must first delineate the "total speech situation" before we can know the force of an illocution is "beset by a constitutive difficulty" (3).

> [H]ow does one go about delimiting the kind of "convention" that illocutionary utterances presume? . . . As utterances, they [illocutionary utterances] work to the extent that they are given in the form of a ritual, that is, repeated in time, and hence, maintain a sphere of operation that is not restricted to the moment of the utterance itself. The illocutionary speech act performs its deed *at the moment* of the utterance, and yet to the extent that the moment is ritualized, it is never merely a simple moment. (3)

That is, if we are to know whether something counts as an injurious speech act, we need to be able to pin down the social context and give a static account of the conventions and rituals that govern that context. Butler suggests that this is in principle impossible, since conventions and rituals are always subject to change—even the history and current understanding of them is open to reinterpretation.

Butler takes her criticism of the static account of social structure and applies it to the theorists who view hate speech as illocutionary. On a general level, she implies that any attempt to define the "total speech situation," or to describe the social context in which a speech act occurs, will automatically suggest that there are enduring structures that are permanent and "static." More specifically, she suggests that the particular accounts that are offered by these hate speech theorists are themselves "static" accounts of power. Describing the work of MacKinnon and Matsuda, Butler writes: "The listener is understood to occupy a social position or to have become synonymous with that position, and social positions themselves are understood to be situated in a static and hierarchical relation to one another. By virtue of the social position one occupies, then, the listener is injured as a consequence of that utterance" (18).

Butler's argument suffers from at least two problems. First, it is not the case that MacKinnon, Matsuda, or Langton views the social structure as static or unchanging; second, it is not necessary that the context be unchanging in order for it to be given some characterization as the "context" or "total speech situation" in which a speech act occurs. I first briefly discuss this second (and more general) point, and I then move to a more lengthy consideration of the first. In emphasizing the need to provide an account of the "total speech situation," Austin need not be understood as requiring that the account of the context be static. To say that the context can be given any particular description right at this moment only means that there is some way that the context can be characterized at this point in time. To the extent that an action that occurs within that context (such as an utterance) has any meaning at all, its meaning must be located in some understanding of the context, conventions, or "total speech situation." If future actions or events change the understanding we have of this particular context, we may come to understand the "speech acts" that occurred within this context differently. This is not to say that the speech act has no meaning, but it does suggest that meaning can shift over time and that what we once thought meant one thing can actually later be discovered to have meant something else.

Despite Butler's contention, none of the hate speech theorists she describes holds a static or unchanging view of the social structure. In fact, all three (Langton, MacKinnon, and Matsuda) attempt to call attention to the context itself as something that desperately needs to be changed. Structures such as racism, sexism, classism, and heterosexism are all social in nature and are not—especially not according to the accounts offered by these theorists—eternal or unchanging; the very point of much of their work is to change these structures and eliminate these oppressive hierarchies. However, because Butler fails to distinguish between an analysis of the context that is, for the most part, accurate at present time, and one that would hold for all of eternity, she suggests that the attempt to give a description of current structures of social power amounts to the assertion that these are unchanging structures.

Interestingly, there seems to be an inconsistency in the way that Butler reads Austin and in the way that she understands the account of illocution provided by Langton, MacKinnon, and Matsuda. On the one hand, she suggests that all these theorists think that it is the words themselves that must constitute the injury in an illocution, and on the other hand, she acknowledges that their view of illocutionary harm relies on particular analyses of the social structure. These two conceptions of illocutionary acts are inconsistent, because the first, in focusing only on the words themselves, precludes the second. Butler disagrees with both views, and she alternatively faults Austin, as well as the recent hate speech theorists, for holding one or the other of them. Her own argument would be clearer if she were to distinguish between these two perspectives and point out their incompatibility. As I argued above, the three theorists reject the first view, that the injury of an illocutionary act adheres in the speech itself. It is the second that they hold: they believe that an account of illocution must make reference to the total speech situation, which includes an account of the social structure.

Recognizing that each speech act must be understood according to some assessment of its "total speech situation" entails acknowledging that the context in which the speech act occurs matters. Thus, the structures of power present in that context—and embodied in the conventions and rituals—play a significant role in determining the meaning of speech acts. And this is true regardless of the fact that the structures of power, conventions, and rituals are subject to change. Thus, in response to a question raised by Butler—"what gives hate speech the power to constitute the subject with such efficacy?" (18–19)—one could say that it is social structures of power. For racist and sexist social structures to serve as the context that enables hate speech to work, it need only be the case that language spoken in this context will very likely function in a way that subordinates, oppresses, or unjustly discriminates. This is not to say that the authority of these structures is absolute, or that an utterance that constitutes hate speech in one context would function as hate speech in another context, or at some point in the future. All that is required of the theorists Butler criticizes is that they establish that the structures of racism and sexism—and those who speak with the force of these structures behind them—do have a certain degree of power and authority under current social, political, and historical conditions.

One of the most serious problems with Butler's work on hate speech and pornography seems to be her evasion of questions of "power" and "authority" on the level of empirical, social reality. She suggests that because the context is never fully definable (it cannot be pinned down and fully understood), there is no way that racism, sexism, or homophobia can be thought of as having the power or authority they would need for racist and sexist hate speech to be considered injurious illocutions. In fact, according to Butler, the possibility that these contexts could change, or be interpreted differently in the future, suggests that there is not much that can be said about the context of race, sex, gender, or class oppression in current society. Is there any sense in which pornography has authority? Is there any sense in which racist hate speech is backed by institutional relations of power? To answer these questions, one must look at the actual power relations in society. Butler stops short of doing this, instead suggesting that because the context is always shifting, and because there are "gaps" between intention and effect, no speech act can be backed by the needed authority to be reliably thought to cause injury.

In two different articles devoted to pornography and hate speech, Rae Langton raises this issue of authority and submits that the question of whether pornography subordinates rests in part on the question of whether it has the authority to do so.[30] She considers an argument by Leslie Green, for whom the problem with taking an illocutionary view of pornography's harm is the following: "if saying simply *is* doing, there is no need to worry about the contingent causal connection and the problematic evidence of it. The evidence of the harm is the evidence for the saying."[31] But this overlooks the importance of the social context, which must be examined to see if there is indeed evidence for the authority of pornography.[32] In response, Langton comments that causal questions are not the only ones that are contingent and that require evidence. Although questions about whether or not an umpire or an elected official has the authority to rule a ball out of bounds or to pass a law might be answered easily, this does not mean that the illocutionary speech acts of these officials are not contingent on certain conditions: "one can imagine cases in which the authority of an alleged umpire, an alleged legislator, is in dispute. And in the case of pornography, evidence for the authority is much more controversial than evidence for the saying. So the question about pornography's illocutionary force inevitably involves evidence and contingent connections: if pornography had no authority, then I think it would not subordinate."[33] Thus, in order to determine whether pornography has the authority to subordinate, one needs to examine the role that it serves in society, its relation to the status of women, its effect on the sexuality of both women and men, and a number of other such questions. These are crucial issues and are not ones that can be settled "from the philosopher's armchair"; one must look to empirical studies and to arguments about the effects of pornography in the actual world.[34] How prevalent is pornography? Whose interests does its proliferation serve? Does it have any effect on the way that men and women view sexuality? Does it cause, contribute to, or in any way affect women's subordination? Many of those who advocate restrictions on pornography—and on hate speech—make extensive reference to the findings of empirical studies that the social context is such that the injurious material does have the authority to injure. While these studies certainly can be disputed, and while some empirical evidence exists to argue for the opposing view, this evidence must at least be offered up in defense of the claim that pornography and racist hate speech do not have the needed authority.

Interestingly, Langton notes that liberal theorists often presuppose that pornography is the speech of "a powerless minority, a fringe group especially vulnerable to moralistic persecution."[35] She points out that if this is the view that you hold, of course you will think that pornography does not have the needed authority; part of MacKinnon's project, suggests Langton, is to persuade us that this view of pornography is false and that "pornography's voice is the voice of the ruling power."[36] Both Langton and MacKinnon cite numerous empirical studies concerning the effects of pornography, and both conclude that there is a great deal of evidence suggesting that pornography does have the authority to subordinate women in the context of our current society. To illustrate its influence, Langton cites studies that show that people "have their attitudes and behavior altered by [pornography] in ways that ultimately hurt women: they can become more likely to view women as inferior, more disposed to accept rape myths (for example, that women enjoy rape), more likely to view rape victims as deserving of their treatment, and more likely to say that they themselves would rape if they could get away with it. This in turn means that some women are hurt by it."[37] Similarly, many of the advocates of legal regulation of racist hate speech cite empirical evidence of the harmful effects of such speech.[38] Unfortunately,

Butler generally avoids addressing questions about what the authority of pornography, or racist hate speech, actually is in the empirical world.[39] She suggests only that it *could* be otherwise, that there is the possibility that pornography or racist speech could end up meaning something slightly different, something liberatory.[40] But how great is this possibility, given current social structures, norms, and relations of power? Is liberation located in this slight, and perhaps even random, chance that social structures of power could suddenly fail to operate in predictable ways, could come to mean something else?

Restaging, Resignifying, and "Deriving Agency" from Injury

Rather than examining the social context, by evaluating empirical studies or by considering and rebutting arguments about who has power over whom, Butler focuses on the *possibility* that speech could be "restaged" or "resignified" by the recipient responding in unanticipated ways. In fact, she goes so far as to suggest that "agency" can be "derived from injury"[41] when hate speech is not legally restricted but is countered by a response from the recipient. Why does she make so much of this possibility? When and how is such resignification possible? What are the conditions in which hate speech will be productive of this agency that Butler invokes? In this section, I argue that she provides very little guidance in explaining *what* exactly should be resisted, *how* one should go about this resistance, and when—or why— "resignifying" language will work as an effective means of social change.

Before considering Butler's own proposals for change (restaging and resignifying injurious speech), it is important to note a couple of reasons that she has for favoring her own approach over the legal regulations proposed by Matsuda and MacKinnon. According to Butler, the law works in a way that places blame and responsibility on the individual subject who utters the speech, and not on the larger political forces: "The legal effort to curb injurious speech tends to isolate the 'speaker' as the culpable agent, as if the speaker were at the origin of such speech. The responsibility of the speaker is thus misconstrued."[42] She thinks that it is wrong to place blame and responsibility on the individual who utters the speech, because speech gets its power from the force of repetition, not from the single act of any speaker.

> When the scene of racism is reduced to a single speaker and his or her audience, the political problem is cast as the tracing of the harm as it travels from the speaker to the psychic/somatic constitution

of the one who hears the term or the one to whom it is directed. The elaborate institutional structures of racism as well as sexism are suddenly reduced to the scene of utterance, and utterance, no longer the sedimentation of prior institution and use, is invested with the power to establish and maintain the subordination of the group addressed.[43]

As I have argued, however, Matsuda, Langton, and MacKinnon do not think that it is the words—or the utterances—themselves that injure; rather it is the uttering of these words in some particular social context. Taking legal action against hate speech can work to call attention not only to the action of the individual perpetrator but also to the structures of oppression that give the perpetrator's speech its injurious force. Thus, Butler is wrong to suggest that these theorists *reduce* the structures of racism and sexism to the scene of utterance and prosecute *only the utterance*; rather, what they are doing is holding individuals who utter racist, sexist, and homophobic hate speech responsible for perpetuating these structures of oppression. Subjecting such individuals to legal regulation is one way of challenging and attempting to alter oppressive structures of power. This does not amount to the claim that an individual is fully and completely at fault—the structures of oppression out of which a speech act arises are not entirely, or even mostly, the individual's own fault—but it is to say that in order to change hierarchical structures, social and legal pressures must be brought to bear on those who perpetuate them.

On a similar note, Butler argues that legal attempts to regulate language are problematic because they wrongly presuppose that the "gap" between intention and effect could be closed and that language can—and should— operate in a more straightforward manner. She suggests that the proposed legal regulations attempt to create a world in which the words people speak *do* mean what they intend, and she contends that this is problematic, since it would both restrict the possibilities for resignification and establish a "normative view of the person" (which she finds inherently problematic). She objects to MacKinnon on these grounds: "[MacKinnon] presupposes that one ought to be in a position to utter words in such a way that the meaning of those words coincides with the intention with which they are uttered, and that the performative dimension of that uttering works to support and further that intended meaning. . . . Presupposed by this conception of the utterance is a normative view of a person with the ability and power to exercise speech in a straightforward way."[44] First, it is not entirely clear to what Butler is objecting. Does she believe that language *should not* work in a straightforward way? Clearly, she thinks that language *cannot* work this way, since it is always to some extent unpredictable.[45] I have argued, however, that MacKinnon, Langton, and Matsuda actually agree with Butler's suggestion that language does not *always* succeed, but they do not agree that the way that language fails is as random or arbitrary as Butler suggests. According to their analysis of hate speech, certain groups of people have more power than others to make their speech heard and understood; the chances that one's language will "misfire" are greatest if one is deprived of certain forms of social power. For example, Langton asserts that the speech of women about matters of sex can be affected by pornographic images that imply that when women say no to sex, they really mean yes. She refers to this as "illocutionary disablement" and describes it as one of several ways in which pornography can work to silence women. Illocutionary disablement occurs when a woman says no but her statement "does not *count* as the act of refusal. The hearer fails to recognize the utterance as a refusal; uptake is not secured. . . . She says 'no.' She performs the appropriate locutionary act. . . . But what she says misfires."[46] Thus, in a context in which such an ideology about women's sexuality has taken hold, when it comes to matters of sex the speech of women will be more likely to misfire than the speech of men. Both Langton and MacKinnon object to this situation, but on the grounds that the current situation is unequal. Men benefit from the way that language is systematically understood and misunderstood, according to their analysis. Contrary to Butler's interpretation, the aim of their arguments is not to suggest that everyone should always be understood exactly as they intend; rather, these theorists seek to equalize the systematic inequalities in the ways that different groups of people have their speech understood. They object not to the unpredictability of speech, but to the fact that it tends to fail (or misfire) in predictable ways, according to lines of social and political hierarchy. They seek to equalize power and to undo these hierarchies so that people all have a more equal chance to have their speech mean what it says.

In contrast to the social, political, and legal changes advocated by Langton, MacKinnon, and Matsuda, Butler offers a far more dubious plan for resistance. In a recent review of a number of Butler's books, Martha Nussbaum finds that this failure to provide an account of resistance is one of Butler's most significant problems. According to Nussbaum, even if we grant Butler's claim that the ubiquitousness of the structure of gender should be resisted through "subversive and parodic acts," two important questions remain:

"What would the acts of resistance be like, and what would we expect them to accomplish?"[47] Resistance, in terms of responding to harmful speech, seems to involve restaging and resignifying certain words that otherwise would be injurious. But how are we to know which words should be resignified in this manner? Butler fails to offer any guidance about how to distinguish speech that is oppressive (and that reinforces social hierarchy) from speech that is merely offensive or upsetting. Nussbaum points out that unlike other feminists who have relied on "ideas such as non-hierarchy, equality, dignity, autonomy . . . to indicate a direction for actual politics," Butler does not explain what is supposed to guide one's decisions about what to resist.[48] In the absence of any discussion of the goals of resistance— or of politics, more generally—it is hard to know what would count as desirable change and what would reinforce the status quo. As Nussbaum notes, Butler seems to think that we need to "wait to see what the political struggle itself throws up, rather than prescribe in advance to its participants."[49] On this issue, Butler's view echoes Brown's view that politics is about struggle and that political change proceeds *in the absence of normative conceptions.*[50] Rather than defend this view of politics, however, Butler simply seems to take it as a given, and she proceeds under the assumption that employing any "normative critique" would inevitably reinforce current social norms.

Not only does Butler fail to offer any guidance about what should be resisted, she also does not say much about the process of resistance—how does it happen, what brings it about, and so on. At times she writes as if she need not describe this process because resignification is something that just *happens* given the inevitable "gaps" between the intention of the speaker and the effects that speech has on its recipient. As I noted earlier, she rejects the view (which she wrongly attributes to Langton, MacKinnon, and Matsuda) that hate speech always works. This rejection seems to be at least partly based on Butler's belief that the transformative possibilities of language—and of society more generally—lie in the *inevitable failures* of language to do what the speaker intends. As she explains, "I wish to question for the moment the presumption that hate speech always works, not to minimize the pain that is suffered as a consequence of hate speech, but to leave open the possibility that its failure is the condition of a critical response."[51] At times she writes about this critical response as a mere possibility, as something that might come about from the speech act's failure; at other times she suggests that there is a much stronger correlation between hate speech and this sort of agency, in that "hate speech *does not destroy the agency* required for a critical response. . . . In the place of state-sponsored censorship, a social and cultural struggle of language takes place in which *agency is derived from injury,* and injury countered through that very derivation."[52] Unfortunately, she fails to explain when, why, and how such "agency" can be "derived" from the very injury itself. Is she implying that the injury prompts the individual victim to take action and resignify speech or is she referring to a process of resignification that just occurs on its own?

Although an extensive discussion of Butler's theory of agency is beyond the scope of this chapter, it is interesting to note that there is a tension between her suggestion, on the one hand, that there are inevitable failures in the way that speech works that will lead to change and, on the other hand, that individual recipients can restage or resignify language by simply responding to it differently. The first of these two views seems to be supported by her discussion of agency in her earlier book *Gender Trouble.* There, Butler goes into more detail about the relationship between agency and significa-tion. Signification is not a "founding act," but rather a "regulated process of repetition. . . . In a sense, all signification takes place within the orbit of the compulsion to repeat; 'agency,' then, is to be located within the possi-bility of a variation on that repetition."[53] While this might sound as if it were the subject who simply seizes on this "possibility" and repeats things differently, this is not what Butler seems to have in mind. Describing the processes that result in gender formation, she claims that "new possibilities for gender" arise "only within the practices of repetitive signifying" and that this occurs because "[t]he injunction *to be* a given gender produces necessary failures, a variety of incoherent configurations."[54] Thus, it seems that the agency that Butler describes arises out of "necessary failures" rather than out of the initiative either of individuals or of social and historical movements. This is affirmed elsewhere in the same book when Butler argues that the "ground of gender" is the "stylized repetition of acts through time . . . The possibilities of gender transformation are to be found precisely in the *arbitrary relation* between such acts, in the *possibility of a failure to repeat.*"[55] This idea that changes in language—and changes in political and cultural relations—occur because of failures in language "to repeat" itself properly seems to be an odd account of agency. And yet this does appear to be at least part of what Butler has in mind when, in *Excitable Speech,* she describes the "scene of agency."

The other view of agency Butler invokes in *Excitable Speech* involves the individual recipient taking up the injurious utterance and embracing it as a self-description: "To take up the name that one is called is no simple submission to prior authority, for the name is already unmoored from prior context, and entered into the labor of self-definition."[56] In other words, by taking up the insulting name myself, I have already changed the context of the word's utterance and have thereby caused a shift in its meaning. Thus, "[t]he word that wounds becomes an instrument of resistance in the redeployment that destroys the prior territory of its operation."[57] What Butler neglects to discuss are the conditions of possibility for this "destruction" of the "prior territory." If a word has the power to "wound" and serve as hate speech in the current social context, how will my embracing the epithet alter this fact? From where does this power to resignify emerge, and are there any conditions that might make resignification more or less likely to succeed?

One way to determine how successful an attempt to resignify language will be—and one way to better understand this process of resistance—might be to examine social, historical, and political movements. In her view that hate speech can be easily resignified, Butler seems to underestimate the role that such movements play in this process. Unless certain social, cultural, and political changes have taken place—or are in the process of occurring—the efforts of any single individual to resignify hate speech will not be very successful. In her account of disempowered speech, Jennifer Hornsby argues that because of the "social character of language use," it will not be easy to resignify an utterance.[58] As she explains, "What others have done with words in the past restricts what someone can do with them now. If a word has pejorated, there is nothing that an individual speaker at a moment can do to repair it. We may think that there is something that a woman might do but would only be able to do if gender were constructed differently from how it actually is."[59] Thus, in order to resignify language, we need to work toward changing the structures of gender—which will only happen slowly, over time, and which will involve more than merely resignifying and restaging language. Consider how the meaning of the words *queer* and *dyke* has evolved over time. Fifty years ago, if someone were the recipient of a homophobic speech act that consisted of one of these words, the individual recipient probably would not have been able to simply restage or resignify that word and make it mean something else. And yet in current times, such words are often used within gay and lesbian communities in a positive and reaffirming manner. I would argue that the meanings (and connotations) of these words have shifted primarily because of the efforts of lesbian, gay, bisexual, and transgendered activists who have reclaimed them for themselves and have caused their meanings to evolve. But such changes do not happen suddenly, by the single response of the recipient of an act of hate speech. Rather, they occur over time, through political and collective acts of resistance that increase the power of oppressed groups to define themselves publicly in more positive ways. It seems, then, that what makes these changes possible is the existence of social movements that challenge oppression and demand freedom, equality, and liberation. In sum, contrary to Butler's claim, it is not the *injury* of hate speech from which agency—or the possibility of change—derives.

Conclusion

In this chapter, I have argued that there are a number of ways in which Butler misunderstands the position of the feminist and antiracist theorists whom she criticizes. Although she shares some of their feminist and anti-racist views about the problems in society, she refuses to engage in precisely the sort of political critique that these theorists argue is needed to bring about social change. Furthermore, her own description of how social change occurs—through restaging and resignifying language—fails to acknowledge the importance of social structures of power in making these acts of resistance possible.

As I noted at the beginning of Chapter 6, Butler's work on hate speech in many ways parallels that of Brown on rights; as a result, both postmodern feminists are subject to a number of the same objections. Although I have dealt with their theories separately (in an attempt to avoid generalization and oversimplification), I now wish to mention a few basic similarities. First, both Brown and Butler fail to acknowledge the important role that social construction plays in the work of feminists whom they criticize. Both seem to suggest that offering an analysis of social structures of power amounts to a declaration that these structures are "static" and eternal, and yet this is precisely the opposite of what MacKinnon, Langton, and Matsuda claim. Second, both postmodern feminists suggest that social change is best approached through means that do not involve "moral critique" and that do not appeal to any "normative view of the person."[60] The fact remains, however, that there are structures of domination in our current society that must somehow be addressed and challenged. While it is understandable that Butler and Brown do not trust the power of abstract liberal theory, "normative critique," or "moral" ideals to automatically bring about the destruction of hierarchical structures, they do not offer any evidence for why (or how) all normative criticism should be discarded. Moreover, the very suggestion that all norms *should* be avoided is itself self-refuting. The alternatives they do offer—Brown's vague suggestion that women engage in political battles that proceed without any reference to "established rights and identities" and Butler's suggestion that we need to restage and resignify language—seem to be woefully inadequate solutions to the problems of social, political, and economic hierarchy.[61] Neither theorist offers much evidence that feminists, gays and lesbians, or people of color have enough power to succeed in these sorts of political contests and attempts to redefine language. On a related note, both Brown and Butler reject legal approaches to social change: Brown dismisses attempts to reformulate "rights," and Butler rejects the legal regulation of racist and sexist speech. In similar ways, each understands the law to be opposed to the realm of popular contestation, rather than understanding the law to be one specific institution within society in which such contestation is possible. Of course, there are legitimate concerns about placing too much power in legal institutions, which are primarily run by men and which may be slow to adopt or enact feminist laws and policies. This, however, is a practical concern of which many feminist activists and legal scholars are aware. Driven by these worries, the feminists whose work I discuss advocate legal strategies as only *one part* of larger social movements against oppression.

Finally, I should note that although much of my discussion in this and the preceding chapter has focused on pornography, as well as—to a lesser extent—other forms of hate speech, I have not advocated any *particular* legal approach to these issues; I have not offered a specific defense of MacKinnon and Dworkin's proposed antipornography ordinance or of any particular legislation regulating racist hate speech. An argument that aimed to defend a specific proposal would have to focus on the actual context in which the proposal would be implemented, it would have to consider its likely effects, and it would need to analyze alternate proposals. I have asserted only that it is wrong to simply dismiss all use of legal methods—as well as all normative concepts—in arguments for social change.

In rejecting the law, normative concepts, and moral critique, Brown and Butler seem to end up supporting the institutions of the status quo. Rather than an analysis and critique of power, they advocate what amounts to personal, individual acts of resistance. For such acts of resistance to be effective, however, they must be backed by larger social movements against oppression. For instance, as I suggested earlier in this chapter, an individual's attempt to resignify a racist or sexist comment is unlikely to succeed unless others also engage in similar attempts. Although Butler acknowledges that one speech act cannot alone bring about social change (and she emphasizes the need for others to repeat the act of resignification), she fails to explain why or how any particular act will come to be repeated by others. Contrary to Brown and Butler's contention, political change cannot be brought about by individual acts of resistance that occur in a vacuum, nor can it be achieved through the mechanistic failure of language to repeat itself in the same way over time. Rather, political change requires some kind of collective engagement of groups of people who work toward changing various forms of social hierarchy and oppression.

Conclusion

Toward a Feminist Approach to Political Theorizing

In the preceding two chapters, I have illustrated how attempts to reject legal discourse, normative concepts, and moral critique can end up reinforcing the status quo. Although Butler and Brown do not intend to convey support for current arrangements of power, their plan to bring about change through individual acts of resistance will be ineffective without larger cultural, political, and economic movements for social change. Advocating more systemic and wide-scale resistance, however, requires a critical analysis of social power structures. In fact, such an analysis is a crucial component of normative criticism: without it, one cannot provide an account of what is wrong with the status quo, nor can one work toward enacting social change.

I have examined Brown and Butler to distinguish my own critical analysis of liberalism from their more wide-scale rejection. The indeterminacy of liberal concepts (such as rights, equality, and privacy) cannot be addressed simply by rejecting these concepts and proceeding as if they had no importance. Because people are officially entitled to certain rights, and because laws affect how persons interact, view themselves, and treat others, we must not simply dismiss legal concepts such as rights and equality. Furthermore, without some vision or ideal of how things could be improved, and without some concepts (such as equality, rights, or justice) guiding social change, systems of oppression are unlikely to be eroded.

Despite the importance of appealing to some form of moral ideal, and to some version of equality, rights, or justice, I have argued that there are a number of problems with the way that liberal theorists typically employ these concepts. Although I focused my criticisms on Ronald Dworkin and Rawls, I suggested that similar problems arise in other versions of liberal theory. The problem is not with the very concepts of equality or rights (as Brown and Butler suggest), but rather with the way that liberals define and apply these concepts.

While I have raised a number of problems with liberalism, my criticisms center around two specific aspects of liberal theory: (1) its individualism, or focus on the preferences and choices of individuals; and (2) its methods of abstraction, or focus on defining ideals and concepts in abstraction from an analysis of social power. Although I suggest that the preferences individuals express, and the choices they make, should play a less central role in normative theory, I do not claim that they are wholly unimportant, nor that they should play no role whatsoever in moral and political theory. Instead, I contend that preferences are always informed by certain social structures, including structures of sexual, racial, and class oppression. Liberal theory goes wrong when it attempts to isolate the current preferences of individuals without acknowledging the extent to which social forces have shaped these preferences.

Likewise, I do not advocate that normative theory refrain from all "abstraction," at least not if we accept O'Neill's definition of abstraction as the bracketing of certain features. As O'Neill rightly notes, all theorizing requires some forms of bracketing. The problem is not that liberalism makes use of abstraction in this very general sense; rather, it is that liberal methods of abstraction often permit objectionable features of the social structure to enter into a theory despite the bracketing. I illustrated this problem in my discussion of Dworkin's theory of distributional equality and in my treating Rawls's theory of justice. For instance, despite Dworkin's attempt to bracket many features of our actual society, these features nonetheless enter into his theory unacknowledged. In addition, I suggested that the liberal procedures of abstraction are not the most apt for rooting out patterns and structures of oppression. Abstract principles and concepts may presuppose facts about individuals that are not true, or that are not yet true. For instance, theories of autonomy may take for granted that individual agents actually *are* autonomous, and they may assume that these individuals formulate their preferences in accordance with a conception of the good that is truly *theirs*. This may not be the case, however, in situations characterized by oppression.

In response to my arguments, a liberal could acknowledge that I describe legitimate problems, while nonetheless contending that one need not move away from liberalism to address them. The liberal could raise the following points: After realizing that the theory has abstracted from certain features of the social structure that *are* relevant to the issue under consideration, the theorist can alter this, and only "bracket" those features that should be bracketed. Likewise, assumptions about individuals could be modified once the theorist discovers that the context is one of oppression in which the autonomy or individuality of the members of certain groups has been compromised. Furthermore, there is nothing, in principle, about liberalism that prevents it from being able to acknowledge and object to the structures of male dominance. In other words, liberals might claim that their theory is flexible enough to answer my feminist objections, once they have been raised.

Even if the liberal could accommodate radical criticism in these ways, however, merely accounting for such criticism offers no guidance in rooting out problems that stem from systems of oppression. If normative theory is to do more than allow us to justify the ideas that we already hold regarding the acceptability of current arrangements of power, this may not be a problem. But if normative theory is to enable us to uncover previously unrecognized injustices, it must offer more than a mere mechanism of justification. While some liberals might claim that it is not the job of political theory to uncover and expose structures of domination, I provide numerous examples of how inattention to power structures can reinforce and perpetuate sexism, racism, and class oppression. Making a similar point in a different context, Cheshire Calhoun notes that questions of justification are not the only ones that are important in doing theory:

> Our being motivated to raise questions of justification in the first place and our ability to address those questions once raised depends at least partially on the social availability of moral criticisms and of morally relevant information. . . . Without an equal theoretical stress on the social determinants of moral knowledge—particularly the potential alignment of moral and factual beliefs with social power structures—the very reflective processes that were designed to criticize cultural prejudices may simply repeat those prejudices.[1]

Although Calhoun is discussing the relationship between the ethics of *care* and the ethics of *justice*, she raises an important point about the theoretical significance of social power structures. My argument that liberal theorists typically focus on the individual in problematic ways—and that their allegedly abstract methods often embody problematic assumptions—posits that liberalism is centered on the wrong sorts of factors. The focus, or emphasis, on certain aspects of situations (rather than others) is not an insignificant matter, since the features one emphasizes strongly affect the theory one produces. Calhoun argues elsewhere in this essay that "concentration on only some moral issues" has "ideological implications."[2] More specifically, she explains, "Even if the ethics of justice could consistently accommodate the ethics of care, the critical point is that theorists in the justice tradition have not said much, except in passing, about the ethics of care" and that they are not likely to do so "without a radical shift in theoretical priorities."[3] This is problematic because concentrating on certain sorts of rights—such as impartiality, rationality, and autonomy—"creates an ideology of the moral domain which has undesirable political implications for women."[4] Although my point does not concern what Calhoun calls the "ethics of justice," and I do not advocate the "ethics of care," Calhoun's commentary on this debate illuminates my own analysis of liberalism: Even if liberalism could remain logically consistent if it were to endorse elements of my feminist critique, this does not mean that liberalism is likely to do this without radically altering its theoretical priorities. Moreover, by placing so much emphasis on individuals, and on the need to devise very abstract principles and ideals, liberal theory fosters an ideology that is antithetical to feminist concerns. Thus, while we cannot do without the concepts typically employed in liberal theory—such as rights, equality, and justice—we must find ways of interpreting and employing them that do not lead to the various problems I have described.

The problems associated with reducing political issues to questions of justification based on abstract principles and ideals are clearly in evidence in the case of pornography. Even among feminists, pornography is controversial. Some propornography (or "sex-positive") feminists maintain that there is nothing wrong with pictures that portray transgressive sexual acts and activities. In the context of society's puritanical and repressive views about sex, they say, the proliferation of pornography might even pose a challenge to conservatives who argue that sex outside marriage is always immoral. Citing the benefits of pornography, Lisa Duggan, Nan Hunter, and Carole Vance contend that

> the existence of pornography has served to flout conventional sexual mores, to ridicule sexual hypocrisy, and to underscore the importance

of sexual needs. Pornography . . . advocates sexual adventure, sex outside of marriage, sex for no reason other than pleasure, casual sex, anonymous sex, group sex, voyeuristic sex, illegal sex, public sex. Some of these ideas appeal to women reading or seeing pornography, who may interpret some images as legitimating their own sense of sexual urgency or desire to be sexually aggressive.[5]

Furthermore, some women who work in the "sex industry" as models for pornography, as strippers, or as prostitutes, argue that their work is a job like any other and should not be stigmatized by feminists.[6] After describing her work as an erotic dancer, Debi Sundahl explains, "stripping is traditional women's work as much as waitressing, teaching and secretarial work is. Consequently, it suffers from the same low pay. . . . The working conditions, overall, are also poor; many theaters are run on a quasi-legitimate financial basis, and are not clean or safe."[7] According to Sundahl, the "anti-sex attitudes of the anti-porn movement" further stigmatize women who are already facing many of the same obstacles as other low-income women.[8] Against these claims, feminist antipornography activists argue that certain forms of pornography are oppressive to women because they reinforce, perpetuate, and promote the already prominent view that women are sexual objects available for male use and consumption. Pornography that portrays male violence against women sexualizes this abuse and thus contributes to a culture in which rape, domestic violence, sexual harassment, and other forms of sexist oppression are more likely to occur.[9]

Although I cannot examine all the arguments on each side of this debate, I highlight the benefits of employing an approach that begins with a reconstructed ideal of equality, understood not as abstract sameness, but as a feminist principle of nondomination grounded in the concrete experiences of women. More specifically, I claim that important feminist arguments against pornography cannot be fully understood if one begins theorizing by attempting to "abstract" from actual power relations to focus on questions of what individual persons could agree to accept.

In the Kantian liberalism of O'Neill, the basic principles of political and moral theory must be ones to which all agents can agree. As I noted in Chapter 4, O'Neill contends that these principles must be ones that "leave the agency of each member of the plurality intact."[10] Applying this criterion to questions about the acceptability of pornography, one might find pornography acceptable if it does not "violate the agency" of either the persons who are used to make it or those who view it, sell it, and produce it. In fact, some who argue in favor of pornography contend that it is unproblematic insofar as women consent to work in the pornography industry and some women actually choose to purchase and use pornography. In other words, although not all women like pornography, those who find it offensive do not have to watch or read it, nor do they have to work as models in the industry. Thus, it seems that this liberal method could be used to promote the idea that as long as no one is "forced" to model for or watch pornography, its production and sale are unproblematic.

Beginning with individuals and employing a liberal method of abstraction does not necessarily lead one to the conclusion that pornography is unobjectionable. One could argue that it actually does affect people who do not explicitly "consent" to it. Many of the pornography models work in the industry because they lack other well-paying jobs, and some are more directly coerced into doing sex work. Nonetheless, unless the women working in the sex industry were actually forced to take their jobs, assertions about their "lack of other options" fail to hold much weight in a society such as ours, where well-paying jobs are scarce for those without higher education or class privilege. The other claim, that women are subjected to pornographic images without "consenting" to view them, is also not likely to work as a powerful argument against pornography. People generally are not forced to watch pornographic videos, nor are they required to read pornographic magazines. Although it is true that sexualized violence is becoming increasingly common, focusing on the issue of consent—as liberals often do—does not facilitate the development of an analysis of what is wrong with pornography in particular, since much of what people read and view is sexist in some intangible way. We clearly do not specifically "consent" to the existence of many types of cultural media, and suggesting that everyone must consent to all forms of cultural representation would be an impossible and unworkable standard. Thus, claims that certain forms of pornography contribute to women's oppression must derive their force from something other than women's lack of consent to the existence of pornography in our culture.

In contrast to the liberal method of beginning from very abstract principles and asking whether individual members of a plurality could each consent to these principles in a way that would preserve their agency, feminist arguments against pornography focus instead on questions of women's subordination and inequality. Feminism begins not from principles that are entirely abstract and neutral, but from the idea that women are subject to various forms of sexist oppression and from the commitment to challenge and eliminate such oppression. Guided by a feminist ideal of equality, whereby equality is understood to require that no one be oppressed based on membership in a social group, the feminist question becomes, Do particular social institutions and practices (such as pornography) reinforce, perpetuate, or contribute to women's inequality? It is from this particular perspective, and from this ideal of equality, that feminist critiques of pornography can be seen to emanate.

Thus, rather than asking whether pornography is something to which individuals each "consent," feminists examine the effects that pornography has on the larger society and on the status of subordinated social groups. Beginning with a concern to end violence against women, and to stop sexual harassment and discrimination, feminists consider whether and how certain forms of pornography contribute to these problems. As Gail Dines, Robert Jenson, and Ann Russo explain in the introduction to their book, *Pornography: The Production and Consumption of Inequality,* "The feminist analysis of the pornography industry begins with the problem of pervasive violence against women. . . . The compelling issues and questions have to do with mistreatment, harassment, rape, battery, and murder, not sex per se. The imaginative feminist vision is a society free of inequality and violence, not a society free of sexual desire and expression."[11] Thus, while liberal analyses of pornography tend to treat questions of whether the sexually explicit nature of pornography is "offensive" to persons who might view it, feminists who oppose pornography highlight questions of equality and examine the effects of pornography in the context of male dominance.

Unlike liberal theorists who ask questions about individual consent and employ principles that aim to be "merely abstract," feminist critics of pornography seek to remedy specific forms of social inequality—sexism, as well as racism, classism, heterosexism, and other types of oppression that are also often manifested in pornography.[12] In this sense, feminism offers an analysis that is not "neutral" or "abstract," but that instead aims for a particular social ideal, women's substantive equality. Achieving this ideal would require reducing various forms of cultural oppression, since some forms of culture (such as sexist pornography and advertising) promote and encourage practices that are oppressive. While this need not require the "banning" or "censorship" of pornography, it does suggest that we attempt to reduce the production and distribution of such materials and that we think critically about the effects of various media images, as well as about the conditions of their production and consumption. Such questions are more likely to be considered when one approaches the issue with the feminist methodology

I have described, rather than relying on the abstraction and individualism assumed by liberalism.

Feminist Alternatives to Liberal Methodology

Although my work here has been primarily critical, I will now outline several elements of a positive approach implicit in my critique and in my discussion of feminist alternatives to liberal methodology: Political theorizing must (1) focus more attention on social groups, (2) analyze actual sociopolitical structures, and (3) examine and critique male dominance as a form of oppression that intersects with other forms—such as racism and classism—but that is not reducible to them.

Central to my feminist approach is the idea that political theory must focus more attention on social groups. In contrast, liberals typically begin theorizing by asking questions about what kind of society *individuals* could agree to form. Liberals often consider the following sorts of questions: To which social arrangements is it rational for individuals to consent? Under what conditions would persons agree to such arrangements? In what circumstances is the state justified in interfering with the liberty of individuals? Although they are by no means the only ones to challenge this approach, feminists have long raised questions about the assumptions liberalism makes when it poses these questions as *the* central problems of political theory and when it frames politics as that which concerns the relationship between individuals and the state.[13] As many feminists have noted, people do not spring from the earth like mushrooms, but rather are born into families, communities, and complex political, economic, and cultural milieus.[14] A social context exists prior to the arrival of any particular individual, and individuals are always to some extent products of their specific social, historical, and cultural environments. In downplaying the significance of social context and focusing mainly on individuals, liberal theorists imply that the family is not important (thereby devaluing women's traditional work of bearing and raising children), they suggest that the only "political" relationships are ones that concern the individual and the state, and they reinforce a model of individual rationality that has long been associated with men rather than women. For these reasons, feminists often object to this sort of "individualism" in liberalism.

What makes feminism different from some other critical analyses of liberal individualism (such as communitarianism or conservativism) is that feminists reject the individualism of liberalism not in favor of a focus on the entire "community" or its "traditions," but rather in favor of a focus on specific *groups*, and in particular on the group "women." For instance, while liberal theorists tend to view the controversy over pornography as a conflict between the rights of individuals and the moral values of the community, feminists raise questions about how the industry, culture, and socioeconomic workings of pornography affect women *as a group*. Only by considering how members of the group *women* are affected by pornography can we understand the feminist objections that I have raised.

In recent years, feminists have vigorously debated the usefulness of analyzing women's situation in terms of the category "women as women." In particular, women of color have questioned the extent to which this category functions to entrench the interests and concerns of privileged white women as being those of "women" more generally.[15] Nonetheless, much feminist theorizing begins by examining social, political, sexual, and economic structures from the perspective of some particular group or the vantage point of those situated at the intersection of various different groups (for instance, examining what it is like to be a working-class African American woman). While many debate the usefulness of developing an analysis from the perspective of *women* as an unmodified term, most feminists agree that theorizing must begin with attention to social *groups*, whether these groups are understood on only one axis (such as sex) or defined in more complex ways, as those situated at the interstices of various axes of social power.[16]

In her essay "Gender as Seriality: Thinking About Women as a Social Collective," Young argues that one reason that feminists need to think about women as a group, and specifically as a "collective," is that we need to "maintain a point of view outside of liberal individualism," since the discourse of liberal individualism "denies the reality of groups":

> According to liberal individualism, categorizing people in groups by race, gender, religion, and sexuality, and acting as though these ascriptions say something significant about the person and his or her experience, capacities, and possibilities, is invidious and oppressive. The only liberatory approach is to think of people and treat them as individuals, variable and unique. This individualist ideology, however, in fact obscures oppression. Without conceptualizing women as a group in some sense, it is not possible to conceptualize oppression as a systematic, structured, institutional process.[17]

Because feminism is centrally concerned with uncovering and altering the structures of women's oppression, it must employ an analytical framework that makes visible these structures. Understanding women as a "group" of some sort seems necessary to this process. Other feminists echo this connection between oppression and social groups. For instance, Marilyn Frye defines oppression as "a system of interrelated barriers and forces which reduce, immobilize and mold people who belong to a certain group, and effect their subordination to another group."[18] Thus, one is not oppressed as an individual, but rather as a member of some particular group, and the effect of such oppression is that another group somehow benefits or gains power from the oppressive system. Because oppression is a group-based phenomenon, social forces must construct, shape, and mold people into different categories, or groups. In fact, these groups are often so well-defined that they appear natural, which makes people less likely to question or challenge the system of oppression that they serve. As Frye notes, "Such a system could not exist were not the groups, the categories of persons, well defined . . . they must be not only distinct but relatively easily identifiable; the barriers and forces could not be suitably located and applied if there were often much doubt as to which individuals were to be contained and reduced, which were to dominate."[19] In other words, if women's oppression is to exist, it must be that "women" and "men" are constructed as distinct groups, marked off in various ways. Thus, the very groups feminism takes as its focus—women and men—are not themselves natural categories that pre-exist the structures and forces of oppression. Nonetheless, because these social groups are central to the functioning of oppression and domination, feminist analysis and critique must focus on them, although with an awareness of the intersectionality of oppressive forces and the complexity of group categories.

Beginning with the social group *women*, feminists focus not on abstract rational agency, nor on theorizing about what persons could agree to under ideal conditions, but rather on the social groups that already exist in our current society and in recent history. In light of this, the second prong of my feminist approach is that political theorizing must be situated in an analysis and critique of actual power structures. Throughout this book I have emphasized the importance of examining social relations of power and not attempting simply to "abstract" from knowledge of social, political, and economic structures. In discussing oppression, feminists necessarily refer to forces of history, culture, politics, and economics, not to a merely "abstract" ideal. Coming to see the workings of patriarchal oppression requires questioning whether various actions and structures function as part of a *system* of *barriers* to some particular group of people. As I argued in Chapter 4, this cannot be determined by thinking only about abstract questions of what rational agents could agree to, nor about what would be the case in an ideal or hypothetical state of affairs. While such counterfactual questions may have some place in theorizing, they are not the most appropriate starting point for feminism.

Unlike much philosophical analysis, feminist theory has arisen out of the concrete practices and struggles of women's everyday experiences. As I noted in Chapter 5, feminists often begin by looking critically at actual phenomena that affect women—practices such as sexual harassment, rape, domestic violence, and women's struggles for reproductive rights. Through examining how gender and the structures of sexism affect women's lives, feminists have developed theories that critically analyze male dominance, and they have devised strategies for challenging and changing these structures. Thus, feminist methodology involves taking up the viewpoint of women, analyzing various phenomena from the perspective of women living within structures of male dominance. From this perspective, "equality" is not a matter of abstract "sameness" (nor is it a struggle to become "just like men"), but rather is understood to require remedying the unjust hierarchies of domination that structure, confine, and shape women's lives. Theorizing does not proceed by bracketing all questions about actual society, but rather begins with an examination of power relations in an attempt to understand, criticize, and ultimately change these arrangements.

Of course, many liberals would agree that understanding specific issues such as rape or sexual harassment requires studying actual social practices. The difference between my proposal and liberalism is that under my approach, an examination of the structures of power—and the recognition that there *are* structures of power, oppression, and inequality—must be a starting point of the *theory*. In contrast, liberals generally attempt to separate out the application of a theory from its conceptual origins, acknowledging structures of power primarily at the level of application.

Applying this second element of my feminist approach to the issue of pornography, one can see that some feminist analyses of pornography begin by examining women's experiences (acknowledging their complexity) and by asking how the practice of pornography functions in the context of current structures of male dominance. Rather than beginning with Ronald Dworkin's abstract question "Do we have a right to pornography?" feminists investigate the effects that pornography has on the lives of women—and not only the lives of women who work in the industry, or who choose to watch and read pornography. Feminists are also concerned with the effects that pornography has on how men view women, on how women perceive themselves, and on how sexuality is practiced more generally. Does pornography make rape, domestic violence, or sexual harassment more likely? How does it affect women's economic status in our society? Questions such as these—which are concrete and concern our *actual* society—must be central to feminist theorizing and not merely taken into account after an abstract theory of rights or equality has been devised and justified.

Critically examining power relations at the level of theory construction opens the theorist to the charge of bias. Beginning with the understanding that women are oppressed, or with the assumption that we live in a country where various forms of racism are systemic and entrenched, one may be accused of philosophizing from a point of view that is not "neutral," but rather is biased toward particular (feminist, antiracist) positions. However, as I argued above, theorizing with the aim of being "merely" abstract, and attempting to avoid appeals to any specific ideals, often results in theories that presuppose and implicitly reinforce dominant social norms. The problems one takes as a matter of interest, and the ways that one formulates the questions on which political theory focuses, all presuppose some understanding of social relations of power—economic, political, sexual, and other such systems. Feminism begins in the midst of these structures, with the life experiences of those living under conditions of various forms of hierarchy.

Unlike liberals who attempt to abstract from actual power relations, the postmodern theorists—of whom I mainly have been critical—do begin their work in the midst of the complexity of various forms of sociopolitical, economic, and sexual power. Although I examine their work primarily to contrast it to my own approach, Brown, Butler, and other postmodern feminists do make significant contributions to feminist theorizing—and to political philosophy more generally—by emphasizing the pervasiveness of power and the inability of theorists to remove themselves from the complex nexus of power in which they are embedded. While postmodern feminists may pay insufficient attention to the ways that oppression systemically benefits and harms persons on the basis of their membership in certain social groups, they are fully aware of the ways that people's lives, identities, and even selves are shaped and constructed by various forms of power, and their insights add important contributions to feminist theories of power.[20]

The third element of my alternative feminist approach, the focus on male dominance, is one that I have not explicitly described, though it is perhaps implicit in all feminist social theory. Throughout this book, I critically analyze two troubling aspects of liberalism—its individualism and its abstraction—and I advocate an alternative feminist methodology that centers on social groups and proceeds by analyzing actual structures of power. These two elements are by no means specific to feminism. Radical theorists of a variety of stripes argue that we must examine society in terms of its social groups and power structures. Most obvious in this is Marxism, which also studies the relations between groups of people—capitalists and workers. Although the point may be self-evident, what makes feminism distinctive is its attentiveness to the situation of women, not just as a group of persons living within some other type of power structure (such as class relations), but as a category of persons shaped and created by male dominance, which is itself a form of power.

During the second wave of the women's movement, feminists engaged in lengthy debates about the exact nature of the connection between male dominance and capitalism.[21] Although these discussions are less common today (perhaps because socialism is not the vibrant movement in this country that it was in earlier times), questions about the ways that feminism meshes with various other social movements persist. Many issues affecting women, people of color, and other oppressed people, can be viewed as matters of class and economic power, and yet feminists argue that class is not the only form of hierarchy. While women's problems are often connected to and exacerbated by economic injustice, it is crucial that they not be seen as reducible to this.

In very different ways, both liberals and socialists/Marxists tend to see power in terms of economics and class. Although classical liberals pay less attention to class differences between individuals (and instead examine the state's power over individuals) most contemporary egalitarian liberals, such as Dworkin and Rawls, take seriously the ways that economic structures affect an individual's ability to realize the formal freedom and equality granted in a liberal society. For instance, in discussing inequality, both Rawls and Dworkin focus on questions of class and economic power. Because neither endorses a radical critique of capitalist economic structures, both believe that some class differences are justified yet support the reduction of economic inequalities. While Rawls discusses gender in some of his most recent work (responding primarily to Okin and other feminist critics), he generally does not suggest that gender is itself a form of "power." He acknowledges that gender differences work to women's disadvantage in our society, but he is ambivalent about whether such disadvantages are fundamentally part of the "basic structure" of society; many gender inequalities occur within "associations" such as the family, which makes them less directly subject to political regulation.[22] Of course, there are differences in men's and women's economic situation—for instance, women receive less pay for comparable work, and the domestic work women typically perform is undervalued. These economic inequalities are clearly unjust and are important aspects of women's oppression. But women's oppression must not be seen as reducible to economic issues.

Although Marxists offer a more radical analysis of society, and a very different understanding of the meaning of class and economic power, they often share with liberals a failure to fully grasp the ways that gender is itself a form of social power. Of course, feminists have long criticized "mechanical Marxists" for their unwillingness to see class and power in anything but economic terms.[23] While concerned with the status of women's work, including that which they frame as the labor of bearing and raising children, as well as other unpaid labor in the home, Marxism offers no independent critique of the situation of women as an oppressed class or group. Rather, Marxists focus on women's work as laborers or as "reproducers" of labor and on the various ways that class oppression affects women.

What makes feminism distinctive, and different from both Marxism and liberalism, is its understanding of women as a group or class of persons who suffer from a particular type of oppression: male domination. Certainly, structures of male dominance are bolstered and reinforced through capitalism, but they cannot fully be understood without acknowledging that they have their own dynamic, which necessitates studying their workings in a somewhat independent manner. Thus, feminists emphasize issues concerning sexual oppression: rape, sexual harassment, abortion and reproductive rights, pornography, and a host of other problems that affect women in a way that is not reducible to economic exploitation. Feminists also call attention to areas of life that were not formerly considered to be either "political" or sites of exploitation: the family and personal/sexual relations of all sorts. As my discussion in Chapter 5 makes clear, approaching issues from a feminist perspective—with an understanding of gender as a hierarchy of power—uncovers new problems and suggests novel solutions. For instance, on a liberal view (one that does not take an explicitly feminist perspective), abortion may appear to be a matter of balancing conflicting rights: the "privacy right" of the pregnant woman to choose what to do with her body versus the fetus's "right to life," if it can be established that such a right exists. Similarly, issues of pornography appear as questions about "free speech" versus "censorship" and focus on whether pictures of naked people having sex are "obscene." When questions of social power have been incorporated into nonfeminist discussions of these issues, they primarily have been questions of economics. Nonfeminist debates about pornography might consider the economic vulnerability of those who work in the industry, or the rights of entrepreneurs and consumers to make and purchase pornographic materials. Or they might examine the state's power to regulate individuals' decisions about what jobs to accept or what materials to produce and purchase. In contrast, a feminist approach calls attention to the fact that male dominance is itself a form of social power that works in conjunction with both state power and economics, while at the same time intersecting with racism, class oppression, and myriad other social forces.

In short, I have argued that as an alternative to liberal abstraction and individualism, feminists focus on women as a group, analyze actual relations of social power while constructing theories, and view male dominance as itself a form of social power. The feminists whose work I draw upon in developing my critical analysis of liberalism—MacKinnon, Langton, Anderson, Young, Babbitt, and others—all employ these methods in their own analyses. Rather than offering a complete theory that would replace liberalism, I suggest, following these theorists, that the concepts typically employed by liberals, including the notions of rights, justice, and equality, must be defined and applied with an attention to social structures of power. If the liberal response to my project is that this is perfectly consistent with liberalism, then this is not necessarily a problem. What is problematic is the suggestion that this vindicates anything other than a very abstract version of "liberalism." What is logically consistent with liberal theory is not necessarily the same as—and might be quite different from—the actual versions of liberalism that have been put forth in recent years, as well as in the history of modern philosophy. As has been demonstrated here, it is not only the former (the issue of logical consistency) that matters philosophically.

Notes

Introduction

1. For an overview of feminist objections to the public/private split in liberal political theory, see Pateman, "Feminist Critiques of the Public/Private Dichotomy," 103–26.

2. For one example of the "abstract" critique, see Jaggar, *Feminist Politics and Human Nature*. In recent years, feminist philosophers have focused critical attention on the liberal conception of autonomy and have challenged the tendency of much mainstream philosophy to assume that individuals are rational and autonomous individuals. For contemporary feminist perspectives on this issue, see Mackenzie and Stoljar, eds., *Relational Autonomy*.

3. For instance, see Gilligan, *In A Different Voice*; and Kittay and Meyers, eds., *Women and Moral Theory*.

4. Nussbaum, *Sex and Social Justice*, "The Feminist Critique of Liberalism," 63. In support of feminist liberalism, Nussbaum contends that the "deepest and most central ideas of the liberal tradition are ideas of radical force and great theoretical and practical value," and that liberalism provides feminists with better theoretical tools than other available theories (56).

For an excellent anthology of work by contemporary feminists writing in defense of feminist liberalism, see Baehr, *Varieties of Feminist Liberalism*.

5. Onora O'Neill explicitly defends "abstraction without idealization" as a useful method for feminist theorizing about justice. In particular, see "Justice, Gender, and International Boundaries." I critically analyze O'Neill's discussion of abstraction in Chapter 4.

Jean Hampton is one scholar who argues for a feminist version of social contract theory. One benefit of contractarianism, according to Hampton, is that it values each individual person's right not to be exploited, which is important to feminism. Thus, she explains that contractarian theory can "help the feminist cause, and it can do so because it unabashedly insists on the worth of each of us. The reliance on self-interest in my formulation of the contract test is not an unfortunate remnant of Hobbes's moral theory; rather, it is a deliberate attempt to preserve what may be the only right-headed aspect of Hobbes's thought—namely, *the idea that morality should not be understood to require that we make ourselves the prey of others.* The self-interested concern that each party to a Kantian social contract brings to the agreement process symbolizes her morally legitimate concern to prevent her exploitation and have the value of her interests and her person respected" (Hampton, "Feminist Contractarianism").

6. Friedman claims that "although women still have occasion to fear *men's* autonomy, it seems that many women have good reason to welcome our *own*. When a woman is the one who is exercising autonomy, even if its exercise disrupts relationships in her life the value of her gain in autonomous living might well make the costs to her worth her while" ("Autonomy, Social Disruption, and Women," 47). The other essays in the volume containing Friedman's work also provide critical insights into the ways that the concept of autonomy functions in moral and political discourse, and the book highlights important debates within feminist theory about the potential for reformulating this central liberal concept.

7. Schneider, "The Dialectic of Rights and Politics," 322.

8. Schneider, "The Violence of Privacy," 52.

9. Ibid., 53.

10. For instance, Martha Nussbaum contends that "liberalism of a kind can be defended" against these charges (*Sex and Social Justice*, 56). Nussbaum explicitly responds to the radical feminist attacks on liberal abstraction and individualism, and she argues that "liberal individualism, consistently followed through, entails a radical feminist program" (67). I discuss and reply to Nussbaum's arguments in Chapter 5.

11. In cases where state neutrality permits or promotes injustices, some liberals reject strict "neutrality" on the grounds that it prevents some persons from being able to form or to pursue their own conception of the good.

12. Will Kymlicka explains that "no life goes better by being led from the outside according to values the person doesn't endorse. My life only goes better if I'm leading it from the inside, according to my beliefs about value" (*Liberalism, Community, and Culture*, 12).

13. For a classic elaboration of this aspect of liberalism and of the importance of civil liberties, see Mill, *On Liberty*.

14. As Elizabeth Anderson observes, while "[v]irtually all egalitarians" accept the claim that the state should treat each of its citizens with "equal respect and concern," only rarely do these theorists critically examine what this entails. "Instead, they invoke the formula, then propose their favored principle of egalitarian distribution as an interpretation of it, without providing an argument proving that their principle really does express equal respect and concern for all citizens" ("What Is the Point of Equality?" 295).

15. Nussbaum, *Sex and Social Justice*, 57.

16. Rawls, *A Theory of Justice*, 505. I discuss Rawls's work in more detail in Chapter 3.

17. Kymlicka, *Liberalism, Community, and Culture*, 12. See also R. Dworkin, "Comment on Narveson," 26.

18. R. Dworkin, "Liberalism," 62.

19. For a discussion of some important differences between feminism and communitarianism, see Friedman, *What Are Friends For?* esp. chap. 9, "Feminism and Modern Friendship: Dislocating the Community," 231–55.

20. In Chapters 4 and 5, I argue that both Onora O'Neill and Martha Nussbaum sometimes conflate these criticisms and fail to address adequately what I take to be the main feminist objections to liberalism's abstraction and individualism.

21. In recent years, Jaggar's analysis of liberalism has been the target of several theorists who argue that feminism and liberalism *are* compatible. For instance, Nussbaum's response to the feminist critique of liberalism focuses particular attention on Jaggar (see Nussbaum, *Sex and Social Justice*, esp. chap. 2, "Feminist Critique of Liberalism"). Will Kymlicka also cites Jaggar's work as representative of the feminist critique of liberalism. For Kymlicka's claim that liberalism can respond to Jaggar's critique, see Kymlicka, *Liberalism, Community, and Culture*, 14–19.

22. Jaggar, *Feminist Politics and Human Nature*, 28–29.

23. Nussbaum explains the individualism of liberalism in this way: "Liberalism holds that the flourishing of human beings taken one by one is both analytically and normatively prior to the flourishing of the state or the nation or the religious group . . . Putting things this way . . . just asks us to concern ourselves with the distribution of resources and opportunities in a certain way, namely, with concern to see how well *each and every one of them* is doing, seeing each and every one as an end, worthy of concern" (*Sex and Social Justice*, 62–63).

24. Following Marilyn Frye, I understand oppression to be "a system of interrelated barriers and forces which reduce, immobilize and mold people who belong to a certain group, and effect their subordination to another group" (Frye, *The Politics of Reality*, 33).

25. Rawls, *A Theory of Justice*, 9.

26. Rawls, *Political Liberalism*, 45–46.

27. See R. Dworkin, "What Is Equality? Part 2: Equality of Resources."

28. Note that Brown and Butler, like many other postmodern feminists, are influenced by the work of Michel Foucault, and in particular by his conception of power as "something which circulates . . . is never localised here or there," and is "never in anybody's hands" (Foucault, "Two Lectures," 98).

Chapter 1

1. Feminists have identified a variety of problems with liberal rights theory and have come to somewhat different conclusions about its usefulness for women. See Schneider, "The Dialectic of Rights and Politics"; Brennan, "The Liberal Rights of Liberal Feminism"; Williams, "The Pain of Word Bondage"; Brown, *States of Injury*, esp. chap. 5, "Rights and Losses"; Peters and Wolper, *Women's Rights, Human Rights*; and Minow and Shanley, "Relational Rights and Responsibilities."

2. MacKinnon and A. Dworkin, *Pornography and Civil Rights*, 17–18.

3. Ibid., 17.

4. Hereafter, except in references, the name Dworkin, when not prefaced by a first initial, should be understood as indicating Ronald Dworkin (not Andrea Dworkin).

5. R. Dworkin, *Taking Rights Seriously*, 82, 90.

6. R. Dworkin, "Rights as Trumps," 153.

7. R. Dworkin, "Liberalism," 62.

8. "Since the citizens of a society differ in their conceptions [of the good life, or of what gives value to life], the government does not treat them as equals if it prefers one conception to another" (ibid., 64). Further page references to this work appear in the text.

9. R. Dworkin, *Taking Rights Seriously*, 192.

10. Ibid., 197.

11. As Rae Langton notes, Dworkin is not entirely consistent in how he defines "external" preferences. She specifically highlights Dworkin's dramatic extension of the notion of an external preference in his discussion of the *Sweatt* case from the discussion of it at work in "What Rights Do We Have?" (Langton, "Whose Right?" 322). In the *Sweatt* case, the University of Texas Law School rejected the application of a Black man, Heman Marion Sweatt, on the basis of its whites-only admissions policy. In 1950, the Supreme Court ruled (in *Sweatt v. Painter*) that the state law restricting university access to whites violated the Equal Protection Clause of the Fourteenth Amendment and was therefore unconstitutional.

12. R. Dworkin, "Liberalism," 70.

13. R. Dworkin, *Taking Rights Seriously*, 205.

14. See R. Dworkin, *A Matter of Principle*, esp. chap. 17, "Do We Have a Right to Pornography?" 335–72, 335.

15. R. Dworkin, *Taking Rights Seriously*, 237.

16. Langton, "Whose Right?" 338.

17. For Langton, in the current context of women's inequality, it is at least "difficult to disentangle personal preferences about pornography . . . from external preferences, difficult to answer the hypothetical question about the dependence of the desire on the prejudice" ("Whose Right?" 346). Given this difficulty, according to Dworkin's own formulation of external preferences in his discussion of the *Sweatt* case, Langton asserts that we must conclude that the preferences to view pornography are "external."

18. R. Dworkin, "Women and Pornography," 36; emphasis added.

19. Ibid., 38.

20. Ibid., 41.

21. For instance, see MacKinnon, *Toward a Feminist Theory of the State*, esp. chap. 8, "The Liberal State"; *Feminism Unmodified*; and *Women's Lives, Men's Laws*.

22. MacKinnon, *Toward a Feminist Theory of the State*, 161.

23. For an excellent account of this problem, and for further discussion of the specific problems that women of color face in getting their claims of discrimination addressed, see Crenshaw, "Demarginalizing the Intersection of Race and Sex."

24. Zia, "Where Race and Gender Meet," 234–35.

25. MacKinnon, "Pornography as Defamation and Discrimination," 797. For additional examples and analyses of how pornography can reinforce racism as well

as sexism, see Cowan, "Racism and Sexism in Pornography"; Gardner, "Racism and Pornography in the Women's Movement"; and Zia, "Where Race and Gender Meet."

26. MacKinnon, *Toward a Feminist Theory of the State*, 169. For a detailed and compelling example of how formal legal rights can work against the interests of women, see MacKinnon's discussion of women in prostitution in her "Prostitution and Civil Rights."

27. MacKinnon, *Feminism Unmodified*, 157–58.

28. Ibid., 158. MacKinnon explains this in more detail in *Only Words*: "censorship occurs less through explicit state policy than through official and unofficial privileging of powerful groups and viewpoints" (77). One specific example that she discusses is the way in which publishing decisions are made by powerful individuals, who are both wealthy and privileged. She explains that "publishing decisions, no matter how one-sided and cumulative and exclusionary, are regarded as the way the system of freedom of expression is supposed to work. Legal accountability for these decisions is regarded as fascism; social accountability for them is regarded as creeping fascism; the decisions themselves are regarded as freedom of speech" (77–78).

29. MacKinnon, *Toward a Feminist Theory of the State*, 164.

30. Ibid., 164–65.

31. MacKinnon, *Feminism Unmodified*, 101.

32. R. Dworkin, "Women and Pornography," 38.

33. R. Dworkin, *Taking Rights Seriously*, 227.

34. R. Dworkin, "Liberalism," 71.

35. MacKinnon, *Toward A Feminist Theory of the State*, 208.

36. Ibid., 209.

37. Ibid., 207.

38. R. Dworkin, "Two Concepts of Liberty," 106.

39. Ibid. Dworkin goes on to state this even more conclusively: "Sadistic pornography . . . is greatly overshadowed by these dismal cultural influences as a causal force" (ibid.). He also makes claims nearly identical to these in his review of *Only Words*, writing that "the view[s] of women presented in soap operas and commercials . . . are much greater obstacles to that equality than the dirty films watched by a small minority" (R. Dworkin, "Women and Pornography," 36).

40. This is not to say that MacKinnon does not seek to alter the sexist portrayal of women in the media, in advertising, or in other aspects of culture. She seems to focus on pornography because it is, in her view, the most extreme example of the ways that women's sexual oppression is constructed and reinforced. Perhaps she would also acknowledge that it would be difficult to simply ban ads and other forms of media that harm women in less obvious ways. Unfortunately, MacKinnon does not focus much attention on this question of what exactly she thinks should be done about these other less extreme but nonetheless pervasive ways in which women's sexual subjection is perpetuated.

41. MacKinnon, "Pornography as Defamation and Discrimination," 799.

42. MacKinnon, *Only Words*, 15.

43. MacKinnon and A. Dworkin, *Pornography and Civil Rights*, 22.

44. There is insufficient space here for me to undertake a more thorough explication of MacKinnon's particular conception of equality, which differs significantly

from Dworkin's. In contrast to the liberal emphasis on procedures for neutral treatment (which frequently amount to treating "likes" alike and treating those who are "different" differently), for MacKinnon "[t]he question of equality . . . is at root a question of hierarchy" (MacKinnon, *Feminism Unmodified*, 40). For a more detailed description of her conception of equality, see *Toward a Feminist Theory of the State*, esp. chap. 12, "Sex Equality," 215–34. Also see Chapter 5 below, where I summarize MacKinnon's "dominance" approach to equality and contrast it to the mainstream liberal "sameness" approach.

45. MacKinnon, *Only Words*, 87.

46. MacKinnon and A. Dworkin, *Pornography and Civil Rights*, 29.

47. Ibid., 31.

48. MacKinnon and Andrea Dworkin describe the way in which civil rights became defined in the civil rights movement: "Our contemporary understanding of civil rights—what they are, what they mean—comes out of the Black experience" (ibid., 11). They explain that the civil rights that Blacks won were ultimately also secured for some other oppressed groups, but that this, too, occurred through political struggle: "This broadening of civil-rights protection to many stigmatized groups was the result of political activism, legislative initiatives, and many, many lawsuits" (11).

49. Note that Langton does not commit herself to a position about what exact conclusion is to be drawn from the fact that Dworkin's liberal theory can be made to yield non-liberal conclusions.

50. R. Dworkin, "Women and Pornography," 42.

51. Ibid., 36.

Chapter 2

1. Kymlicka, *Contemporary Political Philosophy*, 87.

2. R. Dworkin, "What Is Equality? Part 2: Equality of Resources," 311.

3. Ibid., 285.

4. R. Dworkin, "What Is Equality? Part 1: Equality of Welfare," 186.

5. R. Dworkin, "What Is Equality? Part 2: Equality of Resources," 283.

6. Ibid., 285.

7. Ibid., 306.

8. Ibid., 293.

9. Mapel, *Social Justice Reconsidered*, 50–51.

10. For an extended discussion of the prevalence of "luck egalitarianism" in the work of contemporary political philosophy, see Anderson, "What Is the Point of Equality?"

11. R. Dworkin, "What Is Equality? Part 2: Equality of Resources," 331; emphasis added.

12. Ibid., 307.

13. R. Dworkin, "Liberal Community," 481.

14. Susan Babbitt has argued that liberal theorists neglect to consider the ways in which individuals themselves would be transformed if social structures were to change radically. In contrast to the liberal assumption that the interests of individuals are defined by what the individuals can currently endorse "from the inside,"

Babbitt contends that the "objective interests" of individuals are best defined "in terms of interests and desires an individual *would* have in more just and humane social circumstances" (Babbitt, *Impossible Dreams*, 7).

15. See Elster, *Sour Grapes*, esp. 109–40.

16. Ibid., 117.

17. Ibid., 110.

18. "Character planning, although neither a necessary nor a sufficient condition for autonomy, is at least much more compatible with autonomy than are either manipulated preferences or adaptive ones" (ibid., 127–28). Note that Elster uses the term "adaptive preferences" here to refer to the specific phenomenon of sour grapes.

19. For Dworkin's discussion of the problem of expensive tastes, and for his argument that this is one good reason to reject "equality of welfare" and to favor "equality of resources," see his "What Is Equality? Part 1: Equality of Welfare."

20. "Under equality of resources . . . people decide what sorts of lives to pursue against a background of information about the actual cost their choices impose on other people and hence on the total stock of resources that may fairly be used by them" (R. Dworkin, "What Is Equality? Part 2: Equality of Resources," 288).

21. Elster explains that while "one can distinguish operationally between intentional adjustment of preferences to possibilities by meta-desires and the similar causal adjustment by drives, actual cases may not be clearcut enough to persuade sceptics of the reality of this distinction" (*Sour Grapes*, 111).

22. R. Dworkin, "What Is Equality? Part 2: Equality of Resources," 290.

23. Ibid.

24. Whereas *personal preferences* are the preferences an individual has regarding his or her "own enjoyment of some goods or opportunities," *external preferences* are preferences regarding "the assignment of goods and opportunities to others" (R. Dworkin, *Taking Rights Seriously*, 234).

25. Ibid., 276.

26. R. Dworkin, "The Roots of Justice: Part 2," 17–18.

27. Ibid., 20.

28. Ibid.

Chapter 3

1. For a useful overview of feminist analyses and critique of Rawls's work, see Nussbaum, "Rawls and Feminism."

2. For Okin's most comprehensive work on the justice of the family, including a very important critique of Rawls, see *Justice, Gender, and the Family*, esp. chap. 5, "Justice as Fairness: For Whom?" For her other analyses of Rawls, see "Justice and Gender"; "Reason and Feeling in Thinking About Justice"; and "*Political Liberalism*, Justice, and Gender."

3. See Okin, "*Political Liberalism*, Justice, and Gender."

4. Okin, *Justice, Gender, and the Family*, 108–9.

5. Ibid., 89.

6. See Rawls, "Fairness to Goodness," 267–85.

7. Okin, *Justice, Gender, and the Family*, 100–101.

8. Ibid., 101.

9. Okin, "Reason and Feeling in Thinking About Justice," 246.

10. Ibid., 248.

11. Okin, *Justice, Gender, and the Family*, 91, 102–3.

12. "Social and economic inequalities are to be arranged so that they are both (a) to the greatest benefit of the least advantaged and (b) attached to offices and positions open to all under conditions of fair equality of opportunity" (Rawls, *A Theory of Justice*, 83).

13. Ibid., 96.

14. Ibid., 97–98.

15. Ibid., 99.

16. For instance, Rawls explains that there are circumstances in which "[c]ompensating steps must . . . be taken to preserve the fair value for all of the equal political liberties" (ibid., 225).

17. I thank Ann Cudd for urging me to consider this line of argument.

18. Rawls, *A Theory of Justice*, 246.

19. Ibid., 351.

20. Rawls, "The Law of Peoples," 5.

21. Ibid.

22. Okin, "Reason and Feeling in Thinking About Justice," 245.

23. Note, though, that Kittay argues for the addition of these social positions only after maintaining that we need to make other additions to the list of moral powers and to the list of primary goods described by Rawls: "If . . . we add to the other moral powers the capacity to give care, and if we include goods related to our interdependence in states of vulnerability in the index of primary goods, we can make a case for adding the dependency worker and the dependent to the short list of social positions from which to consider issues of fairness and just distributions" (Kittay, "Human Dependency and Rawlsian Equality," 252).

24. Kittay explains: "If the second principle is to ensure a fair distribution of goods to those in dependency relations, it must be interpreted in such a way that (a) the group that is least advantaged includes paid dependency workers and that (b) fair equality of opportunity precludes all forms of sex discrimination that restrict women to poorly paid or unpaid work" (ibid., 250).

25. Also see Green, "Rawls, Women, and the Priority of Liberty"; and Trout, "Can Justice as Fairness Accommodate Diversity?"

26. Rawls comments that "in the simplest form of the difference principle the individuals who belong to the least advantaged group are not identifiable apart from, or independently of, their income and wealth. The least advantaged are never identifiable as men or women, say, or as whites or blacks, or Indians or British. They are not individuals identified by natural or other features (race, gender, nationality, and the like) that enable us to compare their situation under all the various schemes of social cooperation it is feasible to consider" (*Justice as Fairness*, 59n26).

27. Rawls, *A Theory of Justice*, 151.

28. For instance, in another passage he explains, "No one deserves his greater natural capacity nor merits a more favorable starting place in society. But it does

not follow that one should eliminate these distinctions. There is another way to deal with them. The basic structure can be arranged so that these contingencies work for the least fortunate" (ibid., 102).

29. Okin, *Justice, Gender, and the Family*, 171.

30. Ibid., 105.

31. Rawls, *A Theory of Justice*, 137, cited in Okin, *Justice Gender and the Family*, 91; Okin, *Justice Gender and the Family*, 91; ibid., 102–3.

32. "Numerous commentators on *Theory* have made the objection that 'the general facts about human society' are often issues of great contention" (Okin, *Justice, Gender, and the Family*, 196n11).

33. Rawls, *A Theory of Justice*, 137.

34. Ibid.

35. Ibid. One feminist commentator, Deborah Kearns, claims that it is very unlikely that persons in the original position would agree on subjects as controversial as these Rawls lists: "I can hardly imagine four more debatable topics. Rawls recognises the diversity of theories on these topics but still implies that only one will be generally available (which economic theory? what laws of human psychology?). Besides diversity at any one time, historically the leading principles of economic theory and the dominant understanding of social organisation have changed" (Kearns, "A Theory of Justice—and Love; Rawls on the Family," 37).

36. Interestingly, Kearns argues that rather than having knowledge of women's oppression, it seems more likely that the parties in the original position would have the very common knowledge that women and men are simply "different" and that women's differences typically indicate their inferiority: "One of the only theories that can be identified in most cultures and periods is a theory of sexual difference. In modern western [*sic*] culture, this has been a theory of sexual inequality and would permeate the information which Rawls makes available to the contracting parties" (ibid.).

37. Okin, *Justice, Gender, and the Family*, 180.

38. According to the "fact of reasonable pluralism," free institutions tend to generate "a diversity of reasonable comprehensive doctrines . . . that reasonable citizens affirm and that political liberalism must address . . . they are in part the work of free practical reason within the framework of free institutions . . . the fact of reasonable pluralism is not an unfortunate condition of human life" (Rawls, *Political Liberalism*, 36–37).

39. Ibid., 36.

40. Ibid.; emphasis added. Note, too, that Rawls claims explicitly that "[p]olitical liberalism counts many familiar and traditional doctrines—religious, philosophical, and moral—as reasonable even though we could not seriously entertain them for ourselves" (ibid., 59–60).

41. Okin, *Justice, Gender, and the Family*, 180.

42. Ibid., 174.

43. Rawls, *Political Liberalism*, xvi. Further references to this work appear in the text.

44. See his discussion of these two factors in Rawls, *A Theory of Justice*, 102–3.

45. Ibid., 102. Note that Rawls does go on to argue that there are just and unjust ways of dealing with these "contingencies," even though he does not explain the structure of positions itself as being a matter of injustice:

> What is just and unjust is the way that institutions deal with these facts. Aristocratic and caste societies are unjust because they make these contingencies the ascriptive basis for belonging to more or less enclosed and privileged social classes. The basic structure of these societies incorporates the arbitrariness found in nature. But there is no necessity for men to resign themselves to these contingencies. The social system is not an unchangeable order beyond human control but a pattern of human action. . . . In justice as fairness men . . . undertake to avail themselves of the accidents of nature and social circumstance only when doing so is for the common benefit. (Ibid.)

In other words, Rawls does aim to change the social system, yet he still suggests that the positions into which one is born are "accidents of social circumstance" rather than the products of socially created structures.

46. I am bracketing difficult questions about the extent to which talents and skills, and other matters often considered "natural endowments," can be said to be truly "natural." Rawls does acknowledge that talents require cultivation, and that those who are born into circumstances of privilege will have better opportunities for developing their natural talents and abilities: "The extent to which natural capacities develop and reach fruition is affected by all kinds of social conditions and class attitudes" (ibid., 74).

47. Anderson, "What Is the Point of Equality?" 288.

48. Ibid., 288–89.

49. For Young's discussion and criticism of the "distributive paradigm," see Iris Marion Young, *Justice and the Politics of Difference*, esp. chap. 1, "Displacing the Distributive Paradigm," 15–38.

50. According to Rawls, the "basic structure" is "a society's main political, social, and economic institutions, and how they fit together into one unified system of social cooperation from one generation to the next" (*Political Liberalism*, 11). Although the question of whether the family is included in Rawls's "basic structure" is an important issue in feminist interpretations and analyses of Rawls, an extensive discussion of this matter is beyond the scope of this chapter. Rawls attempts to clear up questions about whether the family is part of the "basic structure" (or whether it is merely an "association") in his 1997 essay, "The Idea of Public Reason Revisited." Unfortunately, section 5, "On the Family as Part of the Basic Structure," is somewhat confusing. Rawls initially states clearly, "The family is part of the basic structure, since one of its main roles is to be the basis of the orderly production and reproduction of society and its culture from one generation to the next" (Rawls, "The Idea of Public Reason Revisited," 595). However, he immediately proceeds to qualify this claim, explaining that the principles of political justice "are not to apply directly to the internal life of the many associations within it [the basic structure], the family among them" (596). Thus, it seems that the family is an "association" within the basic structure, much like churches and other voluntary organizations. In fact, "[w]e wouldn't want political principles of justice—including principles of distributive justice—to apply directly to the internal life of the family" (598). Although Rawls argues that political principles do place some limitation on

what family members can do to one another (for example, they cannot violate one another's basic liberties), feminists have argued that such restrictions do not go far enough in promoting women's equality. For an insightful analysis of Rawls's failure to answer feminist criticisms of his treatment of the family, see A. F. Smith, "Closer but Still No Cigar."

Chapter 4

1. O'Neill, *Towards Justice and Virtue*, 40; "Justice, Gender, and International Boundaries," 309; "Ethical Reasoning and Ideological Pluralism," 711.

2. O'Neill, *Towards Justice and Virtue*, 40.

3. O'Neill, "Abstraction, Idealization, and Ideology in Ethics," 57, 58.

4. Ibid., 56.

5. Ibid.

6. O'Neill, "Justice, Gender, and International Boundaries," 305.

7. Ibid.

8. O'Neill, "Abstraction, Idealization, and Ideology in Ethics," 56.

9. Ibid.

10. Ibid.

11. O'Neill, *Towards Justice and Virtue*, 43.

12. Ibid.

13. Ibid.

14. O'Neill, "Justice, Gender, and International Boundaries," 312; emphasis added.

15. Ibid., 305.

16. O'Neill, *Constructions of Reason*, 210. Further references to this work appear in the text.

17. O'Neill, "Ethical Reasoning and Ideological Pluralism," 718.

18. Ibid., 719.

19. As I noted above, O'Neill argues that we can apply abstract principles to determinate cases without "privileging certain views of gender" (O'Neill, "Justice, Gender, and International Boundaries," 305).

20. In a commentary on an essay of O'Neill's, Martha Nussbaum contrasts O'Neill's approach to the issues of justice and gender to another approach (Nussbaum's own), one that is based on a particular conception of human functioning that arises out of discussions in Aristotle (Nussbaum, "Onora O'Neill," 324–35). Nussbaum argues that her own human functioning approach is superior to O'Neill's Kantian emphasis on ethical consistency. According to Nussbaum, it is "essential to focus on *content* . . . the actual doings and beings of people . . . not just what traffic rules will police their doings and beings. Indeed, it seem[s] hard to say anything meaningful about traffic rules until we know who the parties are and what they are doing" (ibid., 330). Although I do not find Nussbaum's particular Aristotelian discussion of human functioning entirely convincing, her general point against O'Neill is a powerful one. One need not support the specific Aristotelian approach that Nussbaum advocates to agree that normative theory requires holding some particular conception of the person.

21. O'Neill, "Ethical Reasoning and Ideological Pluralism," 718.

22. Wood, "Review of *Constructions of Reason*," 650.

23. He actually puts this more strongly: "This deceptive movement from pretended agnosticism through abstract formalism to pernicious idealization is so typical of traditional liberal thinking as to be almost its defining trait. At her best, O'Neill often exposes liberalism on this score, so it is too bad that as a good Kantian she must at last succumb to it herself" (ibid.).

24. Although O'Neill suggests that abstraction without idealization could get around this problem of ideology, or "false consciousness," it is not at all clear that it provides the best method for dealing with these deep-seated hierarchies and inequalities. Note that my claim is not simply that the principles that an abstract method produces could be *applied* in ways that are problematic (this is another problem); rather, I argue that the principles devised from a method that claims to be "abstract" may themselves turn out to be infected with oppressive and hierarchical thinking. The mere attempt to be abstract, and to avoid false idealizations, does not guarantee that one will achieve this goal.

25. Hill, *Autonomy and Self-Respect*, 5.

26. For a similar discussion of this example of Hill's, see Babbitt, *Impossible Dreams*, 43–46. Babbitt's treatment of the case of the Deferential Wife focuses more on questions of personal integrity and on the problems of appealing to idealized accounts of the person (which O'Neill claims not to do, since she rejects such idealizations). Nonetheless, many of Babbitt's points can also be applied to an analysis like O'Neill's, despite O'Neill's rejection of idealization.

27. O'Neill, *Constructions of Reason*, 213.

28. Ibid, 213n.

29. See Babbitt, *Impossible Dreams*, 43–46.

30. O'Neill, "Ethical Reasoning and Ideological Pluralism," 718.

31. Babbitt, *Impossible Dreams*, 90.

32. See R. Dworkin, *A Matter of Principle*, "Do We Have a Right to Pornography?" 335–72.

33. Babbitt, *Impossible Dreams*, 93.

34. Ibid.

35. Ibid., 26.

36. Ibid., 54; and Walker, *Meridian*, 199–200, cited in Babbitt, *Impossible Dreams*.

37. Babbitt, *Impossible Dreams*, 55.

38. Anderson, *Value in Ethics and Economics*, 91.

39. For a more extensive discussion of the process of criticizing and justifying normative ideals, see Anderson, *Value in Ethics and Economics*,chap. 5, 91–116. Anderson argues that "(1) criticizing an ideal requires interpreting its associated attitudes; (2) interpretations can be supported by empirical evidence; and (3) interpretations of attitudes undermine or support their endorsement" (95).

40. Anderson, "What Is the Point of Equality?" 287–337. Further references to this work appear in the text.

41. An important feature of Anderson's democratic equality is that it emphasizes "the need to distinguish between goods that society guarantees to all citizens and goods that may be entirely lost without generating any claims to compensation" (ibid., 301). This does not mean that individuals are to be guaranteed certain

"aggregate levels" of goods—either in terms of property or in terms of welfare. Rather, Anderson argues: "Egalitarians must try to secure certain *kinds* of goods for people" (ibid., 302).

42. Ibid.

43. Ibid., 310.

44. Ibid., 304.

Chapter 5

1. Nussbaum, *Sex and Social Justice*, 58. Further references to this work appear in the text.

2. Ibid., 67.

3. For a discussion of some of the tensions and problems between feminism and communitarianism, see Frazer and Lacey, *The Politics of Community*.

4. Nussbaum, *Sex and Social Justice*, 389, n. 63.

5. Ibid., 67.

6. Ibid.; emphasis added.

7. MacKinnon, *Feminism Unmodified*, 42.

8. Nussbaum, *Sex and Social Justice*, 68.

9. In response, Nussbaum would likely claim that even if such problems were as widespread as MacKinnon and other feminist critics attest, liberalism can remedy them by appealing to its "deepest" principles of equality and respect for persons. I address this point below.

10. "Men's physiology defines most sports, their needs define auto and health insurance coverage, their socially designed biographies define workplace expectations and successful career patterns, their perspectives and concerns define quality scholarship, their experiences and obsessions define merit, their objectification of life defines art, their military service defines citizenship, their presence defines family, their inability to get along with each other—their wars and rulerships— defines history, their image defines god, and their genitals define sex" (*Feminism Unmodified*, 36).

11. MacKinnon, *Toward a Feminist Theory of the State*, 219.

12. Ibid., 167.

13. Ibid., 229.

14. Nussbaum, *Sex and Social Justice*, 55. Further references to this work appear in the text.

15. See, for example, Nussbaum, *Women and Human Development*.

16. Other feminists have also addressed important questions regarding the adaptive preferences of women. For a thoughtful treatment of this issue as it relates to liberal feminism, see Cudd, "The Paradox of Liberal Feminism."

17. Nussbaum, *Women and Human Development*, 140.

18. Ibid.

19. Nussbaum, *Sex and Social Justice*, 62.

20. MacKinnon, *Toward a Feminist Theory of the State*, 242.

21. "As feminist method and practice, consciousness raising is not confined to groups explicitly organized or named for that purpose. In fact, consciousness raising

as discussed here was often not practiced in consciousness-raising groups. Such groups were, however, one medium and forum central to its development as a method of analysis, mode of organizing, form of practice, and technique of political intervention" (MacKinnon, *Toward a Feminist Theory of the State*, 84).

22. Ibid., 91.

23. Ibid., 95.

24. For an excellent description of this problem, see Crenshaw, "Demarginalizing the Intersection of Race and Sex."

25. See Harris, "Race and Essentialism in Feminist Legal Theory"; Kline, "Race, Racism, and Feminist Legal Theory."

26. For MacKinnon's own remarks on this issue, see her "From Practice to Theory, or What Is a White Woman Anyway?"

27. MacKinnon, *Toward a Feminist Theory of the State*, 121.

28. As I discussed in Chapter 4, Onora O'Neill defines abstraction as the "bracketing" of certain predicates, or as "detaching certain claims from others," and she claims that it is "a matter of selective omission, of leaving out some predicates from descriptions and theories." See O'Neill, *Towards Justice and Virtue*, 40; "Justice, Gender, and International Boundaries," 309; and "Ethical Reasoning and Ideological Pluralism," 711.

Chapter 6

1. Although Brown and Butler have much in common with other feminists who consider themselves postmodernists, I do not mean to suggest that their work is representative of all who fall under this category. Indeed, there is much disagreement about exactly what postmodernism is. I use the term here because the work of Brown and Butler is usually considered postmodern and because their criticisms of liberalism are echoed in the work of other postmodern theorists. It is beyond the scope of these two chapters for me to take up the work of other postmodern feminist political theorists.

2. For criticism of MacKinnon regarding women of color, see Harris, "Race and Essentialism in Feminist Legal Theory"; and Kline, "Race, Racism, and Feminist Legal Theory." For MacKinnon's response to these charges, see her "From Practice to Theory, or What Is a White Woman Anyway?" For claims of MacKinnon's inadequate attention to the topic of sexual pleasure, see Cornell, *Beyond Accomodation*, chap. 3, 119–64; and *Transformations*, chap. 5, 112–46. For discussion of MacKinnon's formulations vis-à-vis lesbian experience, see Valverde, "Beyond Gender Dangers and Private Pleasures." For the issue of caring and the "radical feminism" of Andrea Dworkin and MacKinnon, see West, "Jurisprudence and Gender," 213–21.

For an interesting defense of the importance of devising a "generalized" analysis of women's oppression—while nonetheless remaining sensitive to the ways in which women differ—see Rapaport, "Generalizing Gender." Although I do not think Rapaport accurately represents all aspects of MacKinnon's theory, she offers a compelling defense of MacKinnon against the charge of "essentialism." She notes that essentialism is considered a problem because it involves "the imposition of false uniformity on the disparate experience of women of different classes, races, ethnicities, and sexual orientations," and she argues that "these deplorable consequences do not necessarily overtake the theorist who seeks to generalize about gender" (127).

3. Brown, *States of Injury*, 37.

4. See MacKinnon, *Only Words*; "Pornography as Defamation and Discrimination"; Langton, "Whose Right?"; "Speech Acts and Unspeakable Acts."

5. Brown, "Suffering Rights as Paradoxes," 239.

6. Ibid., 231.

7. Brown, *States of Injury*, 40–41.

8. Ibid., 97, 100.

9. She announces that this is her intention in writing this essay: "I want to reflect upon the place of rights in the politics of politicized identities—rights of 'inclusion' as well as rights of 'difference' currently sought for people of color, homosexuals, and women in the late-twentieth-century United States" (ibid.).

10. "It would appear that a provisional answer to the question of the value of rights language for women is that it is deeply paradoxical: rights secure our standing as individuals even as they obscure the treacherous ways in which that standing is achieved and regulated; they must be specific and concrete in order to reveal and redress women's subordination, yet potentially entrench our subordination through that specificity" (Brown, "Suffering Rights as Paradoxes," 238).

11. Ibid., 239–40.

12. In fact, of the six sentences in the final paragraph of Brown's essay "Suffering Rights as Paradoxes," only the first sentence (a quote from Karl Marx, with whom Brown expresses disagreement because of his "progressive historiography") is a statement. The essay ends with a string of questions that do not clarify Brown's view on rights but rather raise a series of questions about the political possibilities of "attention to paradox."

13. Brown, *States of Injury*, 130.

14. Ibid., 88, 89.

15. Ibid., 78.

16. MacKinnon, *Toward a Feminist Theory of the State*, 129.

17. Brown, *States of Injury*, 129.

18. MacKinnon, *Feminism Unmodified*, 27.

19. Brown, *States of Injury*, 70.

20. Ibid., 70–71.

21. Brown, "Freedom's Silences," 315.

22. Ibid., 320.

23. Ibid.

24. Ibid., 321.

25. Ibid., 321–22.

26. Elsewhere Brown describes this similarity more explicitly: "[T]hose familiar with Foucault's genealogy of confession will have discerned in this argument an implied homology between the epistemological-political operations of consciousness-raising [as described by MacKinnon and other feminists] and those he assigns to confessional discourse" (Brown, *States of Injury*, 41).

27. Brown, "Freedom's Silences," 314.

28. For a thorough description of how this occurs, see MacKinnon, *Toward a Feminist Theory of the State*, esp. chaps. 5 and 6 (83–125).

29. Brown, "Freedom's Silences," 314.

30. Brown, *States of Injury*, 45.

31. Ibid., 131.

32. For an alternative understanding of categories see Frye, "The Necessity of Differences." Whereas Brown's work suggests that the category "women" may be inherently problematic, Frye argues that there are ways in which the category could be constructed so that it takes differences among women into account: "[I]f the category of women is constructed as a positive self-supporting category not constituted by universal exclusive relation to the-absence-of-it but by self-reliant structures of differentiation and relation, the identity or subjectivity associated with it has no built-in exclusivity or closure against other identity categories, no analytically built-in hostility to multiple category memberships and subjectivities" (ibid., 1004).

33. Brown, *States of Injury*, 97.

34. Ibid., 134.

35. Ibid.

36. In describing and apparently agreeing with Marx's critique of liberal rights, Brown elaborates: "In Marx's account, the ruse of power peculiar to liberal constitutionalism centers upon granting freedom, equality, and representation to abstract rather than concrete subjects. The substitution of abstract political subjects for actual ones not only forfeits the project of emancipation but resubjugates us precisely by emancipating substitutes for us—by emancipating our abstracted representatives in the state and naming this process 'freedom'" (*States of Injury*, 106).

37. Brown, "Freedom's Silences," 324.

38. Brown, *States of Injury*, 37.

39. Ibid.

40. Later in her chapter, Brown defines the "domain of the sheerly political" as "amoral contests about the just and the good in which truth is always grasped as coterminous with power" (*States of Injury*, 45).

41. Ibid., 37.

42. Ibid., 131; emphasis added.

43. Ibid. 27.

44. MacKinnon, *Feminism Unmodified*, 105.

45. MacKinnon contrasts the illegality of sexual harassment to the illegality of rape. Whereas sexual harassment law has been defined by women's experience, rape law has been defined—at least historically—in far more problematic ways. After suggesting that sexual harassment law marks the "first time in history . . . that women have defined women's injuries in a law," MacKinnon goes on to contrast this to rape law: "We have never defined the injury of rape; men define it. The men who define it, define what they take to be this violation of women according to, among other things, what they think they don't do" (ibid.). Noting that, in this country, it has been white men who have had the power to define rape, MacKinnon points out that rape has wrongly been understood as "an act of a stranger (they

mean Black) committed upon a woman (white) whom he has never seen" (ibid.). Noting that most rapes are intraracial and are committed by men the women know, MacKinnon points out how this understanding of rape makes women who actually are raped question and doubt whether their own experience really fits into the socially and legally defined category. When and if it does not, it may not be understood as rape, even by the woman herself.

46. Brown, *States of Injury*, 133.

47. MacKinnon, "Pornography as Defamation and Discrimination," 801–2.

Chapter 7

1. Butler, *Excitable Speech*, 41.

2. Ibid., 14.

3. Ibid., 15.

4. Ibid., 19.

5. Austin, *How to Do Things with Words*, 12.

6. Ibid., 108.

7. Ibid., 99.

8. Butler, *Excitable Speech*, 16. Further references to this work appear in the text.

9. Austin, *How to Do Things with Words*, 5.

10. Hornsby, "Illocution and Its Significance," 187.

11. Ibid., 188.

12. For example, if you and I are planning to go hiking today, and I wake up, look outside, and utter the statement "It looks like it will rain today," the action of uttering this statement could serve as a warning to you to wear your rain gear, it could indicate to you that I do not want to go hiking today, or it could constitute some other speech act.

13. Austin, *How to Do Things with Words*, 8.

14. Ibid., 116.

15. Ibid.

16. Butler writes, "Illocutionary speech acts produce effects. They are supported, Austin tells us, by linguistic and social conventions" (*Excitable Speech*, 17).

17. Austin, *How to Do Things with Words*, 105.

18. Butler, *Excitable Speech*, 48–49.

19. Ibid., 49.

20. Matsuda, "Public Response to Racist Speech," 43.

21. Ibid., 36.

22. Ibid.

23. Ibid.

24. Ibid., 40.

25. MacKinnon, *Feminism Unmodified*, 176.

26. Langton, "Speech Acts and Unspeakable Acts," 305.

27. Ibid., 305–6.

28. Langton, "Subordination, Silence, and Pornography's Authority," 279.

29. Butler, *Excitable Speech*, 2–3.

30. See Langton, "Speech Acts and Unspeakable Acts"; and "Subordination, Silence, and Pornography's Authority." Langton argues that "in order to answer the question 'Does pornography subordinate?' one must first answer another: 'Do its speakers have authority?'" ("Speech Acts and Unspeakable Acts," 311).

31. L. Green, "Pornographizing, Subordinating, and Silencing," 291.

32. Elsewhere in his article, Green himself makes this point: "[W]hether speech has the power to subordinate is not simply a function of what is said but of the whole social context in which it occurs" (ibid., 294).

33. Langton, "Subordination, Silencing, and Pornography's Authority," 263–64.

34. Langton, "Speech Acts and Unspeakable Acts," 312; "Subordination, Silence, and Pornography's Authority," 264.

35. Langton, "Speech Acts and Unspeakable Acts," 311.

36. Ibid.

37. Ibid., 306. The empirical studies to which Langton refers in this passage are discussed in Edward Donnerstein, Daniel Linz, and Steven Penrod, *The Question of Pornography: Research Findings and Policy Implications* (New York: Free Press, 1987).

38. For a variety of arguments about the harm of both racist hate speech and pornography—and for a presentation of a number of empirical studies regarding their effects—see Lederer and Delgado, *The Price We Pay*. For specific discussions of the harmful effects of racist speech, see Lawrence, "If He Hollers Let Him Go," esp. 72–76; also see Delgado, "Words That Wound," esp. 90–96.

39. There is a sense in which Butler's work shares something with the liberal—and even libertarian—approach to issues of pornography and racist hate speech. Although they do so for different reasons, both Butler and liberals who oppose restrictions on hate speech presume that the hate speech/pornography in question does not have the authority to injure in the way that it is said to injure. And yet this is a claim that must be proved with some reference to evidence and argument about what kind of authority pornography has in our actual world (it cannot simply be assumed *not* to have this kind of authority).

40. Once again, note that the analysis of hate speech as illocutionary does not rely on the argument that such speech would have the needed authority in any context. As I argued above, and as Langton points out, "[i]f pornography subordinates women, then it is not in virtue of its content but of its authority that it does so. It need not have that authority. There are imaginable circumstances where material just like pornography in other respects would have no authority, and in such circumstances such speech would not subordinate. MacKinnon's claim is that those circumstances are not ours, though one can hope that someday they will be" (Langton, "Speech Acts and Unspeakable Acts," 313).

41. Butler, *Excitable Speech*, 41.

42. Ibid., 39.

43. Ibid., 79–80.

44. Ibid., 84.

45. Again, note Butler's emphasis on the importance of this point: "If utterances bear equivocal meanings, then their power is, in principle, less unilateral and sure than it appears. . . . The disjuncture between utterance and meaning is the condition of possibility for revising the performative" (ibid., 87).

46. Langton, "Speech Acts and Unspeakable Acts," 321. For a similar analysis of how disempowered groups can find that their speech effectively has been silenced, see Hornsby, "Speech Acts and Pornography"; and "Disempowered Speech."

47. Nussbaum, "The Professor of Parody," 42.

48. Ibid.

49. Ibid.

50. See Brown, *States of Injury*; and "Freedom's Silences." Although Brown opposes the norms of contemporary society, she also objects to political movements that seek to establish new norms: "Freedom requires the capacity of a kind of public speaking that neither demands concurrence from others nor entails the establishment of new norms by which to live" ("Freedom's Silences," 324).

51. Butler, *Excitable Speech*, 19.

52. Ibid., 41, emphasis added.

53. Butler, *Gender Trouble*, 145.

54. Ibid.

55. Ibid., 141, emphasis added.

56. Butler, *Excitable Speech*, 163.

57. Ibid.

58. Hornsby, "Speech Acts and Pornography," 134.

59. Ibid., 136.

60. Brown, *States of Injury*, 45; *Excitable Speech*, 84.

61. Brown, *States of Injury*, 37.

Conclusion

1. Calhoun, "Justice, Care, Gender Bias," 457–58.

2. Ibid., 453.

3. Ibid.

4. Ibid.

5. Duggan, Hunter, and Vance, "False Promises," 156.

6. In a philosophical defense of this position focused specifically on prostitution, Martha Nussbaum argues both that prostitution should not be stigmatized by feminists and that it is not entirely unlike other jobs that women hold. See *Sex and Social Justice*, "'Whether from Reason or Prejudice."

7. Sundahl, "Stripper," 178.

8. Ibid., 179.

9. For a variety of feminist arguments against pornography, as well as numerous other feminist perspectives on this issue, see Itzin, *Pornography*; Cornell, *Feminism and Pornography*; MacKinnon, *Only Words*; and A. Dworkin, *Pornography*.

10. O'Neill, "Ethical Reasoning and Ideological Pluralism," 718.

11. Dines, Jensen, and Russo, *Pornography*, 11–12.

12. For an analysis of the ways that pornography reinforces racism, see Zia, "Where Race and Gender Meet"; Cowan, "Racism and Sexism in Pornography"; and Gardner, "Racism and Pornography in the Women's Movement."

13. Marxists, communitarians, and conservatives also have objected to the individualism of liberalism, but the exact nature of the problem—and the alternative offered—is very different for each of these analyses.

14. Carole Pateman critically discusses Hobbes's view that "men" are somehow "sprung out of the earth, and suddenly, like mushrooms, come to full maturity" (Thomas Hobbes, *Philosophical Rudiments Concerning Government and Society*, the English version of *De Cive*, in *The English Works of Thomas Hobbes of Malmesbury* (London: John Bohn, 1841), vol. 2, 109, cited in Pateman, "Hobbes, Patriarchy, and Conjugal Right").

15. bell hooks warns of the dangers of feminists' focusing only on how they share one common oppression as women. She writes that "feminist emphasis on 'common oppression' in the United States was less a strategy for politicization than an appropriation by conservative and liberal women of a radical political vocabulary that masked the extent to which they shaped the movement so that it addressed and promoted their class interests" (hooks, *Feminist Theory from Margin to Center*, 5–6). María C. Lugones and Elizabeth V. Spelman also question whether feminist theory should focus on "women as women" in their essay, "Have We Got a Theory for You!"

16. Kimberle Crenshaw calls this phenomenon "intersectionality" and advocates that feminists acknowledge the complex ways in which race, sex, class, and other structures of power "intersect" with one another. For an in-depth discussion of this issue, see her "Demarginalizing the Intersection of Race and Sex."

17. Young, "Gender as Seriality," 17.

18. Frye, *The Politics of Reality*, 33.

19. Ibid. For Frye's most recent work on the meaning and significance of the category "women," see her "Categories in Distress"; "Ethnocentrism/Essentialism"; and "The Necessity of Differences."

20. For an extensive discussion of the contributions that Butler's postmodernism makes to feminist theories of power, see Allen, *The Power of Feminist Theory*.

21. For a sampling of this debate, see the essays in Sargent, *Women and Revolution*. Also see the first four chapters of Catharine MacKinnon's *Toward a Feminist Theory of the State*, esp. chap. 1, "The Problem of Marxism and Feminism," and chap. 4, "Attempts at Synethesis."

22. While Rawls claims that the family is "part of the basic structure," he likens it to an "association" within the basic structure and specifies that although political principles do "impose essential constraints on the family as an institution," they "do not apply directly to its internal life" (Rawls, *Justice as Fairness*, 164).

23. For a concise description of "classical Marxist feminism" see Jaggar, "Political Philosophies of Women's Liberation," esp. 9–12.

Bibliography

Alcoff, Linda, and Elizabeth Potter, eds. *Feminist Epistemologies*. New York: Routledge, 1993.

Alexander, Larry, and Maimon Schwarzschild. "Liberalism, Neutrality, and Equality of Welfare vs. Equality of Resources." *Philosophy and Public Affairs* 16, no. 1 (1987): 85 110.

Allen, Amy. *The Power of Feminist Theory: Domination, Resistance, Solidarity*. Boulder, Colo.: Westview Press, 1999.

Altman, Andrew. "Liberalism and Campus Hate Speech: A Philosophical Examination." *Ethics* 103 (1993): 302–17.

———. "Making Sense of Sexual Harassment Law." *Philosophy and Public Affairs* 25, no. 1 (1996): 36–64.

Anderson, Elizabeth S. "The Democratic University: The Role of Justice in the Production of Knowledge." *Social Philosophy and Policy* 12 (1995): 186–219.

———. "Is Women's Labor a Commodity?" *Philosophy and Public Affairs* 19, no. 1 (1990): 71–92.

———. "Knowledge, Human Interests, and Objectivity in Feminist Epistemology." *Philosophical Topics* 23, no. 2 (1996): 27–58.

———. *Value in Ethics and Economics*. Cambridge, Mass.: Harvard University Press, 1993.

———. "What Is the Point of Equality?" *Ethics* 109 (January 1999): 287–337.

Antony, Louise M., and Charlotte Witt, eds. *A Mind of One's Own: Feminist Essays on Reason and Objectivity*. Boulder, Colo.: Westview Press, 1993.

Austin, J. L. *How to Do Things with Words*. Cambridge, Mass.: Harvard University Press, 1962.

Babbitt, Susan. *Impossible Dreams: Rationality, Integrity, and Moral Imagination*. Boulder, Colo.: Westview Press, 1996.

Baehr, Amy R. *Varieties of Feminist Liberalism*. Lanham, Md.: Rowman and Littlefield, 2004.

Bartky, Sandra Lee. *Femininity and Domination: Studies in the Phenomenology of Oppression.* New York: Routledge, 1990.

Bartlett, Katharine T., and Rosanne Kennedy, eds. *Feminist Legal Theory: Readings in Law and Gender.* Boulder, Colo.: Westview Press, 1991.

Baynes, Kenneth. *The Normative Grounds of Social Criticism: Kant, Rawls, and Habermas.* Albany: State University of New York Press, 1992.

Bell, Linda. *Rethinking Ethics in the Midst of Violence: A Feminist Approach to Freedom.* Lanham, Md.: Rowman and Littlefield, 1993.

Benhabib, Seyla, Judith Butler, Drucilla Cornell, and Nancy Fraser. *Feminist Contentions: A Philosophical Exchange.* New York: Routledge, 1995.

Bovens, Luc. "Sour Grapes and Character Planning." *Journal of Philosophy* 89, no. 2 (1992): 57–78.

Brennan, Samantha. "The Liberal Rights of Liberal Feminism." In *Varieties of Feminist Liberalism,* edited by Amy R. Baehr. Lanham, Md.: Rowman and Littlefield, 2004.

Brison, Susan J. "The Theoretical Importance of Practice." In *Theory and Practice,* edited by Ian Shapiro and Judith Wagner DeCew. New York: New York University Press, 1995.

Brown, Wendy. "Freedom's Silences." In *Censorship and Silencing: Practices of Cultural Regulation,* edited by Robert Post. Los Angeles: Getty Research Institute for the History of Art and the Humanities, 1998.

———. *States of Injury: Power and Freedom in Late Modernity.* Princeton: Princeton University Press, 1995.

———. "Suffering Rights as Paradoxes." *Constellations* 7, no. 2 (2000): 230–41.

Butler, Judith. *Bodies That Matter: On the Discursive Limits of "Sex."* New York: Routledge, 1993.

———. *Excitable Speech: A Politics of the Performative.* New York: Routledge, 1997.

———. *Gender Trouble: Feminism and the Subversion of Identity.* New York: Routledge, 1990.

———. "Ruled Out: Vocabularies of the Censor." In *Censorship and Silencing: Practices of Cultural Regulation,* edited by Robert Post. Los Angeles: Getty Research Institute for the History of Art and the Humanities, 1998.

Calhoun, Cheshire. "Justice, Care, Gender Bias." *Journal of Philosophy* 85 (1988): 451–63.

Campbell, Tom. *The Left and Rights: A Conceptual Analysis of the Idea of Socialist Rights.* Boston: Routledge and Kegan Paul, 1983.

Card, Claudia, ed. *Feminist Ethics.* Lawrence: University Press of Kansas, 1991.

Cohen, Joshua. "Freedom, Equality, Pornography." In *Justice and Injustice in Law and Legal Theory,* edited by Austin Sarat and Thomas R. Kearns. Ann Arbor: University of Michigan Press, 1996.

Colker, Ruth. "Feminist Consciousness and the State: A Basis for Cautious Optimism." *Columbia Law Review* 90, no. 4 (1990): 1146–70.

Cornell, Drucilla. *Beyond Accommodation: Ethical Feminism, Deconstruction, and the Law.* New York: Routledge, 1991.

———, ed. *Feminism and Pornography.* New York: Oxford University Press, 2000.

———. *Transformations: Recollective Imagination and Sexual Difference.* New York: Routledge, 1993.

Cowan, Gloria. "Racism and Sexism in Pornography." In *The Price We Pay: The Case Against Racist Speech, Hate Propaganda, and Pornography,* edited by Laura J. Lederer and Richard Delgado. New York: Hill and Wang, 1994.

Crenshaw, Kimberle. "Demarginalizing the Intersection of Race and Sex: A Black Feminist Critique of Antidiscrimination Doctrine, Feminist Theory, and Antiracist Politics." In *Feminist Legal Theory: Readings in Law and Gender,* edited by Katharine T. Bartlett and Rosanne Kennedy. Boulder, Colo.: Westview Press, 1989.

Cudd, Ann E. "The Paradox of Liberal Feminism: Preference, Rationality, and Oppression." In *Varieties of Feminist Liberalism,* edited by Amy R. Baehr. Lanham, Md.: Rowman and Littlefield, 2004.

Delgado, Richard. "Words That Wound: A Tort Action for Racial Insults, Epithets, and Name Calling." In *Words That Wound: Critical Race Theory, Assaultive Speech, and the First Amendment,* edited by Mari J. Matsuda, Charles R. Lawrence III, Richard Delgado, and Kimberlè Williams Crenshaw. Boulder, Colo.: Westview Press, 1993.

Dines, Gail, Robert Jensen, and Ann Russo. *Pornography: The Production and Consumption of Inequality.* New York: Routledge, 1998.

Douglas, Lawrence. "The Force of Words: Fish, Matsuda, MacKinnon, and the Theory of Discursive Violence." *Law and Society Review* 29, no. 1 (1995): 169–91.

Duggan, Lisa, Nan D. Hunter, and Carole S. Vance. "False Promises: Feminist Anti-pornography Legislation." *New York Law School Review* 38 (1993): 133–63.

Dworkin, Andrea. *Pornography: Men Possessing Women.* New York: Perigee Books, 1979.

Dworkin, Ronald. "Comment on Narveson: In Defense of Equality." *Social Philosophy and Policy* 1, no. 1 (1983): 24–40.

———. "Foundations of Liberal Equality." In *Equal Freedom: Selected Tanner Lectures on Human Values,* edited by Stephen Darwall. Ann Arbor: University of Michigan Press, 1995.

———. "Liberal Community." *California Law Review* 77 (1989): 479–504.

———. "Liberalism." In *Liberalism and Its Critics,* edited by Michael J. Sandel. New York: New York University Press, 1984.

———. *A Matter of Principle.* Cambridge, Mass.: Harvard University Press, 1985.

———. "Rights as Trumps." In *Theories of Rights,* edited by Jeremy Waldron. New York: Oxford University Press, 1984.

———. "The Roots of Justice: Part 2." Program for the Study of Law, Philosophy, and Social Theory, NYU School of Law, November 6, 1997.

———. *Taking Rights Seriously.* Cambridge, Mass.: Harvard University Press, 1977.

———. "Two Concepts of Liberty." In *Isaiah Berlin: A Celebration,* edited by Edna Margalit and Avishai Margalit. Chicago: University of Chicago Press, 1991.

———. "What Is Equality? Part 1: Equality of Welfare." *Philosophy and Public Affairs* 10, no. 3 (1981): 185–246.

———. "What Is Equality? Part 2: Equality of Resources." *Philosophy and Public Affairs* 10, no. 4 (1981): 283–345.

———. "Women and Pornography." Review of *Only Words,* by Catharine A. MacKinnon. *New York Review of Books,* October 21, 1993, 36–42.

Elster, Jon. *Sour Grapes: Studies in the Subversion of Rationality.* New York: Cambridge University Press, 1983.

Engstrom, Stephen. Review of *Constructions of Reason: Explorations of Kant's Practical Philosophy,* by Onora O'Neill. *Ethics* 102 (April 1992): 653–55.

Fineman, Martha Albertson, and Nancy Sweet Thomadsen, eds. *At the Boundaries of Law: Feminism and Legal Theory.* New York: Routledge, 1991.

Foucault, Michel. *Power/Knowledge: Selected Interviews and Other Writings, 1972–1977.* New York: Pantheon Books, 1980.

Fraser, Nancy. "Beyond the Master/Subject Model: Reflections on Carole Pateman's Sexual Contract." *Social Text* 37 (1993): 173–81.

———. "From Irony to Prophecy to Politics: A Response to Richard Rorty." *Michigan Quarterly Review* 30, no. 2 (1991): 259–66.

———. *Justice Interruptus: Critical Reflections on the "Postsocialist" Condition.* New York: Routledge, 1997.

———. *Unruly Practices: Power, Discourse, and Gender in Contemporary Social Theory.* Minneapolis: University of Minnesota Press, 1989.

Frazer, Elizabeth, and Nicola Lacey. *The Politics of Community: A Feminist Critique of the Liberal-Communitarian Debate.* Buffalo: University of Toronto Press, 1993.

Freeman, Samuel, ed. *The Cambridge Companion to Rawls.* New York: Cambridge University Press, 2003.

———. *John Rawls: Collected Papers.* Cambridge, Mass.: Harvard University Press, 1993.

French, Stanley G., Wanda Teays, and Laura M. Purdy, eds. *Violence Against Women: Philosophical Perspectives.* Ithaca, N.Y.: Cornell University Press, 1998.

Friedman, Marilyn. "Autonomy, Social Disruption, and Women." In *Relational Autonomy: Feminist Perspectives on Autonomy, Agency, and the Social Self,* edited by Catriona Mackenzie and Natalie Stoljar. New York: Oxford University Press, 2000.

———. *What Are Friends For? Feminist Perspectives on Personal Relationships and Moral Theory.* Ithaca, N.Y.: Cornell University Press, 1993.

Frye, Marilyn. "Categories in Distress." In *Feminist Interventions in Ethics and Politics: Feminist Ethics and Social Theory,* edited by Barbara S. Andrew, Jean Keller, and Lisa H. Schwartzman. Lanham, Md.: Rowman and Littlefield, 2005.

———. "Ethnocentrism/Essentialism: The Failure of the Ontological Cure." In *Is Academic Feminism Dead? Theory in Practice,* edited by the Social Justice Group at the Center for Advanced Feminist Studies, University of Minnesota. New York: New York University Press, 2000.

———. "The Necessity of Differences: Constructing a Positive Category of Women." *Signs: Journal of Women in Culture and Society* 21, no. 4 (1996): 991–1010.

———. *The Politics of Reality: Essays in Feminist Theory.* Freedom, Calif.: Crossing Press, 1983.

Fuss, Diana. *Essentially Speaking: Feminism, Nature, and Difference.* New York: Routledge, 1989.

Gardner, Tracey A. "Racism in Pornography and the Women's Movement." In *Take Back the Night: Women on Pornography*, edited by Laura Lederer. New York: William Morrow, 1980.

Garry, Ann, and Marilyn Pearsall, eds. *Women, Knowledge, and Reality: Explorations in Feminist Philosophy*. New York: Routledge, 1989.

Gauthier, Jeffrey A. *Hegel and Feminist Social Criticism: Justice, Recognition, and the Feminine*. Albany: State University of New York Press, 1997.

Gilligan, Carol. *In a Different Voice: Psychological Theory and Women's Development*. Cambridge, Mass.: Harvard University Press, 1982.

Green, Karen. "Rawls, Women, and the Priority of Liberty." *Australasian Journal of Philosophy* 64 (June 1986): S26–36.

Green, Leslie. "Pornographizing, Subordinating, and Silencing." In *Censorship and Silencing: Practices of Cultural Regulation*, edited by Robert Post. Los Angeles: Getty Research Institute for the History of Art and the Humanities, 1998.

Gutmann, Amy. *Liberal Equality*. New York: Cambridge University Press, 1980.

Hackett, Beth. "Catharine MacKinnon's 'Feminist Epistemology.'"Ph.D. diss., University of Pennsylvania, 1996.

Hampton, Jean. "Feminist Contractarianism." In *A Mind of One's Own: Feminist Essays on Reason and Objectivity*, edited by Louise M. Antony and Charlotte Witt. Boulder, Colo.: Westview Press, 1993.

———. *Political Philosophy*. Boulder, Colo.: Westview Press, 1997.

Hanen, Marsha P. "Feminism, Objectivity, and Legal Truth." In *Feminist Perspectives: Philosophical Essays on Method and Morals*, edited by Lorraine Code, Sheila Mullet, and Christine Overall. Buffalo: University of Toronto Press, 1988.

Hanen, Marsha, and Kai Nielsen, eds. *Science, Morality, and Feminist Theory*. Calgary: University of Calgary Press, 1987.

Harris, Angela. "Race and Essentialism in Feminist Legal Theory." In *Feminist Legal Theory: Readings in Law and Gender*, edited by Katharine T. Bartlett and Rosanne Kennedy. Boulder, Colo.: Westview Press, 1991.

Hartsock, Nancy C. M. *Money, Sex, and Power: Toward a Feminist Historical Materialism*. Boston: Northeastern University Press, 1983.

Haslanger, Sally. "Ontology and Social Construction." *Philosophical Topics* 23, no. 2 (1996): 95–125.

Hawkesworth, Mary E. "From Objectivity to Objectification: Feminist Objections." In *Rethinking Objectivity*, edited by Allan Megill. Durham: Duke University Press, 1994.

Hennessy, Rosemary. *Materialist Feminism and the Politics of Discourse*. New York: Routledge, 1993.

Herman, Barbara. *The Practice of Moral Judgment*. Cambridge, Mass.: Harvard University Press, 1993.

Hill, Thomas. *Autonomy and Self-Respect*. New York: Cambridge University Press, 1991.

Holtman, Sarah Williams. Review of *Towards Justice and Virtue: A Constructive Account of Practical Reasoning*, by Onora O'Neill. *Journal of Philosophy* 95, no. 6 (1998): 317–21.

hooks, bell. *Feminist Theory from Margin to Center*. Boston: South End Press, 1984.

Hornsby, Jennifer. "Disempowered Speech." *Philosophical Topics* 23, no. 2 (1996): 127–47.
———. "Illocution and Its Significance." In *Foundations of Speech Act Theory: Philosophical and Linguistic Perspectives*, edited by Savas L. Tsohatzidis. New York: Routledge, 1994.
———. "Philosophers and Feminists on Language Use." *Cogito* 2 (1988): 13–16.
———. "Speech Acts and Pornography." In *The Problem of Pornography*, edited by Susan Dwyer. Belmont, Calif.: Wadsworth, 1995.
Itzin, Catherine. *Pornography: Women, Violence, and Civil Liberties*. New York: Oxford University Press, 1992.
Jacobsen, Daniel. "Freedom of Speech Acts? A Response to Langton." *Philosophy and Public Affairs* 24, no. 1 (1995): 64–79.
Jaggar, Alison M. *Feminist Politics and Human Nature*. Totowa, N.J.: Rowman and Allanheld, 1983.
———. "Political Philosophies of Women's Liberation." In *Feminism and Philosophy*, edited by Mary Vetterling-Braggin, Frederick A. Elliston, and Jane English. Totowa, N.J.: Rowman and Littlefield, 1977.
Kearns, Deborah. "A Theory of Justice—and Love; Rawls on the Family." *Politics* 18 (1983): 36–42.
Kiss, Elizabeth. "Alchemy or Fool's Gold? Assessing Feminist Doubts About Rights." In *Reconstructing Political Theory: Feminist Perspectives*, edited by Mary Lyndon Shanley and Uma Narayan. University Park: Pennsylvania State University Press, 1995.
Kittay, Eva Feder. "The Greater Danger—Pornography, Social Science, and Women's Rights: Reply to Brannigan and Goldenberg." *Social Epistemology* 2, no. 2 (1988): 117–33.
———. "Human Dependency and Rawlsian Equality." In *Feminists Rethink the Self*, edited by Diana Tietjens Meyers. Boulder, Colo.: Westview Press, 1997.
———. *Love's Labor: Essays on Women, Equality, and Dependency*. New York: Routledge, 1999.
Kittay, Eva Feder, and Diana T. Meyers, eds. *Women and Moral Theory*. Totowa, N.J.: Rowman and Littlefield, 1987.
Kline, Marlee. "Race, Racism, and Feminist Legal Theory." *Harvard Women's Law Journal* 12 (1989): 115–50.
Kymlicka, Will. *Contemporary Political Philosophy: An Introduction*. New York: Clarendon Press, 1990.
———. *Liberalism, Community, and Culture*. New York: Clarendon Press, 1989.
Langton, Rae. "Duty and Desolation." *Philosophy* 67 (1992): 481–505.
———. "Speech Acts and Unspeakable Acts." *Philosophy and Public Affairs* 22, no. 4 (1993): 293–330.
———. "Subordination, Silence, and Pornography's Authority." In *Censorship and Silencing: Practices of Cultural Regulation*, edited by Robert Post. Los Angeles: Getty Research Institute for the History of Art and the Humanities, 1998.
———. "Whose Right? Ronald Dworkin, Women, and Pornographers." *Philosophy and Public Affairs* 19, no. 4 (1990): 311–59.

Lawrence, Charles R. III. "If He Hollers Let Him Go: Regulating Racist Speech on Campus." In *Words That Wound: Critical Race Theory, Assaultive Speech, and the First Amendment*, edited by Mari J. Matsuda, Charles R. Lawrence III, Richard Delgado, and Kimberlè Williams Crenshaw. Boulder, Colo.: Westview Press, 1993.

Lederer, Laura J. "The Case of the Cross Burning: An Interview with Russ and Laura Jones." In *The Price We Pay: The Case Against Racist Speech, Hate Propaganda, and Pornography*, edited by Laura J. Lederer and Richard Delgado. New York: Hill and Wang, 1995.

Lederer, Laura J., and Richard Delgado, eds. *The Price We Pay: The Case Against Racist Speech, Hate Propaganda, and Pornography*. New York: Hill and Wang, 1995.

Lloyd, Elisabeth A. "Feminism as Method: What Scientists Get That Philosophers Don't." *Philosophical Topics* 23, no. 2 (1996): 189–220.

———. "Objectivity and the Double Standard for Feminist Epistemologies." *Synthese* 104 (1995): 351–81.

Longino, Helen. *Science as Social Knowledge: Values and Objectivity in Scientific Inquiry.* Princeton: Princeton University Press, 1990.

Lugones, María C., and Elizabeth V. Spelman "Have We Got a Theory for You! Feminist Theory, Cultural Imperialism, and the Demand for 'The Woman's Voice.'" In *Women and Values: Readings in Recent Feminist Philosophy*, edited by Marilyn Pearsall. Belmont, Calif.: Wadsworth, 1986.

Mackenzie, Catriona, and Natalie Stoljar, eds. *Relational Autonomy: Feminist Perspectives on Autonomy, Agency, and the Social Self.* New York: Oxford University Press, 2000.

MacKinnon, Catharine A. *Feminism Unmodified: Discourses on Life and Law.* Cambridge, Mass.: Harvard University Press, 1987.

———. "From Practice to Theory, or What Is a White Woman Anyway?" *Yale Journal of Law and Feminism* 13, no. 4 (1991): 13–22.

———. *Only Words.* Cambridge, Mass.: Harvard University Press, 1993.

———. "Pornography as Defamation and Discrimination." *Boston University Law Review* 71 (1991): 793–815.

———. "Prostitution and Civil Rights." *Michigan Journal of Gender and Law* 1 (1993): 13–31.

———. *Toward a Feminist Theory of the State.* Cambridge, Mass.: Harvard University Press, 1989.

———. *Women's Lives, Men's Laws.* Cambridge, Mass.: Belknap Press of Harvard University Press, 2005.

MacKinnon, Catharine A., and Andrea Dworkin. *Pornography and Civil Rights: A New Day for Women's Equality.* Minneapolis, Minn.: Organizing Against Pornography, 1988.

Mapel, David. *Social Justice Reconsidered: The Problem of Appropriate Precision in a Theory of Justice.* Chicago: University of Illinois Press, 1989.

Marx, Karl. "On the Jewish Question." *The Marx-Engels Reader.* 2d ed., edited by Robert C. Tucker. New York: W. W. Norton, 1978.

Matsuda, Mari J. "Public Response to Racist Speech: Considering the Victim's Story." In *Words That Wound: Critical Race Theory, Assaultive Speech, and the First*

Amendment, edited by Mari J. Matsuda, Charles R. Lawrence III, Richard Delgado, and Kimberlè Williams Crenshaw. Boulder, Colo.: Westview Press, 1993.

Mill, John Stuart. *On Liberty*. Indianapolis, Ind.: Hackett, 1978.

Minow, Martha. *Making All the Difference: Inclusion, Exclusion, and American Law*. Ithaca, N.Y.: Cornell University Press, 1990.

Minow, Martha, and Mary Lyndon Shanley. "Relational Rights and Responsibilities: Revisioning the Family in Liberal Political Theory and Law." *Hypatia* 11, no. 1 (1996): 4–29.

Minow, Martha, and Elizabeth V. Spelman. "In Context." *Southern California Law Review* 63, no. 6 (1990): 1597–652.

Nozick, Robert. *Anarchy, State, and Utopia*. New York: Basic Books, 1974.

Nussbaum, Martha. "Onora O'Neill: Justice, Gender, and International Boundaries." In *The Quality of Life*, edited by Martha Nussbaum and Amartya Sen. Oxford: Clarendon Press, 1993.

———. "The Professor of Parody." *New Republic*, February 22, 1999, 37–45.

———. "Rawls and Feminism," In *The Cambridge Companion to Rawls*, edited by Samuel Freeman. New York: Cambridge University Press, 2003.

———. *Sex and Social Justice*. New York: Oxford University Press, 1999.

———. *Women and Human Development: The Capabilities Approach*. New York: Cambridge University Press, 2000.

Okin, Susan Moller. "Feminism, the Individual, and Contract Theory." *Ethics* 100 (1990): 658–69.

———. "Gender Inequality and Cultural Differences." *Political Theory* 22, no. 1 (1994): 5–24.

———. "Justice and Gender." *Philosophy and Public Affairs* 16, no. 1 (1987): 42–72.

———. *Justice, Gender, and the Family*. New York: Basic Books, 1989.

———. "Political Liberalism, Justice, and Gender," *Ethics* 105 (October 1994): 23–43.

———. "Reason and Feeling in Thinking About Justice," *Ethics* 99, no. 2 (1989): 229–49.

O'Neill, Onora. "Abstraction, Idealization, and Ideology in Ethics." In *Moral Philosophy and Contemporary Problems*, edited by J. D. G. Evans. New York: Cambridge University Press, 1987.

———. "Autonomy, Coherence, and Independence." In *Liberalism, Autonomy, and Citizenship*, edited by David Milligan and William Watts-Miller. Brookfield, Vt.: Avebury, 1992.

———. *Constructions of Reason: Explorations of Kant's Practical Philosophy*. New York: Cambridge University Press, 1989.

———. "Ethical Reasoning and Ideological Pluralism." *Ethics* 98 (July 1988): 705–22.

———. "Justice, Gender, and International Boundaries." In *The Quality of Life*, edited by Martha Nussbaum and Amartya Sen. Oxford: Clarendon Press, 1993.

———. *Towards Justice and Virtue: A Constructive Account of Practical Reasoning*. New York: Cambridge University Press, 1996.

Pateman, Carole. "Feminist Critiques of the Public/Private Dichotomy." In *Feminism and Equality*, edited by Anne Phillips. New York: New York University Press, 1987.

———. "Hobbes, Patriarchy, and Conjugal Right." In *Social and Political Philosophy: Classical Western Texts in Feminist and Multicultural Perspectives*, edited by James P. Sterba. Belmont, Calif.: Wadsworth, 1995.

———. *The Sexual Contract*. Stanford: Stanford University Press, 1988.

Peters, Julie, and Andrea Wolper, eds. *Women's Rights, Human Rights: International Feminist Perspectives*. New York: Routledge, 1995.

Phillips, Anne, ed. *Feminism and Equality*. New York: New York University Press, 1987.

Rapaport, Elizabeth. "Generalizing Gender: Reason and Essence in the Legal Thought of Catharine MacKinnon." In *A Mind of One's Own: Feminist Essays on Reason and Objectivity*, edited by Louise M. Antony and Charlotte Witt. Boulder, Colo.: Westview Press, 1993.

Rawls, John. "Fairness to Goodness." In *John Rawls: Collected Papers*, edited by Samuel Freeman. Cambridge, Mass.: Harvard University Press, 1999.

———. "The Idea of Public Reason Revisited." In *John Rawls: Collected Papers*, edited by Samuel Freeman. Cambridge, Mass.: Harvard University Press, 1999.

———. *Justice as Fairness: A Restatement*. Cambridge, Mass.: Harvard University Press, 2001.

———. "The Law of Peoples." In *The Law of Peoples, with "The Idea of Public Reason Revisited."* Cambridge, Mass.: Harvard University Press, 1999.

———. *Political Liberalism*. New York: Columbia University Press, 1993.

———. *A Theory of Justice*. Cambridge, Mass.: Harvard University Press, 1971.

Rhode, Deborah L., ed. *Theoretical Perspectives on Sexual Difference*. New Haven: Yale University Press, 1990.

Ring, Jennifer. "Saving Objectivity for Feminism: MacKinnon, Marx, and Other Possibilities." *Review of Politics* 49 (1987): 467–89.

Rorty, Richard. "Feminism and Pragmatism." *Michigan Quarterly Review* 30, no. 2 (1991): 231–58.

———. "Feminism, Ideology, and Deconstruction: A Pragmatist View." *Hypatia* 8, no. 2 (1993): 96–103.

Sadurski, Wojciech. "On 'Seeing Speech Through an Equality Lens': A Critique of Egalitarian Arguments for Suppression of Hate Speech and Pornography." *Oxford Journal of Legal Studies* 16, no. 4 (1996): 713–23.

Sandven, Tore. "Autonomy, Adaptation, and Rationality: A Critical Discussion of Jon Elster's Concept of 'Sour Grapes,' Part I." *Philosophy of the Social Sciences* 29, no. 1 (March 1999): 3–31.

Sargent, Lydia. *Women and Revolution: A Discussion of the Unhappy Marriage of Marxism and Feminism*. Boston: South End Press, 1981.

Satz, Debra. "Markets in Women's Sexual Labor." *Ethics* 106 (October 1995): 63–85.

Scheman, Naomi. *Engenderings: Constructions of Knowledge, Authority, and Privilege*. New York: Routledge, 1993.

Schneider, Elizabeth M. "The Dialectic of Rights and Politics: Perspectives from the Women's Movement." In *Women, the State, and Welfare*, edited by Linda Gordon. Madison: University of Wisconsin Press, 1986.

———. "The Violence of Privacy." In *The Public Nature of Private Violence: The Discovery of Domestic Abuse*, edited by Martha Albertson Fineman and Roxanne Mykitiuk. New York: Routledge, 1994.

Smith, Andrew F. "Closer but Still No Cigar: On the Inadequacy of Rawls's Reply to Okin's 'Political Liberalism, Justice, and Gender.'" *Social Theory and Practice* 30, no. 1 (2004): 59–71.

Smith, Barbara Herrnstein. "The Unquiet Judge: Activism Without Objectivism in Law and Politics." In *Rethinking Objectivity*, edited by Allan Megill. Durham: Duke University Press, 1994.

Spelman, Elizabeth V. *Inessential Woman: Problems of Exclusion in Feminist Thought*. Boston: Beacon, 1988.

Sundahl, Debi. "Stripper." In *Sex Work: Writings by Women in the Sex Industry*, edited by Frédérique Delacoste and Priscilla Alexander. Pittsburgh, Pa.: Cleis Press, 1987.

Sunstein, Cass R., ed. *Feminism and Political Theory*. Chicago: University of Chicago Press, 1990.

Trout, Lara M. "Can Justice as Fairness Accommodate Diversity? An Examination of the Representation of Minorities and Women in *A Theory of Justice*." *Philosophy in the Contemporary World* 1, no. 3 (Fall 1994): 39–45.

Valverde, Mariana. "Beyond Gender Dangers and Private Pleasures: Theory and Ethics in the Sex Debates." In *The Problem of Pornography*, edited by Susan Dwyer. Belmont, Calif.: Wadsworth, 1995.

Waldron, Jeremy. *Theories of Rights*. New York: Oxford University Press, 1984.

Walker, Alice. *Meridian*. New York: Pocket Books, 1976.

West, Robin. "Jurisprudence and Gender." In *Feminist Legal Theory: Readings in Law and Gender*, edited by Katharine T. Bartlett and Rosanne Kennedy. Boulder, Colo.: Westview Press, 1991.

Williams, Patricia J. *The Alchemy of Race and Rights*. Cambridge, Mass.: Harvard University Press, 1991.

Wood, Allen. Review of *Constructions of Reason: Explorations of Kant's Practical Philosophy*, by Onora O'Neill. *Philosophical Review* 101, no. 3 (1992): 647–50.

Young, Iris Marion. "Gender as Seriality: Thinking About Women as a Social Collective." In *Intersecting Voices: Dilemmas of Gender, Political Philosophy, and Policy*. Princeton: Princeton University Press, 1997.

———. *Justice and the Politics of Difference*. Princeton: Princeton University Press, 1990.

Zia, Helen. "Where Race and Gender Meet: Racism, Hate Crimes, and Pornography." In *The Price We Pay: The Case Against Racist Speech, Hate Propaganda, and Pornography*, edited by Laura J. Lederer and Richard Delgado. New York: Hill and Wang, 1994.

Index